Philip Vickerman

Including Children with Special Educational Needs

Training Physical Education Teachers

LAP LAMBERT Academic Publishing

Impressum/Imprint (nur für Deutschland/ only for Germany)
Bibliografische Information der Deutschen Nationalbibliothek: Die Deutsche Nationalbibliothek
verzeichnet diese Publikation in der Deutschen Nationalbibliografie; detaillierte bibliografische
Daten sind im Internet über http://dnb.d-nb.de abrufbar.
 Alle in diesem Buch genannten Marken und Produktnamen unterliegen warenzeichen-, marken-
oder patentrechtlichem Schutz bzw. sind Warenzeichen oder eingetragene Warenzeichen der
jeweiligen Inhaber. Die Wiedergabe von Marken, Produktnamen, Gebrauchsnamen,
Handelsnamen, Warenbezeichnungen u.s.w. in diesem Werk berechtigt auch ohne besondere
Kennzeichnung nicht zu der Annahme, dass solche Namen im Sinne der Warenzeichen- und
Markenschutzgesetzgebung als frei zu betrachten wären und daher von jedermann benutzt
werden dürften.

Coverbild: www.ingimage.com

Verlag: LAP LAMBERT Academic Publishing AG & Co. KG
Dudweiler Landstr. 99, 66123 Saarbrücken, Deutschland
Telefon +49 681 3720-310, Telefax +49 681 3720-3109
Email: info@lap-publishing.com

Herstellung in Deutschland:
Schaltungsdienst Lange o.H.G., Berlin
Books on Demand GmbH, Norderstedt
Reha GmbH, Saarbrücken
Amazon Distribution GmbH, Leipzig
ISBN: 978-3-8383-7850-3

Imprint (only for USA, GB)
Bibliographic information published by the Deutsche Nationalbibliothek: The Deutsche
Nationalbibliothek lists this publication in the Deutsche Nationalbibliografie; detailed
bibliographic data are available in the Internet at http://dnb.d-nb.de.
 Any brand names and product names mentioned in this book are subject to trademark, brand
or patent protection and are trademarks or registered trademarks of their respective holders.
The use of brand names, product names, common names, trade names, product descriptions
etc. even without a particular marking in this works is in no way to be construed to mean that
such names may be regarded as unrestricted in respect of trademark and brand protection
legislation and could thus be used by anyone.

Cover image: www.ingimage.com

Publisher: LAP LAMBERT Academic Publishing AG & Co. KG
Dudweiler Landstr. 99, 66123 Saarbrücken, Germany
Phone +49 681 3720-310, Fax +49 681 3720-3109
Email: info@lap-publishing.com

Printed in the U.S.A.
Printed in the U.K. by (see last page)
ISBN: 978-3-8383-7850-3

Training Physical Education Teachers to Include Children
with Special educational Needs within Mainstream settings

CONTENTS

List of Figures

PREFACE

When I was a child, I acted like a child,
Now I am a man, I act like a man,
If only people would treat me for what I am, rather than what I am not,
Don't change me, understand me

(Anon)

Background And Personal Interest For The Study

The initial interest for this study arises from a personal and professional interest in the field of PE, sport, disability and SEN. To date, my career has involved working in a number of capacities with children and adults with a range of SEN and disabilities in both school and community contexts. My current post as a Senior Lecturer in PE, Sport, Disability and SEN, has enabled me to particularly extend my knowledge and understanding in relation to the training of PE teachers for the inclusion of children with SEN. Since the return of the Labour Government to power in 1997, the inclusion of children with SEN within mainstream settings has risen up both the political and statutory agenda. For example, the Department for Education and Skills (DFES) state:

> *"The education of children with special needs is a key challenge for the nation. It is vital to the creation of a fully inclusive society" (DFES 1999, p1).*

It is within the backdrop of this statement from the DFES that much of my work in inclusive PE for children with SEN has been recently developed. Consequently, this has given me opportunities to work, and present at National and International levels on diverse aspects of inclusive PE for children with SEN. These have involved course delivery, research publications, consultancy, conference presentations, training, and resource materials.

My particular interests focus upon the views and policies of professional PE associations, government and statutory agencies in relation to the impact this has for implementation within ITT institutions, and delivery by teachers in schools. I am particularly interested to examine how government, ITT providers, teachers, and schools can work together to establish a cohesive framework for the training and delivery of inclusive PE to children with SEN. Therefore, it is within this context that I wish to consider how the training of PE teachers for inclusive settings is implemented.

The forthcoming chapters, outlined below provide an overview to how this study will be examined:

Chapter 1. Context for the study: This chapter establishes the framework for the study, and identifies the key themes, issues, purpose, and research questions for the study.

Chapter 2 Education, special education and initial teacher training, is broken into two parts. **Part (one)** gives an overview of the emergence of ITT standards and expectations, whilst examining the implementation and evaluation of these over recent years. This will be examined within the context of the roles played by agencies such as the Teacher Training Agency (TTA), Office for Standards in Education (OFSTED) and DFES. In contrast, **Part (two)** provides a historical critique, and analysis of how SEN has changed and emerged over the years up to the present day position of the government's commitment to inclusive agendas within schools. It examines the changing emphasis and nature of terminology within this area, and how the shift from segregated to inclusive provision has emerged.

Chapter 3. Developments in inclusive physical education and disability sport critically analyses how PE, special education and disability sport has developed to the present day position of empowerment and support for inclusion within all aspects of physical activity. It examines the role that PE as a subject area can play in meeting the government's wider agenda for inclusive education, as well as considering a range of teaching and learning approaches that can facilitate inclusion for children with SEN.

Chapter 4. Methodology: provides a rationale, critical justification and analysis of the chosen research methods within the study, and examines each of the five stages of investigation undertaken within the study.

The **results** section is broken into three chapters based around the 'official line' (stage one), 'professional opinion and practice', (stages two and three) and the 'consumers' (stages four and five). Each chapter draws upon the research findings from the study, and analyses the relationship and impact upon the training of PE teachers for the inclusion of children with SEN.

Chapter 5. Results and discussion of the official line (Stage one), gives a critical overview of the literature related to statutory and professional agencies that have a role to play in the policy and practice of PE for children with SEN. It examines agencies such as the DFES, OFSTED, TTA, Physical Education Association, (United Kingdom) (PEA (UK)) British Association of Advisors and Lecturers in Physical Education (BAALPE), English Federation for Disability Sport (EFDS) and the Qualification Curriculum Authority (QCA). The literature analyses where the current position lies on PE and SEN, and asserts that there is no common approach, or strategy to the delivery of inclusive PE at the official line level. Consequently, there is a need for a much more systematic and cohesive framework of inclusive PE to be developed in which a co-ordinated 'official line' approach is established.

Chapter 6. Results and discussion at the professional opinion and practice level (Stages two and three), Provides a critical overview of how ITT providers prepare trainee PE teachers for the inclusion of children with SEN. This chapter considers the views, opinions, issues, and strategies from the 30 ITT secondary PE providers in England. This is then followed by extensive analysis from 5 selected ITT PE providers who engaged in follow up discussion. The chapter concludes with a summary and critical review of whether inclusive PE is delivered consistently across all ITT courses, and considers the similarities and differences in delivery between one-year PCE and four year undergraduate programmes.

Chapter 7. Results and discussion from the consumer level (stages four and five), Examines the views and opinions of trainee and recently qualified teachers related to the implementation of inclusive PE, and their readiness to teach lessons that meet the needs of children with SEN. The chapter examines the views of trainees in their final year of training, as well as those of recently qualified teachers in schools, and asserts that training experiences, and preparation vary considerably. As a consequence, the chapter concludes by advocating that there is still much work to be done in order to ensure that PE teachers of the future are adequately prepared to deliver inclusive PE for children with SEN.

Chapter 8. Key themes from the five stages pulls together the key themes and issues from the five stages of the research and examines this in the context of the research aims, and discussion from chapters 5, 6 and 7. It analyses whether there is any systematic process of policy through to practice in relation to the training of PE teachers for the inclusion of children with SEN, whilst suggesting a range of strategies to co-ordinate this work better in the future. The chapter concludes with recommendations for future work that needs to be undertaken based upon the research findings, and offers a proposed model for its implementation and delivery.

9

C H A P T E R   O N E :

CONTEXT FOR THE STUDY

In October 1997 the new Labour government launched their green paper on special

needs education, which stated:

> *"We want to see more pupils with special educational needs (SEN) included*
> *within mainstream primary and secondary schools. We support the United*
> *Nations Educational, Scientific and Cultural Organisation (UNESCO)*
> *Salamanca World Statement on Special Needs Education 1994. This calls on*
> *governments to adopt the principle of inclusive education, enrolling all children*
> *in regular schools, unless there are compelling reasons for doing otherwise.*
> *This implies a progressive extension of the capacity of mainstream schools to*
> *provide for children with a wide range of needs" (DFEE 1997a, p44)*

Since the return of the Labour government to power in 1997, the focus on inclusion

has risen up the political and statutory agenda in the United Kingdom (UK) to such an

extent, that there is widespread evidence of policies being embedded across diverse

sectors of society. In education for example, there has been an increased emphasis

on the inclusion of children with SEN through legislation such as the National

Curriculum (NC) (2000) Inclusion Statement (QCA, 1999), SEN and Disability Rights

Act (DFES 2001c) and the Revised Code of Practice (DFES 2001b). In addition the

TTA revised standards for the award of QTS (TTA 2002) and the OFSTED Inspection

Framework (OFSTED 2002) have increased their focus on the scrutiny, competence

and implementation of inclusive education.

Statistical evidence from the DFES (2001c) supports this increased emphasis on

inclusion, and shows year on year rises in the number of children with SEN (i.e.

registered on the Code of Practice) being included within mainstream education

(2001 - 61%, 1997 - 57%, 1993 - 48%). Thus in setting out this context, many

questions related to the readiness of ITT providers to train teachers in schools to deliver this key agenda need to be considered. In addition, there is even greater

pressure for providers and schools to reflect upon these issues because as the NC

(2000) states:

> "... teachers must take action" and "ensure that their pupils are enabled to
> participate" (QCA 1999, p33)

... and be responsive to a diverse range of pupil needs in order to facilitate inclusive

education.

According to Avramadis and Norwich (2002) teachers are recognised as the main

agents of the implementation of inclusive policy and as such:

> "... without a coherent plan for teacher training in the educational needs of
> children with SEN, attempts to include these children in the mainstream would
> be difficult" (Avramadis and Norwich 2002, p139).

Depauw and Doll-Tepper (2000) support this view, and call for agencies such as ITT

providers, schools and teachers to review existing practices, and procedures in order

to provide a systematic approach to this area of their work. However, they question

whether real change will actually occur, or if agencies are merely getting on the

inclusion policy bandwagon, rather than fundamentally reviewing any necessary

adjustment in working practices. Thus, they argue that in order for change to have

impact, ITT providers need to recognise inclusion as a process model in which

associated issues are infused throughout the undergraduate curriculum. Therefore

not merely being addressed at a superficial policy level, but more essentially making

a difference through inclusive delivery in practice.

In order to reflect this shift of emphasis at government level, the recent NC review

(culminating in NC 2000) set out four main priorities, one of which was to ensure that

the curriculum is setting high standards for all pupils including the gifted, talented and

those with SEN. This supports the 1994 Salamanca Statement (UNESCO 1994), which identified a set of beliefs and proclamations relating to the notion that every child has a fundamental right to education. It identified core principles of providing children with the opportunity to learn, an education system designed to take account of diversity, access to regular child centred education and the acceptance of inclusive orientation as a means of combating discrimination and building an inclusive society.

Therefore, through the introduction of recent inclusive legislation within the UK, the notion of education for all, and entitlement, are viewed as central to the government's drive to create a socially inclusive society in which all children are able to participate, learn and reach their full potential. This commitment is underpinned by the statement from the DFES that:

> *"The education of children with special needs is a key challenge for the nation. It is vital to the creation of a fully inclusive society" (DFES 1999 p1)*

1.1 Delivering the Inclusive Agenda

In relation to teacher education, the governments SEN Excellence for All (DFES 1998) document suggests that the educational achievements of pupils with SEN should be delivered through five key action points of: ensuring that high expectations are set for pupils with SEN; providing support to parents; increasing the numbers of pupils with SEN within mainstream; emphasising the need for practical support, rather than procedural guidance; and to promote partnerships in SEN at local, regional and national levels.

Therefore, in regard to how social inclusion is achieved, and the interpretation of its delivery within the curriculum the government introduced 'citizenship' as a curriculum area in its own right from September 2002. According to the NC (1999) handbooks for primary and secondary teachers (QCA 1999b, 1999c), citizenship will be delivered across all four key stages of the curriculum with the intention of facilitating pupils to:

> "... become informed, active, responsible citizens contributing fully to the life of their school communities". (QCA 1999c, p126)

Thus in doing so children will learn about:

> "... their responsibilities, rights and duties as individuals and members of communities" (QCA 1999c, p126)

In interpreting this statement with reference to the inclusion of children with SEN, it appears that the expectation is the establishment of a set of core values that are to be embedded both within the statutory curriculum, and be delivered through proactive strategies by teachers. However, in order to facilitate these processes, teachers need to be given the knowledge and understanding of how to implement this aspect of their work. For example, the definition and interpretation of terminology alone related to the inclusion of children with SEN is often according to Ito (1999) used interchangeably and this adds to potential confusion in the interpretation of the values and principles it is setting out to achieve. The NC (2000) handbook for example, uses the term's disability, inclusion, integration, mainstreaming and SEN within one document, and teachers need to appreciate the differences between these terms and their significance to the wider debate on inclusion. Thus according to Ito (1999), there is a need to place into context how and what the key terms and issues mean in order to clarify appropriate delivery mechanisms, and set about training teachers accordingly to include children with SEN effectively. This belief is further supported by Dyson and Millward (2000) who argue that the:

> "... language which surrounds educational responses to diversity is often confused and conflicting" and "tend to only have the most general meanings unless and until they are defined precisely" (Dyson and Millward 2000, p8)

1.2 Interpreting and Delivering Inclusive Physical Education (PE) For Children With Special Educational Needs (SEN)

The purpose of this study is to examine the inclusion of children with SEN through the subject of secondary PE. In particular it will focus upon the process of training PE teachers to include children with SEN within mainstream settings.

The subject of PE has been at the centre of many changes during the last few years in relation to its recognition, prominence and delivery within the NC. For example, in the primary sector, the introduction of the numeracy and literacy hours in the late 1990's brought about a significant squeeze on the time available for other subjects areas, of which PE is just one of several others. In addition, the implementation of the Key Stage Three Strategy and its focus on English, Maths and Science from September 2002, brings with it similar issues and pressures for PE within the secondary sector. In noting this however, the NC (2000) does advocate an entitlement of two hours physical activity within the school week for all children. This has been further reinforced through the recent 'Game Plan: a strategy for delivering Government's sport and physical activity objectives' (2002). It states that the government:

> "… have prioritised young people, and committed ourselves to ensuring that by 2005, at least 75% of children will have the chance to participate in two hours of high quality sport and PE each week" (DCMS 2002, p5)

Thus through the recent 'Game Plan' objectives' (DCMS 2002) PE and school sport is being viewed as an area to be developed and extended during the coming years. This is being supported with a commitment of:

> "Over £2bn of money from government and the lottery…going into sport over the next three years" (DCMS 2002, p5)

In recognising the current political climate and curriculum pressures of inclusion, and the need to respond to the requirements of citizenship, PE as a subject area has many opportunities to assist in the positive inclusion of children with SEN within mainstream education. However, the critical success factor that lies behind this is the need to review the currency of existing and future training for PE teachers in order that the requirements of the NC (2000) Statutory Inclusion Statement (QCA 1999a) are met. The impact being that ITT providers and agencies involved in the professional development of teachers will have to examine the extent to which their current practices prepare teachers sufficiently for such a high profile aspect of the government and new curriculum's work.

Within this context therefore, the study will look at a main research question of:

"How is the current training of PE teachers for inclusive settings implemented?"

This will be examined in relation to three key areas of policy through to practice. Firstly what is 'the official line' (with respect to professional and statutory agencies), secondly what are the views of teacher training institutions ('professional opinion and practice') and thirdly what is the impact upon the training of PE teachers ('the consumers').

Within each of these three levels of investigation a further sub aim will be examined in relation to the main research question noted above.

1.3   The Official Line

The official line refers to the role and function of both professional (i.e. PE and disability sport associations) and statutory agencies (i.e. government and associated bodies) in relation to the training of PE teachers for the inclusion of children with SEN. This first level of analysis ('The Official Line') sets out to examine the views and policies of the professional PE associations and statutory agencies in regard to their interpretation and implementation of inclusive education. This will be achieved through analysis of agency documentation and policy positions from the DFES, OFSTED, TTA, QCA, BAALPE, PEA(UK) and EFDS.

Through an examination, analysis and review of these agencies literature, areas of commonality and diversity within the official line perspective will be scrutinised. This will be then related to its context, impact and consistency for people at the professional opinion and practice and consumer levels. Thus the sub question at this level is:

"What are the views and policies of government, statutory agencies and PE associations in relation to the delivery of inclusive PE for children with SEN?"

1.3.1 Government and Statutory Agencies

In relation to government and statutory agencies, the four key organisations that impact on the study question are namely the DFES, OFSTED, QCA and the TTA. The DFES acts as the government department:

> *"... established with the purpose of creating opportunity, releasing potential and achieving excellence for all" and "delivers on a range of issues through working closely with other government departments and agencies" (DFES 2002, p1).*

Thus, through a range of legislative and policy-making strategies, they play a central role in setting the agenda for others in the delivery of education, PE and SEN.

In relation to the development, implementation, assessment and relevance of the NC, the QCA acts as:

> *"... a guardian of standards in education and training" and ... "work with others to maintain and develop the school curriculum and associated assessments and to accredit and monitor qualifications in schools" (QCA 2002, p1)*

They are responsible for ensuring that the PE NC meets the needs of all children and reflects the current and future generations needs within society. Therefore they consult widely with others to ensure that the curriculum is both relevant, broad, balanced and in keeping with the requirements of government and wider society.

In the backdrop of teacher training and the inspection of standards, the TTA and OFSTED play central roles within this process. The TTA have responsibility for:

> "... raising standards in schools...and "improving the quality of teacher training and induction for newly qualified teachers" (TTA 2003, p2).

In conjunction with this remit the TTA have established 'Standards for the Award of QTS and recently introduced the National SEN Specialist Standards. The aim being to ensure that teachers are competently prepared through their ITT and future professional development training to maximise the learning and development that takes place with children in schools. In addition, through setting benchmark standards, they seek to ensure that teachers of the future have sufficient training and development opportunities to support children with SEN effectively once they are working in schools.

In contrast, the role of OFSTED is to:

> "... improve the quality of education.. through independent inspection and regulation, and provide advice to the Secretary of State" (OFSTED 2003, p2)

Therefore in the context of the training that takes place in ITT institutions, they are responsible for inspecting and reporting upon the quality and standards of delivery by these providers. Thus in relation to inclusion, the new Framework for Inspection (2002), requires OFSTED to specifically report on the delivery and implementation of aspects of equality of opportunity and inclusion, as well as disseminate any models of best practice that may be observed.

1.3.2 The Professional PE Associations and Disability Sport Organisations

The roles of the professional PE associations and disability sport organisations are central to the successful implementation of the inclusion of children with SEN from policy through to practice levels. Although BAALPE and PEA (UK) do not have any statutory powers and responsibilities their members play a vital role in ensuring that teachers are adequately prepared and supported to deliver the inclusive agenda within PE and school sport. They also play a key role in lobbying government and statutory agencies for effective change or guidance in order to ensure that current educational agendas are sufficiently met. In addition, they seek to produce resources and documentation that will assist their members support children with SEN within mainstream PE.

In contrast, the EFDS aims to:

> "Serve as the main supporting and co-ordinating body for the development of sport for all disabled people" (EFDS 1999, p36).

In working towards this purpose EFDS has the direct support of all major disability sport organisations and aims to; increase the effectiveness of current disability sport structures; promote inclusion within mainstream programmes; access lottery funding; raise the profile of disability sport and create networks and improve communication. Thus they have a central role to play in both lobbying and supporting PE and school sports agencies to deliver the government's inclusion agenda and offer specialist advice, support and guidance to agencies and individuals.

1.4 Professional Opinion and Practice

The second aim, *'Professional Opinion and Practice'*, examines the roles and responsibilities of PE ITT providers in relation to the sub aim of:

"What are the processes and course contents of ITT institutions related to inclusive PE for children with SEN?"

This will consider the analysis of course content, responses to official line documentation and total hours spent on SEN issues. It will also involve an examination of assessment tasks, school experience, underpinning pedagogy, responsibility and delivery mechanisms within departments and work with mentors in school. This scrutiny will be undertaken in the context and recognition that the range of available training to become a secondary PE teacher does vary greatly from four-year undergraduate courses, through to one-year postgraduate provision, and as such the amount of time available and nature of delivery is rather mixed. However, whilst there is a recognised difference in the amount of time in which issues of inclusion can be addressed, it is envisaged that key themes and issues will emerge across the full range of provision. Therefore these themes can then be drawn together in order to provide a picture of the provision that is both available, and necessary to train PE teachers for the inclusion of children with SEN.

In relation to the TTA standards for the award of QTS, the PE ITT providers are responsible for implementing the requirements as set out in the current 2002 framework. This framework, implemented in September 2002 supersedes the previous 10/97 (DFEE 1997c) and 4/98 (DFES 1998a) standards, and has a greater emphasis on issues of inclusion. Thus ITT providers need to ensure that they are both meeting the requirements of the revised standards, and in turn be able to demonstrate that they are preparing PE teachers accordingly. This assessment of whether ITT institutions are meeting the standards and preparing PE teachers for effective delivery of the NC will ultimately be judged through inspection by OFSTED. However, it is worth noting that under the new inspection framework OFSTED are required to consider in more detail aspects of ITT providers preparation of PE teachers to deliver the new inclusive agenda, as well as listen to the views of students in training.

In relation to professional opinion and practice, ITT providers are recognised as playing a central role in ensuring that the PE teachers of the future are adequately prepared to deliver inclusive education. For example in the governments SEN Excellence for All (DFES 1998c) document, one of the aims of the government is to:

> *"... develop the knowledge and skills of staff working with children with SEN"*

... and the programme plans to address this by:

> *"... giving greater emphasis to SEN within teacher training and development"*
> *(DFES 1998c, p7)*

This was further emphasised in December 1999 through the TTA 'National SEN Specialist Standards', which stressed:

> *"The key to unlocking the full potential of pupils in our schools lies in the expertise of teachers and headteachers. Research and inspection evidence demonstrate the close correlation between the quality of teaching and the achievement of pupils" (TTA 1999, p1).*

Thus the document recognises the central role that teachers and schools play, and for the first time began to identify aspects of SEN provision that are needed in order to create expertise and competence within this area of work. The document then goes on to further suggest that:

> *"... all teachers, whether in mainstream schools or in special schools, will need to continue to develop their teaching, pedagogy based on the known features of effective practice in meeting all pupils learning needs" (TTA 1999 p3)*

Thus the need for inclusive education to be based upon recognised research evidence, and an acceptance of a desire to develop teacher's expertise in this area is central to any future success of including children with SEN within PE, and this is central to the purpose of this study.

1.5 The Consumers

As Avramadis and Norwich (2002) advocate, the role of trainee and qualified PE teachers is central to the successful implementation of the government's agenda on inclusive education for children with SEN. Thus in examining any inclusion process at the official line and professional opinion and practice levels, the ultimate success must be judged in terms of the delivery by '**the consumers**' (i.e. the PE teachers). The central feature for the PE teacher is the statement that the NC (2000) is to be inclusive, with the suggestion that the delivery of this will occur through the implementation of three key guiding principles within the Statutory Inclusion Statement. These are to set suitable learning challenges, respond to pupil's diverse needs and differentiate assessment according to individual need.

Thus any effective implementation and delivery of the inclusion statement will rely on the training given to teachers by ITT providers. Therefore, measurement must come through the reflection by teachers that once qualified they feel equipped with the knowledge and understanding to facilitate the inclusion of children with SEN within mainstream PE. Consequently, the sub aim at this level is to examine:

"What are the views and opinions of current student trainees and recently qualified PE teachers related to their training for inclusive education?"

The first principle of the NC Inclusion Statement, 'setting suitable learning challenges', states:

"Teachers should aim to give every pupil the opportunity to experience success in learning and to achieve as high a standard as is possible" (QCA 1999a p32)

This will therefore require PE teachers to adopt flexible teaching and learning approaches and differentiate their lessons according to pupil need. This links to the second aspect of the inclusion statement related to 'responding to pupils diverse learning needs', in which it is stated that:

> "When planning teachers should set high expectations and provide opportunities for all pupils to achieve including…pupils with disabilities and SEN" (QCA 1999a p33).

Thus PE teacher's lessons should be planned to ensure full and effective access, and therefore take specific action to respond to pupils' diverse learning needs. This can be achieved by creating effective learning environments; securing motivation and concentration; providing equality of opportunity through effective teaching approaches and using relevant assessment strategies and targets for learning.

The third principle of the inclusion statement refers to 'overcoming potential barriers to learning and assessment for individuals and groups of pupils' and states:

> "… a minority of pupils will have particular learning and assessment requirements which go beyond the provisions described earlier (sections one and two)" (QCA 1999a, p35)

However, if not addressed this could create barriers to participation and the NC states that this is usually as a consequence of a child's' disability or SEN. Thus, in suggesting methods to overcome potential barriers to participation, the curriculum suggests that in order to create access, greater differentiation on the part of teachers and the use of external agencies or specialist equipment will begin to enable inclusion to occur. Thus teachers need to be equipped with the necessary skills and expertise to facilitate this process to occur.

1.6 Summary

In summary, the three guiding principles within the inclusion statement are fundamental in ensuring that teachers recognise their responsibility of creating accessible lessons that cater for all pupils' needs. However whether this systematic or co-ordinated process is in place remains to be answered within the context of official line policy, professional opinion and practice and ultimately delivery and implementation by the consumers. Therefore in order to examine the issues related to the training of PE teachers for the inclusion of children with SEN within mainstream settings, an analysis of the process from policy through to practice will be undertaken.

This analysis will be undertaken within the context of the chapters outlined earlier within the preface and the re-stated questions set out below:

Main Question:
"How is the current training of PE teachers for inclusive settings implemented?"

Sub Questions:
"What are the views and policies of government, statutory agencies and PE associations in relation to the delivery of inclusive PE for children with SEN?"

"What are the processes and course contents of initial teacher training institutions related to inclusive PE for children with SEN?"

"What are the views and opinions of current student trainees and recently qualified PE teachers related to their training for inclusive education?"

C H A P T E R   T W O :
EDUCATION, SPECIAL EDUCATION &
INITIAL TEACHER TRAINING

PART ONE
THE EMERGENCE OF STANDARDS IN
INITIAL TEACHER TRAINING

2.1.1   Introduction: The Gatekeepers of Teacher Training

The first part of this chapter (part one) examines the changing nature and direction

that ITT has taken over recent years, and the emergence of standards for the award

of QTS. It considers the impact of policy, and legislation developed by agencies such

as the DFES, whilst considering how such directives are implemented, monitored

and evaluated in conjunction with the TTA, OFSTED and PE teacher training

providers. The chapter concludes with an overview of the present QTS standards in

ITT, and examines the specific roles, responsibilities and relationships of the

agencies noted above in relation to their potential to equip teachers of PE to include

children with SEN. According to Trend (1997):

> *"Most professions have their 'gatekeepers', organisations which control entry*
> *into the profession. They have their own distinctive ways of ensuring that new*
> *entrants are able to work at an appropriately high standard. (Trend 1997, p7)*

In the teaching profession the 'gatekeepers' of the profession can be viewed as the

dual responsibility of the DFES and TTA, who (through ITT providers) train teachers

in partnership with schools. Through this multi-agency approach, monitored by

OFSTED, QTS is finally awarded by the DFES. In order to be eligible for QTS status

however, individuals must satisfy the appropriate standards for such an award to be

bestowed upon them.

There is no doubt that over the last few years teaching in schools, and teacher training has become subject to more regulation, monitoring and review than ever before. This has emanated in part from the implementation of the PE NC (QCA 1999a), which emerged as a result of the 1988 Education Reform Act (DOE 1988), through which significant forms of prescription have been placed upon what teachers must deliver at each Key Stage, and within each activity area. In addition through the appearance and increasing influence of agencies such as the TTA and OFSTED, and the implementation of 'standards' for the award of QTS, there is now a more dogmatic approach within which training agencies and trainee PE teachers must now demonstrate their competence. This drive to create standards against set criteria, is following a similar pattern to the governments agenda within schools under the banner of 'school improvement'.

The ever-increasing pressures brought to bear by the government, go back as early as 1984 and Circular 3/84 (DES 1984) which recommended experienced teachers in schools share more of the training responsibility for ITT, as well as the requirement that trainee teachers spend greater time in schools during their training. In conjunction with this announcement, the Council for Accreditation of Teacher Education was established with a remit to review existing course provision and delivery. Since this time, further scrutiny has emerged on the process and practice of teacher training, culminating in the development of the TTA who took over responsibility for teacher training in 1995.

Since Circular 3/84 (DES 1984), there have been several further revisions of the requirements of ITT, through Circulars 24/89 (DES 1989), 9/92 (DES 1992), 14/93 (DES 1993), 10/97 (DFEE 1997c) (DFE 1997b), 4/98 (DFES 1998a) (DFEE 1998a) and now the current 'Professional Standards Framework' (TTA 2002), implemented in September 2002. Each of these changes has brought with it greater regulation and scrutiny both internally by ITT providers, and externally through agencies such as

OFSTED, TTA and the DFES. In fact in recognising the high level of prescription and unprecedented degree of control of ITT, the University Council for the Education of Teachers (UCET) (1997), stated:

"The language used in these documents is steely and uncompromising"
(UCET 1997a, p3)

Consequently, the intention was to provide a strong steer with regard to the manner in which ITT was to be implemented in the future. However, the extent to which this message was clear, systematic, rigorous and part of a multi-agency approach is in need of further analysis.

The key issue in the context of this study therefore, is to examine the role that government and statutory agencies have played in supporting PE teachers to deliver policy objectives that strongly advocate inclusion, as well as assisting them to gain the necessary professional standards for the award of QTS. The DFES SEN Programme of Action (1998) suggests for example, the government:

"... is committed to ensuring that all teachers have the training and support
they need to do their job well and are confident to deal with a wide variety of
SEN" (DFES 1998b, p3)

As a consequence, as policies and legislation change in relation to ITT and SEN, teachers through their training, induction and continuing professional development must be equipped with the necessary skills and support mechanisms to implement such policies effectively.

The DFES 'Schools Achieving Success' (2001a) document, suggests that the Department will help schools to meet the needs of children with SEN through a commitment to inclusion and a recognition of the responsibility placed upon teachers to enable such practice to occur. According to Rose (1998), the central issue of concern is the extent to which ITT providers are helping teachers with the practical skills to deliver policy objectives that strongly advocate inclusion. Thus, the dual

pressure of significant recognition of inclusion within the current 02/02 (TTA 2002)

standards in tandem with increasing scrutiny of professional standards within ITT

brings an acknowledgement that:

> "... effective teaching depends on working well with everyone who has a stake
> in the education of our children" (TTA, 2001a, p1).

As a result, the need for gatekeeper agencies to work effectively together and

provide a clear and consistent message for teacher training and school improvement

is essential - especially if teachers are to be adequately equipped to deliver inclusive

PE to children with SEN.

2.1.2 Government Legislation and Regulation Linked to SEN and Teachers

Historically the UK government has supported, and maintained through legislation

and policies a significant infrastructure of segregated schools. However, there is a

long established tradition of encouraging mainstream schools to make some form of

provision that was recognisably 'special', and guidance has been offered as to what

this provision should consist of. It is not only in ITT that government has set out

policies, but over many years conventional expectations for the provision of schooling

to children with SEN have been apparent. These conventions will be considered

briefly here, prior to more extensive examination in part two of this chapter. It is worth

noting these changes to SEN policy in the context of ITT here, as any changing

educational policy in schools will have an impact on the manner in which teachers

need to be trained to meet the changing agendas of the particular government of the

time. In addition, many of the gatekeeper agencies such as the TTA, OFSTED and

DFES have dual roles to play both within ITT and school improvement related to a

wide range of issues, of which is inclusion is just one element. Therefore, they must consider the impact that policy directives have in both ITT and school based contexts for preparing teachers for inclusion.

Since the emergence of the first significant (in terms of SEN) piece of educational legislation with the 1944 Education Act (DES 1944), it is only in more recent times through introduction of the NC (QCA 1999a) and the 02/02 (TTA 2002) standards for the award of QTS that some synergy of policy in education in schools, and education in ITT related to inclusion has begun to emerge. Thus, in order for the government's inclusion agenda to become a reality in schools, there is a need to ensure that the policies and agendas of respective 'official line' agencies work in tandem, to complement, rather than work against, each other. For example, as the NC (2000) increased its emphasis on SEN through the Statutory Inclusion Statement, this should also be reflected in an increased emphasis within ITT standards.

The 1944 Education Act (DOE 1944) was the first piece of legislation that established separate schooling for pupils of different aptitudes and abilities. These were established through separate forms of special education with different types of schools, for different forms of disability related to a total of eleven medically defined categories of handicap. (Fredrickson and Cline 2002) However, the act placed a duty on Local Education Authorities (LEA) of the time to ascertain the needs of children with SEN, and anticipated that treatment in many cases may be best served in mainstream education.

The reality for many teachers training to work in mainstream schools however was that the issue of disability, handicap, and the education of such children were rarely addressed. At the time this was seen as the role of special school teachers, who had the knowledge to work with such pupils, rather than see them educated alongside their non disabled peers, where mainstream teachers were ill equipped to support them. This situation remained largely the same until the publication of the Warnock

Report in 1978 (DES 1978), which acknowledged that around 18% of school pupils could be expected to have special needs, and reinforced that the majority of these needs should be met in the mainstream. This change in policy, culminating in the 1981 Education Act (DES, 1981), in which 'statementing' (a formal process of identifying, assessing and supporting a child with SEN) was introduced, brought more mainstream teachers into contact with children with SEN. In conjunction with this requirement, there was no formal ITT stipulation for teachers to be trained to support this goal. Consequently, as more children with SEN integrated into mainstream schools, few if any teachers or training providers had spent time adequately considering the needs of these children. As a result, the changing policy directives reflected in schools, were not being developed alongside changes in ITT provision, thus demonstrating a distinct lack of co-ordination and multi-agency working.

In 1994, the Code of Practice on the Identification and Assessment of Children with SEN (DES, 1994) was introduced which brought with it designation of clear roles and responsibilities that schools must adopt in order to support children with SEN. This has since been replaced by the new Code of Practice (DFES 2001b), which takes account of the SEN and Disability Act (DFES 2001c) and puts a stronger emphasis on children with SEN being educated in the mainstream. In addition, rights of statutory assessment and duties on local education authorities to arrange services to support parents and help resolve any matters of conflict were further emphasised. Thus, with the increasing emphasis of inclusion being placed upon schools, the need to ensure teachers were given the appropriate training in ITT is self evident, and this began to be reflected (although only minimally) in the 4/98 (DFES 1998a) standards for the award of QTS which will be consider later in this chapter.

In support of this position, the UCET (1997) response to the government SEN green paper in 1997 stated that:

*"There is some evidence from research and OFSTED reports that pupils
benefit where teachers are trained in SEN. We recommend that there is a need
for research into their training needs for successful inclusion" (UCET 1997b p2)*

In addition, Ainscow et al (1999) suggest:

*"The government green paper 'Excellence for All Children: Meeting SEN'
places the issue of inclusion at the centre of discussions on the development of
policy and practice for pupils with special needs" (Ainscow et al 1999 p9).*

Thus, the need for government educational policy within schools to match the ITT

policy can be seen as a critical success factor in ensuring that the needs of children

with SEN in mainstream schools are adequately met. This further strengthened the

need for agencies such as DFES, OFSTED, TTA, and ITT providers to work together

within a cohesive framework to support PE teachers to deliver inclusion for children

with SEN.

2.1.3   Implementing Teacher Training and SEN Policy in Practice – A Multi Agency Approach to a Multi Agency Challenge for PE Teachers?

The DFES 'Schools Achieving Success' (2001) states:

*"We will not rest until we have a truly world class education system that meets
the needs of every child. Whatever it takes" (DFES 2001a, p7)*

The government seek to realise this desire by aiming to:

*"... develop multi-agency working. Too often different support agencies do not
work effectively together" (DFES 2001a, p22)*

The government, DFES and agencies like the TTA and OFSTED, play a critical role

in ensuring that partnership, collaboration and joined up thinking are fostered in order

to ensure that future generations of PE teachers are equipped to deliver the governments objective of a truly world class education system, which includes

meeting fully the needs of children with SEN.

Specifically in relation to children with SEN in school contexts, the DFES have stated

that:

> "... a framework will be developed to measure the effectiveness of school and
> LEA programmes for raising standards for children with special needs"
> (DFES 2001a, p22)

The DFES will seek to implement this through the development of benchmark

standards and performance tools to compare attainment, so mainstream and special

schools can evaluate how they are doing in relation to other schools. However, whilst

this brings with it further regulation and monitoring of schools, it does give all

stakeholders the opportunity to measure the extent to which progress is being made

to support children with SEN.

The government suggest that in regard to the formal assessment of benchmark

standards:

> "Ofsted inspection will look at schools development of inclusive practice"
> (DFES, 2001a p22)

They will report upon their findings and advise on the quality of delivery and assist in

the preparation of future policy direction, for the government and TTA, in relation to

inclusive schools and the process by which this can be achieved. It was originally

through Circular 3/93 (Higher Education Funding Council for England, 1993) that

responsibility for monitoring quality in ITT moved to the remit of OFSTED. It then

commenced a role of scrutiny and examination of standards through an inspection

framework that began to make judgements on whether trainees were meeting fully

the standards, and that the training received was adequate.

In tandem with school based inspections, OFSTED play a central role in the examination of how ITT providers prepare PE teachers of the future, and the extent to which they are ready once qualified to facilitate inclusive schooling for children with SEN. This dual approach of inspection in ITT, and schools places OFSTED in a strategic position to focus upon all aspects of the inclusion process for children with SEN. As a result, this should assist with the ability to evaluate a range of perspectives, and judge the extent to which there are gaps in current training, as well as ensure that teachers of PE are effectively trained to deliver an inclusive education for children with SEN.

In relation to school inspection, OFSTED believes:

> "An educationally inclusive school is one in which the teaching and learning, achievements, attitudes and well being of every young person matter. Effective schools are educationally inclusive schools. This shows not only in their performance, but also in their ethos and their willingness to offer new opportunities to pupils who have experienced difficulties" (OFSTED 2002 p4).

Therefore, in relation to school contexts, OFSTED will consider whether all pupils get a fair deal, how well schools recognise and overcome barriers to learning, and whether the schools values embrace inclusion and promote it openly and proactively. In addition, they will look at the extent to which teachers have taken account of the three principles of the NC Inclusion Statement, and consider, from an ITT perspective whether trainees, and training providers are meeting the QTS standards to ensure inclusive schooling for children with SEN. This therefore emphasises that OFSTED are well placed to make judgements on the level to which teachers are equipped to deliver inclusion from their inspection visits to schools. As a consequence, if patterns or gaps begin to emerge, they can focus attention were appropriate on the need for ITT provision to be modified and or make recommendations to the TTA to strengthen aspects of SEN within the QTS standards frameworks.

2.1.4 Support Mechanisms for Trainee & Qualified PE Teachers

In looking to support teachers both during training, and once working in schools, various agencies responsible for teacher training have over time published documents to ensure that trainees are sufficiently equipped and prepared to meet the demands of the teaching profession. For example, the development and revision of standards for the awards of QTS, have emerged out of several government circulars, (3/84, 24/89, 9/92, 14/93, 10/97, 4/98 (DFES 1998a)) and have culminated in the current 02/02 'Professional Standards Framework' (TTA 2002). The intention and rationale for further prescription of standards for teacher training in part came out of a desire by the TTA to look at a full codification of training expectations and monitor these through OFSTED. Pring (1996) however, identifies three historical weaknesses of the training process delivered by ITT providers and sees this also as a direct consequence of why there is ever-increasing central intervention and more prescription emerging under the revised QTS standards frameworks. Pring argues therefore, that due to ITT providers being perceived to have not sufficiently responded to the changing nature and demands in schools, questions over the relevance of training by the gatekeeper agencies began to emerge, resulting in a shift towards standardisation of training expectations.

According to Pring (1996), increased regulation emerged in part due to ITT provider's philosophical defects in educational theory, political bias of educational theorists, and the irrelevance of theoretical training to professional practice. Thus it was envisaged that in establishing a series of expectations of ITT providers, teachers would be broadly prepared to meet the diverse needs of children and school environments that they may work in. However, as noted earlier the 'expectations' (UCET 1997a) can be perceived as rather restrictive and over bearing, and as result minimise the flexibility of ITT providers to make their own judgements upon the context within which trainee

33

teachers would be trained. Thus, whilst prescription may bring with it greater

regulation and constraints placed upon the ITT provider, the TTA would argue that

through the standards for the award of QTS, and the requirements placed upon ITT:

> "NQT's (newly qualified teachers) are increasingly well prepared for teaching"
> demonstrated by OFSTED evidence each year on classroom performance"
> (TTA 2001b, p3)

Consequently, the TTA are:

> "... seeking to make sure that, at entry to the profession, each new teacher has
> a good foundation of knowledge and understanding, is able to perform as a
> skilled teacher and can operate within a clear framework of professional values
> and practice" (TTA 2001b, p5)

The current 02/02 'Professional Standards Framework' (TTA 2002) for the award of

QTS, for example, are based around:

> "... outcome statements that set out what a trainee teacher must know
> understand and be able to do to be awarded QTS" (TTA 2002, p2)

The standards are organised in three inter-related sections, which describe the

criteria for the award under which training should take place, which are:

Professional Values and Practice
... the foundation of teacher attitudes and commitment;

Knowledge and Understanding
... shaping of values to be experts in their field of study;

Teaching
... relating to planning, teaching strategies, monitoring,
assessment, class management and inclusion

In setting out these standards for the award of QTS, the TTA argue that they provide:

> "... a rigorous set of expectations and set out a minimum legal requirement ..."
> (TTA 2002, p3)

... through which training must be undertaken. In addition, the TTA acknowledge that in some instances training providers may wish to also provide additional training in specialist areas such as the teaching of children with SEN. Therefore, the TTA suggest some providers may wish to extend their provision and offer specialisms in SEN, however there is no set criteria or expectation as to what this should contain.

The background to the DFES and TTA establishing standards emerged from the DFES publication 'Teaching: High Status, High standards Circular 9/97- (DEE 1997c) Requirements for Courses of Initial Teacher Training'. This established the criteria under which all courses of ITT must be delivered. In relation to specific training requirements placed upon providers and trainee teachers related to SEN, the first significant recognition came through the DFES (1998) SEN Excellence for All publication. This stated that government planned to give:

> "greater emphasis to SEN within teacher training and development" (DFES 1998c, p6)

However on further examination of this, the DFES suggest this policy objective will be delivered at the time through the 4/98 (DFES 1998a) (and now subsequent 02/02 (TTA 2002)) Standards in ITT. Therefore, within the standards, providers were expected to equip teachers in certain aspects of SEN, particularly related to the Code of practice and individual education plans. However there was little consideration of trainee teachers having to demonstrate any evidence and application of this knowledge.

In addition to the standards for the award of QTS acknowledging the need for trainee teachers to be trained in aspects of SEN and inclusion, the TTA began to develop materials to assist schools to develop their specialist knowledge of this area as well. This culminated in the development of the TTA National SEN Specialist Standards (TTA 1999), which were designed as an audit tool to help teachers and head teachers identify specific training and development needs related to the effective teaching of SEN. The TTA state within the National SEN Specialist Standards:

> "As the governments intention to increase opportunities for pupils with severe and or complex SEN to be educated within mainstream school is realised, teachers will need a basic understanding of the range of SEN to be found in most mainstream classes, and more teachers in mainstream schools require the knowledge, understanding and skills to work effectively with pupils with severe and or complex SEN" (TTA 1999, Point 9 p3)

In support of this view, the SEN Excellence for All (DFES 1998) fourth action point is of particular relevance to teacher training in that the document specifically states its intentions to:

> "... develop the knowledge and skills of staff working with children with SEN"
> (DFES 1998c, p4)

As a result, in order to ensure all teachers have the training and support they need to do their job well, and are confident to deal with a wide range of SEN a clearer strategy position was beginning to be formulated. Since this time, further publications have arisen such as the Centre for Studies in Inclusive Education (2000) 'Index for Inclusion', which provides schools with a framework to audit existing practices and plan for the development of fully inclusive cultures within schools. However, the extent to which the various gatekeeper agencies (i.e. TTA, OFSTED and DFES) have come together to share strategy, and jointly plan for expectations on implementation and delivery of inclusion for children with SEN is unclear. As a consequence, this issue will be examined as part of the analysis of 'official line' policy within the study.

2.1.5 The Teacher Training Process From Day One, Through ITT, Award of QTS, Induction and Lifelong Continuing Professional Development

The TTA acknowledges the teaching profession is based upon 'reflective practice', and a recognition that teacher's knowledge and understanding, develops and grows over a lifetime of work with children. As a consequence, in relation to teachers of PE, it is important to recognise that training in inclusive education for children with SEN must involve several agencies working together in partnership to ensure that learning and development processes work effectively. For example, as soon as trainee PE teachers are enrolled onto a course of ITT, their work with training providers and their professional education begins to develop and grow alongside the experiences they gain during school-based experiences. These vital formative stages of a trainee's education are crucial in ensuring that under the guidance, mentoring and scrutiny by the TTA, OFSTED and DFES, their understanding of the needs of children with SEN are moulded to a stage in which they are equipped to enter the teaching profession.

This staged learning and development of trainees is judged in terms of whether they satisfy the requirements for QTS status. Once this has been established, they then begin the 'induction year' in schools. This model of agencies working together recognises the different roles indicated by Depauw and Doll-Tepper (2000) with regard to ensuring inclusion is 'infused' throughout the undergraduate curriculum. In addition, it particularly recognises the vital role in which the gatekeeper agencies link into the provision delivered by ITT providers. Thus demonstrating some evidence of official line policy feeding into professional opinion and practice.

The induction year is an opportunity to build and extend upon the training received in ITT, and assist with NQT's transition towards becoming an experienced teacher. The TTA (2002) suggest:

This process of 'career entry profiles', and 'induction years' demonstrates another vital link between professional opinion and practice and the consumers as teachers in schools.

However, the training process does not end here and teachers will have many opportunities to undertake continuing professional development within their career lifetime, and as such need to be encouraged to undertake these where available. With this in mind, there is some limited evidence of specific courses relating to the inclusion of children with SEN in PE now being delivered by agencies such as the EFDS, Youth Sport Trust and some ITT providers. These courses have to some extent been funded by the DFES or the TTA, which further indicates an emerging link between policy makers, ITT providers, schools and teachers as part of continuing professional development.

2.1.6   Achieving the Standards for Qualified Teacher Status (QTS) and Supporting the Development of Teachers Knowledge and Understanding of SEN in Schools

The DFES publication 'Teaching: High Status, High standards Circular 9/97, suggests:

"To raise the standards we expect of schools and pupils, we must raise the standards we expect of new teachers" (DFEE 1997c, p3)

Thus by establishing what were described as a full and detailed codification of training and competency requirements (4/98 (DFES 1998a) and the recent 02/02 (TTA 2002) standards), it was envisaged student trainees would be given a thorough grounding in all aspects of the teaching profession. The document suggests prior to teachers taking responsibility for their own classes, new teachers will have had to prove their ability in:

> "... wide range of knowledge, understanding and skills including effective teaching and assessment methods, classroom management, discipline and subject knowledge" (DFEE 1997c, p3)

According to the TTA:

> "The standards themselves are the criteria against which those seeking QTS must be judged, and those who assess trainees for QTS must satisfy themselves that all the standards have been met" (TTA, 2001a p2).

However, measurement of whether trainee teachers have met the standards is according to OFSTED, a matter of professional judgement, which leaves interpretation open to some discussion. In relation to aspects of knowledge and understanding of SEN during training, OFSTED and the TTA do offer some direction, by suggesting they are seeking for trainees to demonstrate amongst other things; the core pedagogical skills of interactive teaching, differentiation and assessment of learning, and support for pupils with a diverse range of needs.

The TTA SEN Subject Specialist Standards (TTA 1999) advocate that the 4/98 (DFES 1998a) (and now subsequent 02/02 (TTA 2002)) standards will be the main vehicle for measuring competence within ITT. They argue that as more children with SEN enter mainstream:

> "more teachers in mainstream schools will require the knowledge, understanding and skills to work effectively with pupils" (TTA 1999, point 9, p3).

It goes on to suggest:

> "... all teachers, whether in mainstream schools or in special schools, will need to continue to develop their teaching, pedagogy based on the known features

of effective practice in meeting all pupils learning needs" (TTA, 1999, point 10, p3)

In relation to outcomes of the training process, Cheminas (2000) notes that under the new Code of Practice for SEN (DFES 2001b) implemented in 2002, comes an expectation that OFSTED will have a responsibility to inspect and report upon:

"... the impact of the schools strategies for promoting inclusion" (Cheminas 2000, p52)

In addition Cheminas (2000) notes that in evaluating inclusion within schools, OFSTED will be ensuring that the training teachers receive in ITT is effective once they come to teach in schools.

Thus, OFSTED inspections of the future although based in one educational setting (i.e. school or ITT provider), will look to examine both the ITT and school delivery aspects of inclusion for children with SEN. This indicates recognition that both aspects of this process must work in synchrony if the inclusion agenda is to be fully met.

Through the 4/98 (DFES 1998a), and now 02/02 (TTA 2002) standards, the DFES, TTA and OFSTED have firmly supported the policy that, by establishing standards for NQT's, this will help raise competence. However questions still remain as to the extent of student trainee's knowledge relating to SEN, and the appropriateness of the standards that have been identified as essential pre-requisites prior to qualifying. Therefore, whilst standards give the general area to be developed, it is a matter of professional judgement by the ITT provider and schools as to how this is achieved, and the extent to which competence has been attained. In addition, there is much debate around the use of terms such as 'competence' and how this can be clearly demonstrated, interpreted and evidenced within ITT programmes (Dyson 2001).

Thus whilst there is some formal grading of students against a rating scale, the competence factor is a matter of judgement for ITT providers and schools to judge. However, this is subject to some scrutiny through OFSTED inspection.

The next part of this chapter will now turn to an examination of the two most recent frameworks of standards within which inclusion began to be recognised, namely the 4/98 (DFES 1998a) and 02/02 (TTA 2002) 'Professional Standards Framework' (TTA 2002)s for the award of QTS. In particular it will focus upon how aspects of SEN and inclusion are embedded within the recent 'Professional Standards Framework' (TTA 2002)s, whilst examining the roles that the gatekeeper agencies play in ensuring that teachers of PE are prepared to deliver inclusive PE.

2.1.7   The 4/98 Standards for the Award of QTS

In July 1998, after consultation with a wide range of agencies OFSTED and the TTA published a framework for the assessment of quality and standards in ITT. The purpose was that the revised framework would reflect new requirements from the DFES related to the 4/98 (DFES 1998a) standards for the award of QTS, whilst considering the experience of OFSTED in using the previous 10/97 (DFEE 1997c) standards documentation to inspect ITT provision. In addition, the standards needed to reflect some of the recent changes in educational philosophy since the return of the Labour government to power in 1997.

The framework for the assessment of quality and standards in ITT (1998) suggests that in undertaking such a review TTA and OFSTED are:

> "... required to have regard to inspection evidence and other quality
> assessments provided by HMCI (Her Majesty's Chief Inspector) or other
> assessments by the TTA" (TTA 1998a, p3)

Thus, the 4/98 (DFES 1998a) framework was used by the TTA to:

Monitor compliance of the Secretary of States recommendations

Set ITT targets – linking OFSTED grades to increased numbers in ITT institutions

Publish annual reports

Address weaknesses in provision

Seek to improve standards of delivery by ITT

Address the government's agenda on inclusion and diversity in education

In meeting this agenda, the 4/98 (DFES 1998a) standards resulted in identification of over 60 standards against which an NQT was expected to demonstrate competence across four key aspects of training namely:

Classroom management – The ability to manage pupils and classroom environments

Teaching and learning – Pedagogical practices

Assessment monitoring and reporting – The ability to make effective judgements on pupils learning and plan for future developments

Other professional standards – wider roles within the school and general professional expectations

In examining the standards with regard to inclusion, SEN was only mentioned explicitly twice, and related to issues of planning, and teaching and class management. The standards stated that student trainees had to demonstrate competence in (i) the identification of pupils who have SEN, and (ii) be familiar with the Code of Practice and the role that Individual Educational Plans play. Therefore, whilst other standards could be linked in general terms to SEN, the implicit rather than explicit nature does lead to the potential for the issues of inclusion and SEN to be marginalised alongside the many other requirements placed upon ITT providers. As a result, the 4/98 (DFES 1998a) standards tended to relate to the theory of SEN, and only required trainees to demonstrate knowledge and understanding on general principles and processes, rather than the application of them in practice. Thus for trainees it would be easy to 'tick a box' and suggest that they understand what the Code of Practice is, however they would not have to demonstrate any underpinning appreciation of the philosophy, values or ethos that lies behind such policies. Consequently many trainees within their evidence of standards would submit a copy of an Individual Education Plan or the Code of Practice, but not be required to analyse the context behind this process, or evidence the extent to which they are equipped to support children with SEN.

In conjunction with the 4/98 (DFES 1998a) standards, the DFES produced a document entitled the 'SENCO' (Special Educational Needs Co-ordinator) Guide (1997) aimed at giving support to practising and specialist teachers working with children with SEN. This does begin with the 4/98 (DFES 1998a) standards, and the Code of Practice (DFES 2001c), to offer some specific SEN guidance and particularly supports the notion of multi agency working and offers practical advice in relation to; developing the role of the SENCO, preparing Individual Education Plans and the drawing up of a SEN policy. Consequently to a limited extent a pattern was beginning to emerge from the 4/98 (DFES 1998a) standards in which SEN was beginning to be recognised as an essential aspect of a trainee teacher's preparation for work in schools. Furthermore the development of documentation by the DFES (SENCO guide, and Code of Practice) began to see some synergy of policy emerging.

2.1.8   The 02/02 'Professional Standards Framework' for the Award of QTS

OFSTED aims to: "... *promote high standards in ITT and contribute to raising standards in schools" (OFSTED 2002, p2).*

In addition, it aims to provide a basis for consistency, fairness and validity in ITT inspection and consequently seeks to allow providers to prepare for inspections and work with inspectors to ensure the smooth running of the inspection process as well as support providers self evaluation of their programmes. As a consequence, in relation to the development of professional standards in teacher training, the joint TTA/OFSTED (2001) 'Inspection Arrangements for ITT' note:

> "Inspection remains a spur to the improvement of quality" (TTA/OFSTED 2001, p1)

The main purpose of the inspection of ITT is to ensure public accountability for the quality of ITT, stimulate continuous improvement, provide objective judgement, inform policy, maintain statutory links between funding and quality and check compliance with statutory requirements. Therefore, the TTA, with help from OFSTED aim to work together to develop improvement strategies that identify and disseminate successful practice, monitor policy implementation, identity specific areas of intervention and encourage successful providers to help others.

Therefore, as part of the new OFSTED inspection framework and in conjunction with the 02/02 (TTA 2002) 'Professional Standards Framework' (TTA 2002), OFSTED will consider as part of their scrutiny process five critical aspects of the ITT process namely:

> **Training and assessment quality** – Examining the provision of ITT and how quality is measured and reviewed

> **Standards achieved by trainees** – Focusing on the outcomes and levels of competence achieved by trainees

> **Trainee entry requirements** – Quality and nature of students who enter the profession to train as teachers

> **Management of the ITT partnership** – focusing upon the crucial links between the ITT provider and schools

Quality assurance processes – *Management and quality of the ITT process incorporating official line (gatekeepers) policy, ITT provision, school and trainee delivery and support*

The judgement will be made by OFSTED against the criteria above in terms of a grade ranging from, 'A' (very good), to 'E' (not compliant with requirements). In noting these grade bandings, it is worth acknowledging that in the latest publication of OFSTED inspection results (2003), only one of over 30 PE ITT providers achieved a grade 'A' status, so there is still much work to be done in relation to meeting these standards.

The new 02/02 'Professional Standards Framework' (TTA 2002) has reduced the number of standards from over 60 to now just over 43 aspects that trainees must fulfil. This is not to say however, that there is now less 'prescription', as under the new framework, standards have been made much clearer and explicit in terms of establishing the requirements for the award of QTS. The new framework sets out clear standards and expectations in relation to a range of key aspects of the training process delivered through trainee teachers, ITT providers and schools. These expectations will be met through consideration of:

Trainee Entry Requirements
ITT providers must satisfy themselves that entrants possess the appropriate personal and intellectual qualities to be a teacher

Training and Assessment
Scrutiny of the content, structure and delivery of training

Management of the ITT partnership
Working in partnership with schools

Quality Assurance
Ensuring that provision complies with current requirements for ITT set out by the Secretary of State

In developing a much clearer yet concise range of expectations for trainees, training providers and schools, the TTA (2002) aimed to:

"… establish a common framework of expectations…to promote the highest professional standards for everyone coming into the teaching profession"
(TTA 2002a, p1)

In relation to the new standards, more now relate specifically to SEN, or require trainees to:

"demonstrate that a trainee teacher has met standards relating to inclusion"
(TTA, 2002, p4)

For example trainees must now demonstrate evidence of:

High expectations – Of all pupils including those with SEN

Promotion of positive values

Understand their responsibilities under the Code of Practice

Differentiate teaching – responding to a diverse range of learning needs

Recognise and respond to equal opportunity issues

This begins to address some of the concerns noted with the 4/98 (DFES 1998a) Standards which were at the time not addressing underpinning philosophy and application of aspects of work in SEN. Therefore, if more recognition of SEN issues and inclusion are now being reflected in the standards it will encourage ITT providers to focus more on this aspect of their delivery with trainees and through schools.

2.1.9 Summary: The Role of Higher Education in the Development of the Subject of SEN

An examination of the development and implementation of the DFES standards framework has reinforced the significance of the role of ITT providers to the successful delivery and implementation of the government's inclusion agenda for children with SEN. The standards can be viewed as the medium through which government policy is responded to and delivered in to schools by the future generation of teachers. ITT providers need to consider therefore the extent to which they are currently in a position to impart this knowledge transfer to trainee teachers. The 1997 'TTA Survey of Special Educational Needs Training Provided by Higher Education' survey for example, aimed to review the current provision for the training of teachers within higher education and offered guidance for the future planning and development needs of various aspects of SEN. This survey was the first of its kind to audit existing provision, and focused on a total of 73 institutions, which were surveyed across five areas of their work. These focused upon; outlines of SEN provision, course structures and content, staffing profiles and areas of expertise, monitoring and evaluation of training provided and current SEN led research. From the key findings, it is evident that institutions offered a diverse range of content related to the training of teachers for the inclusion of children with SEN within mainstream settings. However, although the research was not specific to PE, many training providers were beginning to establish strategies to support the development of further work related to generic aspects of SEN.

In relation to PE and SEN, there is still much work to be done in co-ordinating an overview of existing strategies and provision within this area. Training providers and PE teachers need to evaluate the extent to which their existing practices do offer children entitlement and accessibility to the curriculum, particularly as this is now subject to analysis by OFSTED under the new inspection arrangements, as well as scrutiny by the DFES and TTA through statutory and non-statutory guidance. As a consequence whilst many of the frameworks are now in place to ensure SEN and inclusion is addressed, the next stage is for the stakeholders at official line, professional opinion and practice and consumer levels to now work together to make inclusive practice a reality.

PART TWO
Special Needs Education: Past, Present & Future Directions

2.2.1 Introduction

Part two of this chapter maps the history of special needs education from the position of segregation and isolation, through to the emergence, development and future directions of the inclusion movement of today. It examines how legislation and policy directions have transformed special education, and the impact upon children, teachers and schools. The evolvement of terminology and language will also be analysed, with particular reference to its principles and implementation in practice.

The development of special needs education has over time produced a complex picture within which several competing theories have contributed to the modern day 'inclusive' stance. Norwich (2002a) for example, argues:

> *"There is no logical purity in education", (Norwich 2002a, p483) rather there is 'Ideological impurity', in which no single value or principle encompasses all of what is considered worthwhile. As a result, there needs to be recognition of a range of "multiple values" (Norwich 2002a, p483) through which a series of inter-related concepts and ideologies are acknowledged as contributing to contemporary views on inclusion for children with SEN.*

This rather convoluted analysis of developments, definitions and interpretations of inclusion is further acknowledged by authors such as Ainscow et al 1999, Ballard 1997, Barton 1997, Croll and Moses 2000, Dyson 1999, Dyson and Millward 2000, Fredrickson and Cline 2002.

2.2.2 The Context and Emergence of Inclusion

Dyson and Millward (2000) suggest the government Green Paper on SEN (DFES 1997a) was the first time that the UK government had avowedly committed itself to creating an inclusive education system. This was significant in that it indicated a commitment by the government to two central themes. Firstly, it:

> "... signalled an intention to shake special needs provision out of the somewhat complacent state in which, it is arguable, it had rested for the past two decades" (Dyson and Millward 2000, p1)

For example, since the introduction of the Warnock Report in 1978 (DES 1978), culminating in the 1981 Education Act (DES 1981), the notion of children with SEN moving from special into mainstream schools was largely taken for granted. Progress during the period from 1978 to 1997 was in Dyson and Millward's (2000) view ad-hoc, in that it supported integration, but gave no firm steer to how LEA's should implement this. This is broadly in line with policy developments in ITT which prior to the 4/98 (DFES 1998a) and 02/02 'Professional Standards Framework' (TTA 2002), guidance was given through a series of government circulars (i.e. 3/84, 24/89, 9/92, 10/97, but with no firm instructions in relation to SEN. Consequently, some LEA's moved further than others, and as a result since the introduction of the 1981 Education Act, there had been no significant shift towards a more integrated system (Swann 1985, 1988, 1992).

Secondly, the 1997 Green Paper brought alignment with the Salamanca Statement (UNESCO 1994), formulated in an agreement between 94 governments, and 25 International Organisations. This according to authors such as Pijl, Meijer and Hegarty (1997) recognised the extent to which inclusion had now become a 'global agenda', as well as advocating genuine recognition and commitment to the term 'inclusion'. The Salamanca Statement (1994) argued:

"The challenge confronting the inclusive school is that of developing a child centred pedagogy capable of successfully educating all children, including those who have serious disadvantages and disabilities. The merit of such schools is not only that they are capable of providing quality education for all children; their establishment is a crucial step in helping to change discriminatory attitudes, in creating welcoming communities and in developing an inclusive society" (UNESCO 1994, pp6-7)

The emergence of this contemporary position is a far cry from the mid 1800's, which saw the first special schools established (Fredrickson and Cline 2002). These were intended to provide for children with severe hearing or visual difficulty who could not learn in ordinary schools alongside existing school provision, offered only to upper and middle class pupils. In the late nineteenth century as more children were educated from diverse backgrounds, schools were not accustomed to such diversity of learning needs. Increasing numbers of children were therefore excluded, as payment to schools at the time was 'by results'.

This rejection of children who were entitled to an education under the 1870 Education Act (DFE 1870) led to an expansion in special school provision (Fredrickson and Cline 2002). Thus, children who were perceived as 'handicapped', were seen as different from other children, and educated in separate schools. This separate provision remained largely static up until the mid 1960's when authors such as Dunn (1968) acknowledged there was a lack of evidence that disabled children educated in special schools did any better than those who were being educated in mainstream schools. Consequently arguments for 'reverse separation' (Fedrickson and Cline 2002) began to emerge, prompting a move towards more integrated school structures within the UK.

In 1970, the Education (Handicapped Children) Act (DFE 1970) removed the legal distinction between those who were, and were not educable within schools. According to Mitler (1985), this rapidly transformed the educational experience of children with SEN including those with severe learning difficulties, and saw a growth in the skills of teachers and curriculum development, in what Coupe (1986) described as the 'new special schools'. A key feature of this shift in provision was that the education of children with disabilities moved from the responsibility of departments of health to that of education. This follows similar developments in the United States of America (USA) associated with concepts of 'zero reject' and 'entitlement for all'.

The principle of 'normalisation' focusing on commonalities between children rather than differences also began to emerge with ideas that:

> "… the aims of education for children and young people with disabilities and other children are the same as those for all children and young people.. Disabilities and significant difficulties do not diminish the right to and equal access to participation in society" (Inner London LEA 1985).

In addition through the 'Public Law 94-142 Education for All Handicapped Children Act (1975)' in the USA, children were given a fundamental right to access education, and have a clear statement of their SEN, which was subject to regular review. The law also enforced a requirement for states and localities to assess, and ensure the effectiveness of their efforts to educate handicapped children. Consequently, those responsible for the education of 'handicapped' children became accountable for the implementation of an appropriate education, within a context that was mindful of pupil's individual needs.

In the UK, similar developments in the 1981 Education Act (DES 1981) introduced the legally defined term SEN, following advice from the 1978 Warnock Report (DES 1978). Prior to this time, provision focused upon identifying schooling for the 'handicapped'. The Warnock Report, recommended statutory categories of handicap (other than maladjustment) be abolished, and children with SEN to be identified by individual, and detailed profiles of their needs following assessment. Warnock indicated that it was not appropriate to focus attention merely on a small proportion of children with severe difficulties, which gave a sharp distinction between the disabled and non- disabled. Thus, a child should not be assigned to a particular category, but rather acknowledge SEN on a continuum with ordinary needs. Consequently the recommendation was made that school provision should not be either 'segregated' or 'mainstream', but on a dimension, which took, account of children's individual needs.

The 1981 Education Act (DES 1981) (introduced to implement the recommendations of the 1978 Warnock Report), brought a shift towards assessment of SEN, rather than diagnosis of disability, which had been previously used to categorise and isolate children. This supported similar developments at the time associated with the development of 'medical and social models' of disability (Reiser and Mason 1990). Social models of disability acknowledge that once a child's individual learning needs are established through assessment, schools and teachers must respond accordingly and plan to meet their particular learning requirements. In contrast, 'medical models' of disability view the learning difficulty as located with the child and as such, once assessed they would be placed into existing, unchanged provision, or placed in segregated school structures.

2.2.3 Focuses of Causation

The location and cause of SEN has been subject to much debate (Fredrickson and Cline 2002, Reiser and Mason 1990, Farrell 2001, Lloyd 2000), and various approaches have been suggested which consider what or whom the disabling factor in a child's education is. In support of developments in medical and social models of disability, Fredrickson and Cline (2002) indicate that a combination of individual differences, environmental demands and interactional analyses have contributed to differing perspectives on the inclusion of children with SEN.

They propose that models of individual difference (medical models) are embodied in legislation prior to introduction of the 1981 Education Act (DES 1981), and are particularly emphasised in the 1944 Education Act (DOE 1944), which was dominated by disability of body or mind. Consequently, individual differences were considered along a range of biological, behavioural or cognitive domains, with causation located firmly with the child, and no acknowledgement of contributory factors external to the child such as quality of teaching. This rather dated view is distinct from what was acknowledged in the Code of Practice (DFE 1994) on the Identification and Assessment of Children with SEN, which advocated:

> *"… schools should not automatically assume that children's learning difficulties always result solely or even mainly from problems within the child. The schools practices can make a difference – for good or ill" (DFE 1994, Para. 2.19).*

Therefore, the quality of teaching and learning delivered by the teacher, the ability to be equipped with the necessary skills to support children with SEN, and school cultures are significant factors in making inclusion a success or failure (Centre for Studies in Inclusive Education (CSIE) 2000).

In contrast to medical and individual models of disability, **environmental models** emerged which adopted a situation, rather than person centred focus to inclusive provision. This suggests that SEN can only be defined in terms of relationships between what a person can do, and what a person must do to succeed in any given environment. Frederickson and Cline (2002) suggest:

> *"… at one extreme then, the environmentally focused approach holds that there are no children with learning difficulties, only adults with teaching difficulties" (Fredrickson & Cline 2002, p40).*

This supports the work of Hegarty who in the 1980's advocated that children should be placed on a 'continuum of provision', that should equate to discrete categories of need. As a consequence, rather than attempting to adapt the child to the environment and see the disability as located with the child (medical model), schools and teachers conversely should be looking to how they can modify there learning environments (social model) in order that it meets the individual needs of children. As a result this necessitates schools and teachers to be prepared to think in different ways and recognise that there are many methods and strategies that can be utilised to support the inclusion of children with SEN (Ainscow et al 1999, Skrtic 1995, Dyson and Millward 2000).

Interactional models advocate impossibility in separating the learning competencies of individual children from the environment within which they live and function (Booth 1993, Keogh et al 1997). Models of disability, causation and location are seen as a combination of complex interactions between the strengths and weaknesses of the child, levels of support available and the appropriateness of education being provided. Thus, neither environmental, nor individual approaches on their own fit the particular reality of SEN in schools, and:

> "... special educational needs are often not just a reflection of pupils inherent difficulties or disabilities; they are often related to factors within schools which can prevent or exacerbate problems" (National Curriculum Council, 1998, Para. 5)

This view has been further endorsed in the Code of Practice (2001), which suggests:

> "It should be recognised that some difficulties in learning may be caused or exacerbated by the school's learning environment or adult/child relationships" (DFES 2001b, Para 5.6).

In addition the revised Code of Practice (DFES 2001b) seeks for schools to look within existing provision (school action and school action plus), rather than regularly seek external advice and support as a means of addressing individual children's needs.

Therefore, in order to respond to the needs of children with SEN at a more localised level, teachers need as part of their ITT to be given opportunities to examine the impact of school cultures and pedagogical practices on either enabling or restricting inclusive education. This in part is now being addressed through the 02/02

'Professional Standards Framework' (TTA 2002) in which trainee teachers are

required to have high expectations of all pupils, promote positive values, differentiate,

and respond to individual needs, and understand their responsibilities under the

Code of practice. As a result teachers are now required to think in many different

ways about how their teaching approaches can enhance or deny access to an

inclusive education for children with SEN.

2.2.4 Contradictions in Attempts to Plan for Inclusive Practice

In deducing how education systems in schools respond to diversity, Artiles (1998)

suggests there is a 'dilemma of difference' within which fundamental mass education

systems are established to deliver all students an 'education'. Mass education has for

instance, basic features of a common core of skills and knowledge (NC), delivered in

broadly equivalent circumstances, in schools with similar levels of training and

pedagogies which do not vary significantly from school to school.

However, if education is to fulfil the diversity it demands, Artiles (1998) suggests this

can only be achieved by acting at individual pupil levels, which recognise children are

different from each other. Pertinent to this is the need to construct and engage

learning strategies that recognise different interests, aptitudes and expectations. This

dilemma and tension brings with it, difficulties in planning an appropriate education

for children with special needs. As a consequence, there is:

> "a dilemma in education over how difference is taken into account – whether to
> recognise differences as relevant to individual needs by offering different
> provision, but in doing so could reinforce unjustified inequalities, and is
> associated with devaluation; or, whether to offer a common and valued
> provision for all but with the risk of not providing what is relevant to individual
> needs" (Norwich 1994, p293)

This picture recognises the development of educational policy in SEN over many years. The 1944 Education Act (DOE 1944) formalised, a common education structure, in which all children were placed into different forms of schooling. The 1970's then involved increasing exploration of how far all children could be included within the same school, and in the 1980's there was the emergence of the NC, and exploration of mixed ability classes and concepts of differentiation. In the late 1990's and early part of the 21st Century, and as a consequence of this evolving provision, Dyson and Millward (2000) suggest:

> "... it is more helpful to think of inclusion as an outcome of actions within a
> school rather than as an inherent characteristic of the school" (Dyson &
> Millward 2000, p170)

Thus the measure of the extent to which inclusion is demonstrated in practice comes through the observation and charting of 'real life' case studies of children engaged in inclusive schools (Ainscow 1999). As a result, teachers of the future need to be equipped with the knowledge, understanding and strategies to enable inclusion to become a reality, and to be enabled to demonstrate this in outcomes that indicate positive experiences for children with SEN. As a consequence according to Westwood (1997), the place to develop this teaching philosophy is as part of a trainee teachers ITT.

2.2.5 Dilemmatic Resolutions

Inclusive, and SEN provision has been subject to:

> "... a succession of dilemmatic resolutions" (Dyson and Millward 2000, p173)

... which have changed and emerged over many years. In addition, factors such as introduction of the NC, OFSTED inspection and development of the Code of Practice (DFES 2001b) have signalled an ever-increasing scrutiny and control by government on many issues of provision within schools. This brings with it a pressure between the espoused policy of schools, and policies pursued nationally by government and statutory agencies (Dyson 2001, Lloyd 2000). Consequently, the need for joined up and collaborative approaches to inclusive education are essential if they are to become a reality for children with SEN. To some extent, in agencies such as OFSTED having dual roles of inspection of ITT, and school based provision, this does give a better appreciation of what the issues and needs of the future are. Thus, more of this type of dual, or joint agency working is to be further encouraged through the DFES Schools Achieving Success (DFES 2001a) publication in which an increased emphasis is placed on collaboration.

In the post war years, the education of children was largely by groupings of ability, in which 'streaming' was very much the order of the day as a means of integrating all pupils into mainstream contexts. Tansley and Guildford (1960) argue this was with the intention of not segregating people, but providing specialist provision through what at the time were referred to as 'remedial classes'. However, authors such as Carroll 1972, Collins 1972, Galloway and Goodwin 1979, criticised this provision for its segregatory and stigmatising nature, and consequently streaming was seen as limiting the life opportunities to which children with special needs had access to. This led to experiments with remedial work, and a shift in attention to 'whole class approaches' to teaching all pupils. This movement in thinking resulted in an emergence of 'whole school approaches' (Clark et al 1995b), through which teachers would look to accommodate needs within the classroom, rather than through separate (remedial) classrooms and special needs teachers. This necessitated a change in curriculum pedagogy, in which ordinary classes became fully accessible, with additional teacher support, and the role of the remedial teacher began to develop into one of a special educational need co-ordinator (SENCO). As a result, teachers of the future need to be given the necessary support and training within their ITT, and continuing professional development to reflect upon the impact that their pedagogical practices can have in contributing to either positive or negative learning experiences. In addition, teachers as part of their training need to know how to work collaboratively in order to provide a holistic approach to a child with SEN's education involving parents, support workers, health care professionals and the like.

2.2.6 Liberal Principles and Interchangeable Terminology

In moving towards a more integrated structure of SEN provision, Clark et al (1995b) suggests educational developments have been driven through relatively liberal principles. Whilst these principles have been contested, the history and development of special needs education in the UK are in tune with what we now term 'inclusion' (Dyson 1999). Consequently, the education system has been influenced through moderate principles of equity, valuing pupil's individual rights of all to participate, curricula learning experiences, and recognition that:

> "the purpose of education for all children is the same, the goals are the same"
> (Warnock Report DES 1978, 1.4).

The key challenge for educationalists though is how this is interpreted in practice and provision for children with SEN within inclusive environments. Additionally, in relation to ITT providers, the challenge is to be able to equip teachers of the future with the necessary skills to respond to the requirements of the inclusion movement.

Lloyd (2000) suggests:

> "... rather than developing inclusive approaches to practice in mainstream
> education, the integration of pupils with SEN has served to perpetuate and
> reinforce segregated practices, placing the impetus for change on the pupil"
> (Lloyd 2000, p135)

Many factors have contributed to this viewpoint, which have mainly arisen out of:

"... fundamental misunderstanding and confusion about the concepts of
integration and inclusion, and indeed the term SEN itself" (Lloyd 2002, p111)

Dyson (2001) for example, argues there is a lack of consensus on what constitutes

an equal education, failure to recognise all children's rights to learn, lack of how to

identify SEN and the resistance of practitioners to change. As a consequence, there

is a need for significant debate and common ground to be established on what the

related terms mean in policy and practice (Lloyd 2000, Farrell 1998, Dyson 2001,

Dyson and Millward 2002). If this first stage of clarification is not achieved, then the

various stakeholders involved in the inclusion of children with SEN are going to be

potentially working against rather than with each other to promote inclusive

educations (Depauw and Doll-Tepper 2000).

Within the UK, 'SEN' was introduced as a legally defined term in the 1981 Education

Act (DES 1981) and:

> *"... refers to children's learning needs in school...is legally defined and this*
> *legal definition is used to decide whether particular children are eligible for*
> *special educational services" (Frederickson and Cline 2002, p34).*

In contrast 'special needs' is not legally defined, and refers to needs experienced by

pupils from most of the school population (i.e. homeless children, English as an

Additional Language (EAL) and unstable family environments). As a consequence,

the terms 'SEN' and 'special needs' are often used interchangeably (Dyson 2001,

Ainscow et al 1999) and this can:

> *"... cause unhelpful confusion since individuals from groups who have special*
> *needs may or may not have SEN" (Frederickson and Cline 2002, p34).*

In relation to 'integration', Ainscow (1995) suggests this is concerned with making a

limited number of additional arrangements for individual pupils with SEN in schools,

which as an outcome result in little change overall. In contrast, inclusion is concerned with the introduction of more radical changes through which schools restructure themselves in order to embrace all children. Thus integration involves a process of assimilating an individual into existing structures, whilst inclusion is more concerned with accommodation, where the onus is on the school to change (Dyson 2001, Dyson and Millward 2000). However, despite the conceptual distinction between the two terms they are often (like special needs and SEN) used as synonyms to each other (Thomas et al 1998).

Consequently, this is an issue in need of further clarification at the three levels of interpretation within this study. For example, at the official line (policy level) there is a need to be clear about what the terms mean in order to set clear expectations and resource inclusion effectively. At the professional opinion and practice (ITT provider) level trainee teachers need to be equipped with a full appreciation of the history, context and interpretation of terminology. If this is successfully achieved through delivery in schools by PE teachers (the consumers) there is a greater likelihood of inclusion become a reality for children with SEN.

2.2.7 Interpretations of Inclusion

Concepts of inclusion have been subject to extensive debate in terms of there meaning and interpretation related to SEN, especially as Dyson and Millward (2000) suggest it:

"... had its origins elsewhere" (Dyson & Millward 2000, p2)

Ballard (1997) a New Zealand scholar notes for example:

"Inclusive education means education that is non-discriminatory in terms of disability, culture, gender or other aspects of students or staff that are assigned significance by a society. It involves all students in a community, with no exceptions and irrespective of their intellectual, physical, sensory or other differences, having equal rights to access the culturally valued curriculum of their society as full-timed valued members of age-appropriate mainstream classes. Inclusion emphasises diversity over assimilation, striving to avoid the

colonisation of minority experiences by dominant modes of thought and action"
(Ballard 1997, pp244-245)

According to authors such as Booth (1995) and Dyson and Millward (2000) this

definition is highly content specific and refers more to aspects of cultural diversity,

rather than special needs education. They argue that the 1994 Salamanca

Statements interpretation of inclusion refers predominantly to finding basic forms of

education for marginalised street children, working children, and those living in

remote areas. In contrast, Dyson and Millward (2000) suggest inclusion within the UK

has stronger links to its emergence through the work of Skrtic (1991, 1995) and

Fuchs and Fuchs (1994), in which the American notion of inclusion grew out of a

different social policy history based on civil rights, with particular reference to race,

and more recently the philosophy has been transferred to the education of children

with SEN.

Booth et al (2000) suggests:

> *"Inclusion is a set of never ending processes. It involves the specification of the
> direction of change. It is relevant to any school however inclusive or exclusive
> its current cultures, policies and practices. It requires schools to engage in a
> critical examination of what can be done to increase the learning and
> participation of the diversity of students within the school locality" (Booth et al
> 2000, p12)*

As a consequence, Daniels and Garner (1999) argue whilst it is important to

recognise that inclusion can have global agreement (Pijl, Meijer and Hegarty 1997) it

is vital that inclusion is specifically interpreted within each national system. The

development of inclusion and SEN within the UK should be considered therefore in

terms of its particular history, culture and politics of its specific emerging system. As

a consequence, it is:

> *"... dangerous to see the recent adoption of the inclusion agenda by the UK
> government as a straightforward alignment with a policy direction that is both
> globally understood and relatively straightforward" (Dyson & Millward 2000, p4)*

As a result the relationship between inclusion and SEN, needs to be specifically aligned to the UK education system and government provision in order to fully appreciate its underlying philosophies and practices.

2.2.8 Changing School Approaches: The Shift From Integration To Inclusion

The difference between integration and inclusion is that the former applies to ways of supporting students with special needs in essentially unchanged mainstream schools. However, the latter refers to a radical restructuring of schools in order that they are inherently capable of educating all students within their communities (Corbett and Slee 2000, Sebba and Sachdev 1997). However, Dyson and Millward (2000) argue that this interpretation is too simplistic to apply to the UK system, in a background of long standing expectations of mainstream schools to educate children with SEN. As a result, these expectations have involved the exploration of 'whole school approaches', in which teachers were required to consider:

> "... fundamental changes in practice and organisation" (Dyson & Millward 2000, p8)

This exploration has led to the dissolving of boundaries between special and mainstream education, as well as categories of special and ordinary children:

> "... and whole school response will essentially be a response to meeting the individual needs of children" (Dessent 1987, p121)

In examining the concept of 'whole school approaches', the emergence of the NC (2000) (QCA 1999a) has added impetus to this shift, with its emphasis through the Statutory Inclusion Statement on setting suitable learning challenges, responding to individual diversity and differentiating assessment. Consequently, in the years following the introduction of the NC, a number of schools were:

"... moving 'beyond the whole school approach' in this sense towards what we chose to call 'innovatory practice' in schools' approaches to special needs" (Dyson and Millward 2000, p10)

Thus according to Dyson and Millward (2000) school provision centred upon conceptualising approaches in terms of responses to student diversity as a whole, rather than simply a response to special needs; merging of special needs infrastructures within the mainstream; promoting differentiation through transformation of the curriculum and pedagogy; and redefining the role of SENCO's. (Clark et al 1995a, Dyson, Millward and Skidmore 1994, Dyson and Millward 2000)

The development of inclusive practices has seen some schools pushing back the boundaries of whole school approaches and exploring even further methods of enhancing teaching and learning for all pupils. This led Dyson, and Millward (2000) (and Dyson, Millward and Skidmore 1994) to note that in some schools:

"... quite dramatic transformations were evident - schools which dismantled their special needs departments, abandoned all forms of segregated provision, reinvented their SENCO's as teaching and learning co-ordinators, embarked on intensive programmes of staff development, set up quality assurance programmes to enhance teaching and learning across the school and invested heavily in resource based learning in order to create flexible learning environments across the school" (Dyson & Millward 2002, p11)

"The inclusiveness of English schools has to be defined therefore not simply in terms of which students they educate, but in terms of how they educate them" (Dyson & Millward, 2000, p11)

Consequently, inclusion is not about the mere presence of children with SEN, it has to lead to participation, be guided by notions of equity, and a fundamental recognition that the school system needs to adapt to meet the individual learning needs of the pupils it serves. In order to examine these changes in emphasis, Clark et al 1995a advocates that the practicality of inclusion, as well as the theoretical frameworks that underpin it must be fully considered in order to arrive at a comprehensive appreciation of all the key issues of provision. This position is to some extent now being reflected in the 02/02 'Professional Standards Framework' (TTA 2002) in which both knowledge of SEN and inclusion is required, but significantly, trainee teachers are expected to be able to demonstrate its application in order to meet the requirements for the award of QTS.

2.2.9 Moving Towards an Understanding of Inclusion

It is recognised that in recent years (along with many other aspects of SEN terminology), we have become used to the terms inclusion, inclusive education and inclusive schools being used inter-changeably (Dyson and Millward 2000, Barton 1998, Depauw and Doll-Tepper 2000). In attempting to unpack the similarities and differences, it is relevant to note that within this study the complexities of inclusion need to be considered within a context that reflects official line policy (government and statutory agencies), professional opinion and practice (teaching pedagogy) and consumer levels of classroom practice involving curriculum structure, experiences and outcomes. Thus Clarks (1995a, 1997) view of interpretation of theoretical and practical contexts is of particular relevance, and in considering this approach, Lipsky and Gartner (1999) suggest:

> "... while there is no single educational model or approach, inclusive schools tend to share similar characteristics and beliefs" (Lypsky & Gartner 1999, p17)

For example:

> **School wide approaches** - in which the philosophy and practice of inclusive education is accepted by all the stakeholders.

> **All children learn together** – reflecting a continuum of learning needs within contexts of 'whole school approaches'

> **A sense of 'community' within schools** – through which children and teachers are valued. (In addition, trainee teachers are required to demonstrate evidence of the promotion of positive values within the 02/02 (TTA 2002) 'Professional Standards Framework' (TTA 2002)).

Services based on need, rather than category – recognising and responding
to individual need as a starting point for supporting inclusive practice

Extensive teacher collaboration – Involving recognition of multi-agency
working, and thus linking with the desire of the DFES Schools Achieving
Success (2001) publication to promote collaborative working.

Curriculum adaptation - through which inclusion provides adaptations to
enable all pupils to benefit from a common school curriculum.

Enhanced instructional strategies – Encouraged and developed within ITT
and CPD, then facilitated in practice by teachers in schools

Standards and outcomes - linked and drawn from those expected of children
in general.

Whilst Lipsky and Gartners (1999) list helps to identify a number of important

inclusive school factors, Dyson and Millward (2000) argue that it also poses many

problems with the belief that all stakeholders will accept a particular philosophy or set

of inclusive practices. In reality these:

*"… fly in the face of what we know about the complexity of school life" (Dyson
and Millward 2000, p18)*

This contrasting view of the inter-relationship of theory and practice is one of many

offering schools guidance on how to become more inclusive and indicates the extent

to which inclusive education is both complex and problematic to implement (Booth

and Ainscow 1998, Clark et al 1995a, Porter 1997, Ainscow and Tweddle 1998,

Rouse and Florian 1996, Thomas, et al 1998).

In attempting to draw perspectives together, Dyson (2001) argues that in order to

understand what inclusion stands for in principle and practice, the detail of many

authors views are weak on underpinning theoretical frameworks, organisational

structures and processes that lead to either inclusion or exclusion. Consequently, in

order to arrive at a thorough appreciation of inclusion for children with SEN there is a need to examine the combined strengths of 'theoretical' and 'applied' views on inclusive practice. In Dyson's view this can be best achieved through a collective critique of two authors work, namely 'Skrtics theoretical models of inclusive practice' and 'Ainscow's examination of applied inclusive practice' in schools. Therefore in order to arrive at a coherent view of the fundamental principles, processes and practices concerned with inclusion, by examining the work of Skrtic and Ainscow a clearer picture should begin to emerge.

2.2.10 Skrtic's Adhocratic Schools

Skrtic (1991) argues from a position of 'crisis in modern knowledge', and a loss of confidence in the current state of special education understanding. He believes that in arriving at the inclusive standpoint of today, the profession has been subject to a range of sociological, philosophical and political critiques. From a sociological perspective, Skrtic suggests professionals operate in a manner that realises the interests of its members, within the context of the organisations in which they operate, and consequently impose their own constraints and imperatives to suit their, rather than children's needs. In contrast, philosophical perspectives refer to a wide-ranging transformation in the way in which knowledge and certainty have come to be understood and recognise there is not one paradigm through which knowledge is universally transferred. Skrtic indicates that Interpretivist, radical humanist and radical structuralist paradigms have challenged the previously dominant functionalist paradigm of the 1960's, and as a direct consequence there are now many competing theories on special education (Pijl, Meijer and Hegarty 1997, Clark et al 1995a, Clark 1997, Dyson 2001).

Skrtics political critique recognises that in the past, the profession has argued from a position of access to privileged knowledge. However, this knowledge and understanding is now subject to scrutiny and questioning by competing theories, resulting in a diminishment of the power that they exercise over other people. In addition the emergence of agencies such as OFSTED and the TTA have contributed to the diminishing power base originally dominated solely by the teaching profession. In appreciation of the changing nature of inclusive education, Skrtic takes the view that special education is grounded in four assumptions and these are that:

> *Disabilities are pathological;*

> *Differential diagnosis is objective and useful;*

> *Special education is a rationally conceived and co-ordinated system of services that benefit diagnosed pupils;*

> *Progress results from incremental technological improvement in diagnosis and instructional interventions (Skrtic 1995, p54)*

The special education field cannot be therefore grounded in foundational knowledge, and this view complements the UK position in which many researchers (Thomlinson 1982, 1985, Oliver, 1988, 1990, and Barton 1988) have indicated that disability has been constructed in a manner that serves the purposes of the profession, rather than the client and is subject to a range of views and opinions. This supports the earlier views of Pring (1996) and UCET (1997a) who note that many agencies and individuals have a role to play in determining what the nature of education, standards in ITT, and the government's drive for 'school improvement' should consist of.

As a consequence, Skrtic suggests that whilst radical theorists claim to have changed the nature of SEN and inclusive provision, they have not sufficiently challenged the bureaucratic configuration of schools and the convergent thinking of the professional culture in a sufficiently fundamental manner (Skrtic 1995). Thus whilst there has been a call for the dismantling of separate special schools, the bureaucracy still establishes systems that do not sufficiently respond to diversity, and Skrtic (citing Mintzberg 1979, 1983) designates this as an 'adhocracy'.

In considering this 'adhocracy', Skrtic explains:

> "The professional bureaucracy is non adaptable because it is premised on the principle of standardisation, which configures it as a performance organisation for perfecting standard (rather than flexible) programmes. An adhocracy is premised upon principles of innovation, rather than standardisation; as such, it is a problem-solving organisation configured to invent new programs. It is the organisational form that configures itself around work that is so ambiguous and uncertain that neither the programs nor the knowledge and skills for doing it are known" (Skrtic 1991, p182).

The adhocratic organisation has therefore many advantages in that Skrtic argues it encourages collaboration between professionals with different kinds of expertise; involves discursive coupling through which teams reflect upon practice; team approaches in which theory and practice are unified through informal communication; professional-political accountability and a community of common interests. As a result:

> "A school configured in this way would see the diversity of its students not as a disruption to be minimised by 'pigeonholing' the students into existing or separate programmes, but as a problem to be solved through a collaborative commitment to innovation" (Dyson and Millward 2000, p25)

This supports the view of the TTA who see teaching as a reflective based profession and therefore this needs to be encouraged and fostered with trainee teachers as part of their ITT.

In summarising the adhocracy, Dyson & Millward (2000) suggest that Skrtics views:

> "… ultimately are philosophical rather than empirical. In particular they are grounded in the theory of knowledge rather than in studies of actual schools" (Dyson & Millward 2000, p27)

However, Skrtic argues the empirical realties of schools are intentionally not addressed, in order that they do not interrupt the open and free flow of his thinking, rather than establish arguments around constraints of existing structures. Thus, it is for others to look to how the adhocratic models can be implemented structurally (official line) and delivered in practice (professional opinion and practice and the consumers).

In response, Dyson and Millward (2000) cite the work of Ainscow, and his notion of 'the moving school' in which he documents 'good inclusive practice' in schools as an answer to the need to provide empirical substance to the inclusion debate. Consequently, Ainscow is concerned with documenting not only the good practice, but also more significantly, what, why and how it is deemed to be good inclusive practice. As a result, Ainscow's documented practice is grounded in wider circumstances of institutional development, professional development and special education.

2.2.11 Ainscow's Documentation of Inclusive School Practice

Ainscow (1999) defines inclusion as:

> "... a process of increasing the participation of pupils in, and reducing their exclusion from, the cultures, curricula and communities of their local schools, not forgetting, of course, that education involves many processes that occur outside of schools" (Ainscow 1999, p218)

He suggests inclusion is often viewed as involving movement from special, to mainstream contexts under a belief that once there; they will be 'included'. Inclusion should however be considered:

> "... as a never ending process, rather than a simple change of state, and as dependent on continuous pedagogical and organisational development within the mainstream" (Ainscow 1999, p218)

This view is of particular interest to Dyson and Millward (2000), as Ainscow links pedagogical development, to teacher development, and then assimilates this to the organisational development of schools. This standpoint is at the centre of Ainscow's model of inclusive practice in which he advocates a desire to move away from views of locating the problem with the child, and look to an examination of curriculum

adaptation and modification (social model). Consequently, inadequacies of learning

environments should be seen as generating the learning difficulty, rather than the

individual characteristics (medical model) of the pupil (Ainscow 1994). In order to

develop the theme of curricula, rather than pupil adaptation, Ainscow (1999) believes

that schools must become 'moving schools', which are in a constant state of inclusive

development and change in order to adapt to the individual needs of all its pupils.

Schools should therefore be looking to develop their inclusive practice around a

number of core areas namely:

> *Effective leadership* – *incorporating a clear vision and strategy for making inclusive practice work;*
>
> *Involvement of all staff students and the community* – *and this supports notions of citizenship in the National Curriculum (2000) in which all people understand their rights and responsibilities to respect and value diversity;*
>
> *Commitment to collaborative planning* – *in which through multi-agency working children with SEN receive an holistic approach to their education;*
>
> *Attention to the benefits of enquiry and reflection* – *supporting teachers as reflective practitioners, constantly prepared to modify and adapt their teaching and learning approaches;*
>
> *Policies for staff development that focus on classroom practice* – *through which all staff are offered opportunities for continuing professional development to enhance their knowledge and understanding*

The fundamental premise of inclusive school practice is designed therefore to

support Ainscow's notion of a changing school, responding flexibly to the individual

need of its pupils, rather than the other way around in which children have to adapt to

fit pre-existing educational settings. As a result of the notions of constantly changing

schools, Dyson and Millward (2000) argue that due to the empirical basis of

Ainscow's views there is significant credence in supporting his models of inclusive

practice in schools. Consequently ITT needs to be constructed within a framework of creating reflective teachers who are responsive and adaptable to the individual needs of pupils that they serve in schools.

2.2.12 Common Themes – An Inclusive Approach to Teaching Children with SEN

The work of Skrtic and Ainscow has made significant contributions toward articulated theoretical accounts of the relationship between principles and processes of inclusive practice and school organisation (Lloyd 2000, Dyson and Millward 2000, Dyson 2001, Frederickson and Cline 2002). Within this context, attempts have been made to identify 'common themes' that have emerged in schools with reference to inclusive principles and practices, whilst identifying potential threats to this movement. Thus, whilst classes and schools may be very different in their approaches, it is possible (Dyson and Millward 2000) to establish characteristics of a 'model of the inclusive school', which can then be used as a basis for all the key stakeholders to work towards the creation of inclusive schools. In reflecting on the work of Skrtic and Ainscow, inclusive schools can be characterised by:

Effective leadership - in which all people in positions of responsibility (whether that be at government, ITT or school level) drive forward the belief of inclusive practice;

Clear vision – in which all stakeholders work together to promote inclusive practice;

Dismantling of structures and barriers – through which agencies and individuals are prepared to review, modify and change policies and practices whether they be physical, attitudinal or financial barriers and constraints;

Response to diversity – In which difference is valued as an essential component of the make up of schools and wider society;

Senior management responsibility – in which people in positions of responsibility ensure that the visions of inclusive practice become a reality;

Reliance on in-class support – in contrast to separate or segregated provision;

Emphasis on the professional development of staff – *as the future of inclusive provision rests with the skills, expertise and determination of staff to make inclusive practice a reality for children with SEN.*

2.2.13 Conclusion and Future Directions in Inclusion for Children with SEN

Dyson and Millward (2000) argue that through a combination of Ainscow and Skrtics inclusive models, and their own case studies of common themes lending empirical weight, an:

> "... illuminating explanation" (Dyson & Millward 2000, p149)

... of the nature of inclusive education for children with SEN begins to emerge. Thus, in taking account of:

> "... the multiple values" (Norwich 2002a, p484)

... offered by the authors above, a clearer picture on the nature of training required to equip teachers of PE begins to emerge.

In support of a clearer picture emerging on the nature of inclusive practice, Reynolds et al (2001) notes that two paradigms have dominated school improvement over recent years, and consequently have assisted with development of teaching and learning approaches for children with SEN. The first is concerned with a 'top-down process' (official line), which is centrally designed, through which innovation and change is transmitted to schools. In contrast the 'bottom-up process' (consumers) involves building upon the professional development of teachers and involving them fully in the development of school improvement and inclusive practice. Dyson and Millward (2000) additionally suggest that the development of educational policy:

> "... cannot simply be seen as a technical-rational process of formulation and implementation" (Dyson & Millward 2000, p157).

73

Consequently ITT providers (professional opinion and practice) need to act as the catalyst to constantly review the emerging professional development needs of teachers. As a result, the ITT providers are in a significant position to respond, react and drive forward inclusive practice in partnership with their official line and consumer stakeholders.

Dyson and Millward (2000) state that educational progress is fraught with conflict, contest and compromise out of which may come policy positions that are far from coherent. In contexts of top down and bottom up change processes therefore and the nature of conflict, it is easy to appreciate why apparently well intentioned models of inclusion, integration or whole school approaches for children with SEN seem to often deliver less than they initially promise (Lloyd 2000, Croll and Moses 2000). This conflicting picture:

> "... has illuminated the way in which such policies, both in formation and in
> practice, are shaped by, inter alia, ambiguous and contradictory national
> imperatives, interacting with the competing interests of head teachers, parents
> and others with a vested interest in the nature of that provision" (Dyson and
> Millward 2000, p157).

School improvement, and inclusive theories and practices become ever more complex and problematic to disentangle (Rouse and Florian 1997, Vincent et al 1994, Visle and Langfeldt 1996). As a result, Feiler and Gibson (1999) argue that within this background there are four potential threats to the inclusion movement, which need to be addressed as a matter of urgency prior to any further developments in relation to the education of children with SEN, which are:

A lack of consistency in definition and understanding of inclusion

Lack of empirical data

Notions of internal exclusion (i.e. streaming or grouping)

Tendency to describe individual needs in a manner that implies the problem resides with the child, rather than the school structure.

In reflecting upon the four threats indicated by Feiler and Gibson (1999), the future development of special needs education needs to move towards a coherent framework within which government policy is reflected, delivered and implemented within a structure that ensures all agencies and individuals are clear about what the vision of inclusive schooling involves. In summary with regard to future visions Dyson (2001) succinctly makes the following statements, which act as a point for further reflection:

> "Special needs education so patently has a past and that past – like the present – is highly fluid and even turbulent" (Dyson 2001, p24)

In coming to terms with the future:

> "It is my contention that the inherent instability of the present means that it is incumbent on us to look carefully at what the future might hold. Even as the 'new' resolution of 'inclusion' struggles to establish its hegemony, we should, I believe, try to understand how it will ultimately fragment and what possibilities might open up for alternative resolutions" (Dyson 2001, p27)

C H A P T E R   T H R E E :

DEVELOPMENTS IN INCLUSIVE PHYSICAL EDUCATION AND DISABILITY SPORT

This chapter examines the characteristics of PE, within the context of strategies to include children with SEN. The subject of PE will be analysed in relation to its structure, organisation and delivery, and potential to link to wider sporting opportunities as part of an examination of 'disability sports' activities. The chapter concludes by highlighting a range of issues and themes that are emerging related to ensuring that PE teachers are sufficiently equipped to include children with SEN within mainstream settings.

3.1   Defining and Interpreting PE

According to QCA, PE:

> "... is the process of developing pupils knowledge, skills and understanding so that they can perform reflectively and with increasing physical competence and confidence. This process requires pupils to think as well as perform" (QCA 1999a, p1)

PE is concerned with involvement and development of physical skills, knowledge of the body in action, and attitudes to engagement in physical activity. Consequently, PE requires children to be predominantly physically active in order to improve skilfulness, and develop learning in which growing competence leads to personal confidence, and increased self-esteem.

The purpose of the PE curriculum is to provide:

> "the range of tasks, contexts and environments so that an individual's skills can be tuned, adjusted, adapted, modified and refined. The challenge of teaching is

to provide information, ideas and encouragement for each pupil to become competent and confident in each new task, context and environment and then extend them again" (QCA 1999a, p1).

Within this backdrop, the PE curriculum is delivered through six activity areas of; dance, games, gymnastics, athletics, outdoor and adventurous activities, and swimming and water safety. This broad, balanced and relevant curriculum 1988 Education Reform Act (DOE 1988) seeks to provide children with a diverse range of experiences in order to develop and extend their physical and personal development, as well as their general well-being.

This provision, as part of the NC 2000 (QCA 1999a) should be made available to all children, including those with SEN. As a result, teachers of PE will often need to think in different ways about what and how they are going to teach, whilst making best use of their differentiation, teaching and learning strategies. Sugden and Talbot (1998) support this view, and suggest that teaching children with SEN is merely an extension of teachers mixed ability teaching. Thus, flexibility of teaching and learning strategy is central to successful inclusive PE. This view is similar to that of Dyson and Millward 2000, Ainscow et al 1999, and Skrtic 1995, which focuses the emphasis of change with teachers and the need to be pro-active and adapt the curriculum to meet the individual needs of children with SEN.

In the context of the NC (2000), PE is divided into four content areas of; acquiring and developing skills; selecting and applying skills, tactics and compositional ideas; knowledge and understanding of fitness and health; and evaluating and improving performance. These sections, delivered through the six areas of activity, and with acknowledgement of the principles of the Statutory Inclusion Statement (i.e. setting suitable learning challenges; responding to pupils diverse learning needs; and overcoming potential barriers to learning and assessment) establish the context for the implementation of the PE curriculum in primary, secondary and special schools.

3.2   The National Curriculum for PE and Children with SEN

The revised NC for PE (2000) suggests teachers should consider assessment in alternative activities, with flexible judgements and contexts in order to facilitate accessibility to the curriculum for pupils with SEN. It states:

> "... teachers must take action" and "ensure that their pupils are enabled to participate" (QCA 1999a p33)

... and be responsive to a diverse range of pupil needs in order to facilitate inclusive education. In meeting this requirement, teachers of PE will need to actively review their pedagogical practices in order to ensure they meet the statutory requirements to facilitate entitlement and accessibility to inclusive activities for all pupils including those with SEN. In order to satisfactorily address the needs of pupils with SEN, Farrell (1998) suggests teachers must be willing to move beyond an acknowledgment of inclusion policies and be prepared:

> "to reconsider their structure, teaching approaches, pupil grouping and use of support" (Farrell 1998 p81)

This position supports earlier work noted by Ainscow 1999 who advocates a notion of 'moving schools' that are constantly evolving and changing to be responsive to the needs of the pupils it serves.

The four key principles related to equality, identified in the 1992 NC for PE (DOE 1992) still hold true today as guiding principles to be considered when including pupils with SEN within mainstream PE (Vickerman 1997, Vickerman et al 2003). These are **entitlement, accessibility, integration** and **integrity**, and have acted as the corner stones upon which the NC for PE (2000) has been revised and extended. In relation to **entitlement**, the premise is to acknowledge the fundamental right of pupils with SEN to access the PE curriculum. This is of particular relevance with the emergence of the SEN and Disability Rights Act (DFES 2001c), which gives pupils a fundamental right to inclusive activity, and the revised Code of Practice (DFES 2001b) implemented in January 2002. The Code of Practice now focuses much more on the action of schools and teachers to implement and deliver inclusive PE through further delegation of centralised SEN budgets and a requirement to think in different ways about their teaching provision (Dyson 2001, Dyson and Millward 2000, Skrtic 1995).

Teachers of PE are expected to therefore take action within their individual school contexts, and modify and adapt practices in order to facilitate full entitlement to the curriculum for pupils with SEN. This shift in legislation recognises the philosophy of positive attitudes and open minds (Vickerman 2002), and the commitment to a process that offers inclusive education, in which teachers overcome potential barriers through consultation and the adoption of diverse learning, teaching and assessment strategies (Ainscow 1999, Dyson 2001, Dyson and Millward 2000, Sugden and Talbot 1998). This position is to some extent now being reflected in the 02/02 (TTA 2002) 'Professional Standards Framework' (TTA 2002) with the expectation that trainee teachers will demonstrate evidence of differentiated teaching, response to equal opportunities and diversity, and the promotion of positive values.

In terms of **accessibility**, it is the responsibility of teachers to make PE lessons accessible and relevant to the child with SEN. This supports the social model of disability (Reiser and Mason 1990) in which teachers adjust their teaching in order to accommodate the needs of individual pupils rather than the child's disability (medical model) being seen as the barrier to participation. In examining the need to make PE lessons relevant and accessible, it is important to acknowledge the earlier view of Sugden and Talbot (1998) who advocate teaching pupils with SEN is part of an extension of mixed ability teaching. Teachers should therefore, possess (from their ITT) many of the skills necessary to facilitate inclusive PE, and consequently may only occasionally require specialist advice and guidance.

Thus, the fundamental factor in a successful inclusive activity for pupils with SEN is a positive attitude, suitable differentiation and a readiness to modify existing practice within PE lessons (Farrell 1998). Whilst there may be a few difficulties for teachers to embrace more inclusive approaches, the PE profession is well placed to embrace inclusive practice and, to a large extent, the process has begun with the increased focus on aspects of inclusion within PE, education and society in general (Fredrickson and Cline 2002, Dyson 2001, Vickerman et al 2003). However, the critical success factors in the drive to more inclusive PE will be the training and support given to trainee, qualified teachers and schools within process models which reflect implementation of 'policy through to practice' (Depauw and Doll Tepper 2000, Watkinson 1997). As a result, ITT providers, schools and statutory agencies need to ensure that future teachers of PE are adequately prepared to deliver this inclusive agenda. Consequently, as part of the drive to a more co-ordinated approach, the DFES Schools Achieving Success (DFES 2001a) publication advocates greater levels of multi-agency and collaborative working practices need to evolve in the years ahead.

The third principle of *integration* recognises the benefits of disabled and non-disabled pupils being educated together and the positive outcomes, which can be achieved for all pupils through such approaches. Whilst concepts of integration have moved on since 1992 (now embracing concepts of inclusion) these can be seen as fundamental stepping-stones towards inclusive practice, (Slinger et al 2000) ultimately recognising difference, but treating pupils appropriately and according to their learning needs. This also begins to address the UK government's citizenship agenda in which pupils are to be educated to have mutual understanding and respect for individual diversity as part of their involvement and participation within a socially inclusive society. PE is an ideal vehicle for this to occur with many activities involving teamwork and co-operation.

PE teachers need to underpin their learning and teaching practice with *integrity*, and a recognition that they value and believe in the adaptations and changes that are made to the activities they teach. As part of this personal commitment, they should ensure that inclusive PE for pupils with SEN is of equal worth, challenging, and in no way patronising or demeaning to the individual child concerned. PE teachers should therefore, adopt approaches which set appropriate and challenging tasks (NC 2000 Statutory Inclusion Statement) to pupils who have additional learning needs whilst avoiding the 'cotton wool' approach, which often assumes that these pupils cannot cope with some of the demands that a challenging curriculum may offer (Goodwin and Watkinson 2000, Sherril 1998, Vickerman et al 2003). Consequently, this may involve schools and teachers re-examining their present teaching philosophies, attitudes, values and cultures with the intention of establishing flexible yet challenging educational experiences for children with SEN. (Centre for Studies in Inclusive Education 2000).

3.3   Adapted PE and Sport

In conjunction with definitions, interpretations and contexts related to the PE curriculum in the UK, extensive work has been undertaken in the development of 'adapted PE', 'adapted sport' and 'disability sport' both here and within the USA. These strategies support and extend provision within the formal school curriculum, and have to a certain extent shaped the delivery of present day PE and school sport for children with SEN. Winnick (2000) suggests:

> "Adapted physical education is a sub-discipline of physical education that allows for safe, personally satisfying and successful participation to meet the unique needs of students" (Winnick 2000, p4).

Adapted PE is designed to meet the long-term (i.e. over 30 days) unique needs of disabled children, and establish common frameworks for their inclusion within PE programmes (Auxter et al 2001, Winnick 2000):

> "Adapted physical education is an individualised program of physical and motor fitness; fundamental motor skills and patterns; and skills...designed to meet the unique needs of individuals (Winnick 2000, p4)

In contrast:

> "Adapted sport refers to sport modified or created to meet the unique needs of individuals with disabilities. Adapted sport may be conducted in integrated settings in which individuals with disabilities interact with non-disabled participants or in segregated environments that only include those persons with disabilities" (Winnick 2000, p5).

The use of the term 'adapted sport' is preferred to 'disability sport' as it stimulates and encourages participation and excellence in a variety of settings, rather than categorising activity that specifically caters for disabled people alone (Auxter et al 2001, Depauw and Gavron 1995, Winnick 2000). This supports modern day shifts towards inclusive activity in which children with SEN participate within the same inclusive environment as their non-disabled peers. To some extent this is also being seen within National, and International disability sport where adults in the recent Sydney 2000 Olympics and the Manchester 2002 Commonwealth Games competed at the same venue and at the same time.

Auxter et al (2001) argues within the contexts of adapted PE and sport that it is crucial for teachers to assume responsibility for all children and adults that they work with regardless of individual needs. Winnick (2000) supports this view in suggesting:

> "A good teacher and/or coach of children places the development of positive self esteem as a priority and displays an attitude of acceptance, empathy, friendship and warmth, while ensuring a secure and controlled environment. The good teacher or coach of adapted physical education and sport selects and uses teaching approaches and styles beneficial to students, provides individualised and personalised instruction and opportunities, and creates a positive environment where students can succeed" (Winnick 2000, p8)

This supports the current evolving thinking on the practice, structure and delivery of inclusion within the UK in which flexibility, adaptation and openness to change are seen as critical success factors (Dyson and Millward 2000, Ainscow 1999, Skrtic 1991, 1995).

3.4   Evolving Practice in Inclusive PE and Sport

Whilst the most significant progress in adapted activity has recently focused on educational services for disabled children and adults, the use of physical activity as part of exercise and therapy for treatment is not a new concept and dates back to as early as 3000 BC in China. The Romans and Greeks also recognised the benefits of therapy and the value of exercise as a means of assisting with mobility and general health and well-being (Winninck 2000, Auxter et al 2001). Developments in physical activity and remedial therapy date back many years and have contributed to arriving at more contemporary approaches to inclusive PE and sport for children with SEN. Sherill (1998) notes that the 1800's and early part of the 1900's for example, were initially characterised by medical orientation of therapy, prevention, rehabilitation and cure.

However, there was a shift from the 1930's onwards to the modern day position in which orientation has shifted from medical to 'whole person' approaches which run in tandem with educational developments moving from segregated to inclusive, person centred strategies. Within the context of 'whole person orientations', Winnick (2000) suggests individuals who require physical activity programmes, as part of their disability should be assessed according to their particular needs, then seek to establish programmes that best fit their particular needs. This is in line with modern day concepts of inclusive practice within schools, in which teachers and schools change and adapt their provision to meet the individual needs of children with SEN, rather than the other way around (Ainscow 1999).

In shifting to more inclusive practices, Winnick established a framework of 'alternative instructional placements' within the PE curriculum that were based on strategies moving from conventional medical models of treatment and separate centres which he described as 'most restrictive', through to 'regular' inclusive placements which were 'least restrictive' in terms of developing the child with SEN as a whole. Winnick posits that teachers should start from the premise of full inclusion (level 1), and then move only if necessary to more specialised or separate provision (levels 2-9) as a secondary option.

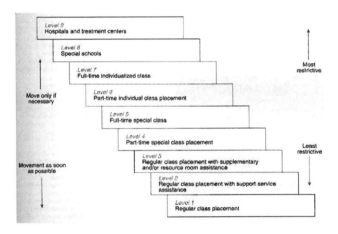

Figure 3.1 Continuum of alternative instructional placements in
physical education (Winnick 2000)

In developing 'least restrictive environments', Winnick (2000) offered teachers guidelines for instruction, which focus upon the curriculum, teaching styles and organisational strategies. In facilitating an inclusive (least restrictive) curriculum for example, lessons should be based on developmentally appropriate activities, centred according to Winnick upon 'Crafts (1996) four curricula options' namely:

Same curriculum – *Access to the same activity areas within the curriculum;*

Multi-level curriculum – *pursuing different objectives, but within the same lesson;*

Curriculum overlap – *Involving modification of the curriculum;*

Alternative curriculum - *separate or disability specific activities.*

Thus, there is an expectation that teachers adopt a range of flexible teaching, learning and organisational approaches to deliver inclusive PE for children with SEN (Farrell 1998, Sugden and Talbot 1998, QCA, 1999). This expectation is now being reflected within the 02/02 (TTA 2002) 'Professional Standards Framework' (TTA 2002) in which trainee teachers are expected to consider a diverse range of differentiated teaching and learning strategies.

Crafts (1996) 'Curricula Options' complement recent thinking in the development of the 'inclusion spectrum', which builds upon Winnick's notion of flexible teaching and learning strategies and has been extended by the Youth Sport Trust and the EFDS. The inclusion spectrum offers a range of strategies that teachers of PE can move in and out of during their lessons in order to ensure maximum participation and access to physical activity for children with SEN. These strategies are not solely however related to including children with SEN and can as many authors have suggested (Wright and Sugden 1999, Farrell 1998) be used to create greater flexibility in teaching and learning to include all pupils. The inclusion spectrum suggests five strategies of open, modified, parallel, separate, and disability sport activities that enable teachers to deliver PE in conjunction with the principles of the NC (2000) Statutory Inclusion Statement (QCA 1999a).

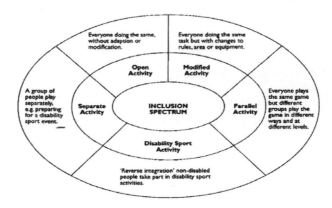

Figure 3.2 The Inclusion spectrum

3.5 Extending and Developing Teaching and Learning Strategies in PE

As part of their general teaching philosophy and practices, teachers of PE should seek to embrace the guiding principles of entitlement, accessibility, integration and integrity. This should be undertaken alongside contemporary notions of inclusion and flexible teaching and learning strategies if they are to make genuine commitments to inclusive PE for pupils with SEN. Additionally, as part of the revised NC for PE (QCA 1999a), teachers need to spend time interpreting the inclusion statement, whilst recognising the need to set suitable learning challenges, respond to pupils diverse needs' and overcome potential barriers to learning and assessment for individuals and groups of pupils. The strategies and models offered in the 'four curricula options' (Craft 1996), 'inclusion spectrum' and 'continuum of alternative instructional placements in physical education' (Winnick 2000) are valuable starting points for teachers to consider their approach to inclusive PE. As a result, these suggested models need to be considered fully as part of trainee PE teachers ITT, and or continuing professional development work.

In relation to '**setting suitable learning challenges'**, the NC for PE (2000) states:

> "Teachers should aim to give every pupil the opportunity to experience success in learning and to achieve as high a standard as is possible" (QCA 1999a p28)

It suggests this can be achieved by teaching knowledge, skills and understanding of PE from earlier key stages, if appropriate, with the aim of ensuring those pupils with SEN progress and achieve. It could be argued, therefore, that inclusion for pupils with SEN is about focusing upon earlier developmental expectations, or adopting a more flexible teaching approach to accommodate individual's needs in terms of learning, teaching and assessment. Sugden and Talbot (1998), for example, support this view through the principles of 'moving to learn' and 'learning to move'. They argue:

> "Physical Education has a distinctive role to play, because it is not simply about education of the physical but involves cognitive, social, language and moral development and responsibilities (Sugden & Talbot 1998 p22)

Thus, to facilitate inclusion, a shift away from the traditional (learning to move) outcome of PE in which skills are taught and learned, to a wider experience of PE (moving to learn) may be one such approach in enabling access to inclusive PE.

PE teachers need to consider their learning outcomes carefully in order to ensure all pupils with SEN have the opportunity to demonstrate a wide variety of movement learning experiences, and this links with the principle of '**responding to pupils diverse learning needs'**. Consequently, the NC for PE (2000) states:

> "... when planning teachers should set high expectations and provide opportunities for all pupils to achieve including ... pupils with disabilities and special educational needs" (QCA 1999a p29)

This section suggests lessons should be planned to ensure full and effective access, and that teachers need to be aware of equal opportunity legislation. This begins to answer some of Dyson's (1999) concerns that the curriculum needs to focus on how outcomes can be differentiated and measured for each child, rather than focusing upon philosophical definitions of equality. A key feature of this occurring will need to be based upon the social model of disability and a commitment to change the activity to fit the child rather than the other way around (Vickerman 1997).

In terms of 'overcoming potential barriers to learning and assessment for individuals and groups of pupils' the NC for PE (2000) states:

> "... a minority of pupils will have particular learning and assessment
> requirements which go beyond the provisions described earlier (sections one
> and two) and if not addressed could create barriers to participation" (QCA
> 1999a p30)

The document indicates this is usually as a consequence of a child's disability or SEN. The curriculum suggests, in order to create access, greater differentiation on the part of teachers and the use of external agencies or specialist equipment will begin to enable inclusion to occur. This statement is fundamental in ensuring that teachers recognise their full responsibility for creating accessible lessons that cater for all pupils' needs, whilst recognising the need to work through a multi-agency approach to deliver inclusive activities (Depauw and Doll-Tepper 2000). This will necessitate teachers to have different expectations of some pupils with SEN, and/or the need to modify assessment in ways that offer children the opportunity to demonstrate development of their knowledge and understanding.

The strategies outlined so far, aim to move in the direction of 'least restrictive' activities within a context of support within 'regular', inclusive environments. This changing teaching philosophy supports many of the legislative changes that have occurred over recent years to support this practice (SEN and Disability Right Act

DFES 2001c) (Code of Practice DFES 2001b) (QCA 1999a). Within this backdrop the modern day approach to physical activity for disabled adults and children with SEN is to work towards an integration continuum for sport participation that supports regular (inclusive), rather than segregated (restrictive) provision (Winnick 1987). The model indicated in the earlier work of Winnick (1987) succinctly emphasises the context within which inclusive education for children with SEN should be established in the future.

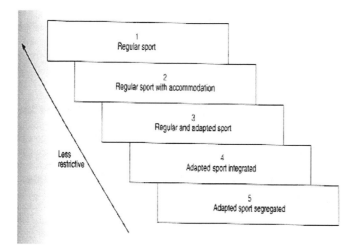

Figure 3.3 An integration continuum for sport participation (Winnick 1987)

3.6 Models for successful inclusion in PE and Sport

Models designed for the inclusion of children with SEN in PE can be grouped into three categories (Block and Volger 1994, Giangreco et al 1993,). These are based around:

Curriculum adaptation - changing what is taught;

Instructional modifications - changing how we teach;

Human or people resources - looking at changing who teaches or supports adapted aspects of PE.

These models have led to the successful inclusion of many children with SEN (Volger and Romance 2000, Slinger et al 2000, Goodwin and Watkinson 2000). As a result statutory agencies, teacher training providers, schools and teachers of PE should structure their future training and development around these three factors in order to progress inclusion for children with SEN. This is beginning to a certain extent to be looked at through the 02/02 (TTA 2002) 'Professional Standards Framework' (TTA 2002) and the inspection evidence gathered by OFSTED in both school and ITT contexts.

Many of the studies undertaken into good practice identify critical success factors related to teaching and learning, yet are more patchy in gauging the views and opinions of children with SEN related to their experiences of inclusive PE (Dyson and Millward 2000, Ainscow 1999, Skrtic 1991, 1995 Volger and Romance 2000, Slinger et al 2000). Goodwin and Watkinson (2000), in their study however identified a distinction between what they refer to as 'good days and bad days' for children with SEN in inclusive PE. The study found children with SEN who were involved in positive inclusive PE experiences described the 'good days' as being engaged in learning contexts with modified practices to accommodate their needs, feelings of progression in skill development, sense of belonging, and the support of teachers who were prepared to adopt flexible approaches to their involvement. These experiences support many of the issues noted earlier based upon curriculum adaptation, instructional modifications and human or people resources. In contrast, 'bad days' involved restricted participation (Winninck 2000) in which due to a lack of flexibility of approach children with SEN felt isolated, de-motivated, lacking in self-esteem and engaged in learning environments were teachers had not planned effectively for their involvement.

Figure 3.4 Thematic summary of inclusive physical education from the perspective of students with physical disabilities (Goodwin and Watkinson (2000)

In support of these findings, Place and Hodge (2001) looked at the behaviour of disabled and non-disabled children when engaged in inclusive PE related to levels of social interaction between the two groups of children. They found inclusive PE can lead to increased social interaction, but only if there is full recognition and due regard for inclusive PE as a process, which is practised within a context of:

Appropriate curricula adaptations – *recognising and valuing diversity, and planning effectively for its implementation;*

Instructional modifications – *based upon sound pedagogical practices that enhance rather than restrict inclusive activity;*

Sound human resources – *Incorporating PE teachers who are well equipped to deliver inclusive PE;*

Informed decision-making – *Based on consultation, reflection, and a readiness to modify and adapt strategies to facilitate inclusive activity.*

Slinger and Sherril (2000) support this view in their advocation of 'contact theory' in which they argue in order to eliminate prejudice, discrimination and establish environments that are conducive to learning; teachers of PE must plan effectively for inclusive lessons. They found that if teachers did not plan inclusive lessons, many shared opportunities for learning and development were missed and the overall success of inclusive learning was limited. This research demonstrates the need for trainee and qualified teachers to spend time planning effectively for inclusion within a context of readiness to change, and modify existing teaching and learning strategies. To some extent this 'culture', and 'attitude of mind' shift needs to be instilled in trainee teachers as part of their ITT if practices are to change and evolve once they begin to teach in schools.

3.7   Practical Examples of Inclusive PE for Children with SEN

When planning inclusive PE for pupils with SEN, it is important to start from the premise of full inclusion, and where this may not be possible, to consider adaptation or modification of learning and teaching activities (Winnick 1987, Winnick 2000). A central success factor for teachers is to consult, where appropriate with the child with SEN and relevant professionals as part of a multi-disciplinary approach. This enables the pupil and teachers to consider, at the planning stage, any differentiation that may be required (Goodwin and Watkinson 2000). This supports principles of equality, and the social model approach, which acknowledges individual diversity, whilst also responding to the needs of pupils with SEN by modifying or adapting activities as appropriate (NC 2000 Statutory Inclusion Statement, QCA 1999a).

An example of this could be in games activities such as hockey, where pupils may initially require lighter, larger or different coloured balls in order to access the activity. Adaptations to rules may need to be considered, such as allowing a player with movement restrictions five seconds to receive and play the ball. If utilising such a strategy, it is vital that all members of the group understand the need for such an adaptation (Slinger and Sherril 2000) in order that they can play to this rule during a game. In dance, activities can be adapted through consultation with the disabled and non- disabled pupils, as part of the requirements of the curriculum to work co-operatively. A pupil in a wheelchair for example can use the chair as an extension of their body to move around a particular area. If group tasks are to be performed, then the group can work together on themes for inclusion in which the movement patterns of the pupils with SEN can be incorporated into the overall group piece being performed. (Vickerman et al 2003).

Another example of inclusive participation in athletic activities with physically disabled pupils may involve one push of their wheelchair, rather than a jump into the sandpit, or reducing distances to run or travel. If there are pupils with visual impairments teachers can organise activities such as a 100-metre race in which a guide stands at the finish line and shouts out the lane number they are in, or a guide runs alongside them for support. Many of the suggestions indicated above support the points noted earlier of, needing to be open to change whilst recognising that this work is as an integral component of a PE teacher's general mixed ability teaching (Sugden and Talbot 1998). Consequently, the attitude of mind and motivation to change existing teaching and learning practices is central to successful inclusive activity (Dyson and Millward 2000, Ainscow 1999, Farrell 1998).

3.8 Opportunities for Pupils with SEN Outside of the Curriculum

Although the focus of this chapter relates to core curriculum matters in PE it is appropriate to highlight how pupils may access activity outside of curriculum time through extra-curricular and/or community based activities. This is of particular relevance as the PE NC (QCA 1999a) has direct links with school and extra curricula sporting activities of which children with SEN are just as entitled to as their non-disabled peers. There are a number of organisations and initiatives aimed at providing activity for pupils who have additional learning needs, and PE teachers as part of their extended inclusive practice should seek to develop partnership links with such organisations to serve the needs of the pupils post curriculum time. This is of particular relevance in the Governments recent 'Game Plan' (DCMS 2002) strategy, which encourages school – community links in order to ensure that the foundations of physical activity within the curriculum are built upon and extended after school into life-long enjoyment and participation in sport.

The structure of disability sport, like developments in inclusive PE is evolving. In 1997 Sport England's Task Force on the future of disability sport (Sport England 1997), recommended the mainstreaming of disability sport into the work of Governing Bodies of Sport. There was a clear recognition, however, that this was not going to occur in the short-term and that a considerable amount of work was going to have to be undertaken to achieve this objective. The EFDS was established in order to achieve the shift towards a more integrated approach to the provision of sport for children with SEN and disabled adults.

EFDS aims to expand sporting opportunities for disabled people and increase the numbers actively involved in sport. It also aims to ensure that people with disabilities are included in sporting opportunities, and to encourage a move towards more inclusive approaches of delivery.

There are currently nine EFDS regions, where teachers can access information about local and national opportunities, each comprising membership of seven National Disability Sports Organisations (NDSO's). The NDSO's are structured around impairment specific groups encompassing: British Amputee & Les Autres Sports Association; British Blind Sport; British Deaf Sports Council; British

Wheelchair Sports Foundation; Cerebral Palsy Sport; Disability Sport England and English Sports Association for People with Learning Disabilities. Whilst this reinforces the medical model of disability (Reiser and Mason 1990), the organisations have long established traditions, and the aim over time is to function through mainstream governing bodies of sport, and one umbrella disability governing body (EFDS). This will be in line with current thinking on evolving inclusive practice both within sport and PE. In addition, by agencies such as EFDS working alongside mainstream governing bodies of sport, and schools, it is envisaged that inclusive activity has real potential for success in the future.

3.9 Classification of Disability Sport and the Paralympic Movement

According to Richter et al (1992) classification systems have been widely used in sports to allow for fair and equitable starting points for competition.

There is a distinction to be made however between definitions and rationales for 'medical' and 'functional' models of classification. Medical classifications are concerned with verifying minimum levels of disability, whilst functional classification considers how an athlete performs in specific sports (Winnick 2000). Consequently, it is through functional classification that the structure of disability sport for competition purposes is organised. The functional classification as Richter et al (1992) indicates establishes a starting point for fair competition that takes account of how disability impacts upon performance in specific sports. The functional classification is characterised by over 40 separate physical profiles, and 3 categories for people with visual impairments. This system, although complex in relation to disabled athletes gaining classification (through assessment by a medical practitioner) has worked well in relation to competition for individuals with a physical disability. (Depauw and Gavron 1995).

The situation is more complex, and less clear when it comes to judgements on how 'intellectual cognition' relates to performance in sport, and this has been subject of much debate at International level, at events such as the Paralympic games. The paralympic games (parallel games) are the equivalent of the Olympic games, but are mainly concerned with provision for the physically disabled and those with visual impairments. Deaf people compete in the World Deaf Games, whilst people with learning disabilities have the Special Olympics and a separate Paralympic movement. This categorised and distinctive organisational approach has served disability sport well over the years. However, in light of more recent moves to inclusive environments there is significant debate on how this should be reflected in relation to competition for disabled groups and individuals. Consequently, at present whilst in school sport and PE the shift is towards inclusive activity, there will always be a place for disability sports activity through which children with SEN can compete on relatively even playing fields. As a result, teachers of PE will need to have a full appreciation of the structures of disability sport and the nature of classification systems if they are to enable children with SEN to access these structures. This is another issue that can be addressed by ITT providers as part of their work with trainee PE teachers.

The development of the Paralympic movement and disability sport is well documented (Depauw and Gavron 1995, Auxter 2001, Winninck 2000), with International competition in disability sport starting in 1948 at Stoke Mandeville as part of the 14th Olympic games held in London. The background to the development of the Stoke Mandeville games was to include sport as part of a rehabilitation process for people with spinal cord injuries. This was within the context of innovatory practice, which acknowledged that disabled people could still participate and compete in sport (and at high levels) despite any limiting mobility factors. The first Paralympics were held in Rome in 1960, and have developed and increased in size significantly culminating in the largest games in Sydney 2000. It was in Sydney that for the first time some disability events were held as part of the mainstream Olympic games, whilst the separate Paralympics had regular crowd attendances of 90,000 spectators. This demonstrated the interest and recognition of how far disability sport had come in recent years and reinforces the shift towards more inclusive approaches to sport and PE. This was further emphasised in the Manchester (2002) Commonwealth Games in which disabled and non-disabled athletes competed at the same event.

3.10 Finding Local Opportunities and Creating School-Community Links

There are two key pathways that can be followed in the development of school-community links for children with SEN as part of an extension to the formal PE curriculum, - disability-specific sports clubs, or mainstream sports clubs (Vickerman et al 2003). As part of Sport England's strategies for sport over a long period of time, most local authorities have established sports development officers who know where local sports clubs meet, and how accessible they are to disabled people. Some local authorities produce directories of sports clubs that provide opportunities for disabled people and sports development officers can act as invaluable links between school PE departments and local sports communities.

Governing Bodies of Sport, in line with Sport England's Disability Task Force, (Sport England 1997), are taking a more inclusive approach to their delivery. Initiatives such as the Amateur Swimming Association Swim 21 programme have ensured that disabled swimmers can access local swimming groups. EFDS' 'Ability Counts Programme' has worked with the Football Association to ensure that professional clubs include young disabled people in their community programmes, and local sports disability groups provide a good way of bridging the link between school and the community. Development work in disability sport is mainly concentrating at present on providing disabled people with more choice on the range of activities that they can become involved in, both within inclusive, adapted, and disability sport settings. Clearly there is still a considerable way to go before total inclusion and mainstreaming of disability sport is fully realised. It is easy to be critical, but it should be recognised that inclusion is becoming a reality (Depauw and Doll-Tepper 2000), and not just a possibility and strategies such as those by Sport England, and the development of EFDS, is complementing similar work being undertaken within the PE curriculum. New initiatives such as the introduction of Youth Sports Trust TOP Sportsability programmes have also added a new dimension to the area of inclusive PE provision. The equipment produced has been aimed specifically at special schools and mainstream schools with pupils with SEN.

Whilst this equipment is aimed at young people with SEN, all young people can join in playing by the same rules as their disabled peers. In addition five separate games were included in the equipment bag issued by the Youth Sports Trust, which can be used to help those pupils with severe disabilities. These games are known as Boccia, (a bowls type game), Table Cricket, Table Hockey, Polybat, (an adapted version of table tennis) and Goalball, (a game played by visually impaired people). Four of these games have pathways for young people to go on and progress from recreational level through to National, International and Paralympic competition which further supports the need to provide clear, consistent and achievable pathways for children with SEN to progress through in PE, school sport, and wider community sporting opportunities.

The tabletop games (although designed primarily to be played on a table tennis table) have the versatility so that they can be played at most tables. Polybat was designed for children with SEN who have control and co-ordination difficulties. The development of a glove bat has ensured that pupils who find it hard to grip a bat can handle the Polybat, and therefore can still participate successfully. In addition, activities such as goal ball (a 3-a-side game developed for visually impaired people) can involve sighted players in which everyone wears adapted goggles. This is an example of 'reverse inclusion' (Auxter et al 2001, Winnick 2000), where sighted people can be included in a disability-specific game as part of a PE teacher's use of the 'inclusion spectrum' noted earlier.

Although these activities go some way to addressing activity levels for people with disabilities, research undertaken by Sport England (2000) has highlighted some interesting differences in sports participation between people with disabilities and their non-disabled peers. For example the research found:

> *Over a quarter of young disabled people had not taken part in sport more than ten times in the past year, compared with 6 % of non-disabled young people;*
>
> *Over 56 % of young people with a disability had taken part in sport outside of school, compared with 87 % for the non-disabled population;*
>
> *37 % of young people with a disability had taken part in sport during their lunch break, compared to 67 % of the overall population of young people.*

Thus, whilst more opportunities are being created for young disabled people to participate either recreationally or competitively in sport, for the teacher of PE, and schools, it is knowing where and how to access the network of provision available at both local and/or national level. This situation could be improved through better-informed partnerships between school PE departments and disability organisations, both nationally and regionally, and should be seen as a developing role within a PE department's inclusive structures (Vickerman et al 2003).

3.11 The Role of Professional PE and Sport Associations

The roles of professional PE associations and NDSO's are vital to the successful development of PE and sporting provision at all levels of the continuum (from foundation, participation, through to performance and excellence). Although these agencies do not have statutory powers and responsibilities they are central to the development and support of the governments principles and desire to promote inclusive practice.

The PEA (UK) do not at present have formal policies related to the training of PE teachers for the inclusion of children with SEN. However, the intention is to establish such a policy statement in the near future. The draft PEA (UK) policy states:

> "... quality PE should be available to all pupils regardless of social background, gender, ability, culture, physique, religion, or race.... acknowledgement should be made of the wider spectrum of pupils fundamental needs regarding physical behaviour and intellect... in consequence all pupils will enjoy and benefit from a policy of physical, psychological, locational and circular inclusion" (PEA (UK), unpublished 2000)

BAALPE have produced a book 'Physical Education for Children with Special Needs in Mainstream Education (1989). In the book it supports the PEA (UK) belief that:

> "All children with special needs should take part in regular physical education lessons, an area of experience which is vital to their growth and development" (BAALPE 1989 p8).

They further emphasise this in advocating that educational policy should be focused around ensuring that as many children with SEN as possible are integrated into mainstream schools. In addition, they suggest teachers need to broaden their skills to accommodate children with a wide diversity of needs. Consequently, these professional associations need to provide advice and guidance to their membership, whilst lobby government to ensure sufficient training and support is given to teachers of PE in the future.

3.12 Concluding Thoughts and a Rationale for inclusive PE

The PE NC (2000) clearly supports the notion of inclusion through a set of statements that are based upon ensuring that teachers set setting suitable learning challenges; respond to pupils diverse learning needs; and overcoming potential barriers to learning and assessment in order to accommodate all children's needs. However, in setting out to achieve such an inclusive approach Dyson (1999) notes some concern with the concept of disability now being:

> "... at the heart of a new and privileged society" (Dyson 1999, p2)

According to Dyson, 'social inclusion' is limited as it only pursues measures to remove difference that focus upon predicted equality, and are not necessarily outcome based. Therefore implementation of policies by official line agencies may appear to be socially and morally right, but the danger is that measurement will be through expectations for statements written into policies. However success should be judged in terms of its impact and effects upon a child's quality of education and achievement. (See Depauw and Doll-Tepper 2000; Dyson 2001, Farrell 2000, 2001 for further issues related to policy implementation and practice). Thus, greater focus in the future must be turned to the development of facilitating inclusive practice through pedagogical practices, rather than simply making policy statements of intent (Dyson 1999, Dyson 2001, Dyson and Millward 2000).

On examining the inclusion statement in relation to PE, these fundamental requirements, in conjunction with recent legislative changes will require PE ITT providers to review their current strategies. They will need to ensure that PE teachers of the future are able to facilitate and empower children with SEN to have a full entitlement, and accessibility to the curriculum. The PE Handbook, which accompanies the revised NC, sets an expectation that the curriculum should be based around the key principle of openness and accessibility and a belief that:

"… equality of opportunity is one of a broad set of common values and purposes which underpin the school curriculum and the work of schools" (QCA 1999b, p4)

Dyson (1999) supports such a move as part of the process model that moves beyond recognition of principles and philosophical standpoints and moves into the practice of action based upon how the curriculum relates to outcomes that can be differentiated and measured for each child. A key feature of this occurring will need to be based upon a strong emphasis of consultation between teachers, pupils with SEN, parents and professionals (Vickerman 1997, Vickerman 2002). This will need to be undertaken with the context of models of best practice in teaching and learning in inclusive education noted earlier (Dyson 2001, Farrell 1998, Winnick 2000, Goodwin and Watkinson 2000).

The PE handbooks (QCA 1999a; 1999b) indicate a minority of pupils will have particular learning and assessment requirements which go beyond the provisions described earlier and if not addressed could create barriers to participation, and this is usually as a consequence of a child's' disability or SEN. In suggesting methods to overcome potential barriers to participation, the handbook states that in order to create access, greater differentiation on the part of teachers and the use of external agencies or specialist equipment will begin to enable inclusion to occur. This statement is fundamental in ensuring that teachers recognise their responsibility of creating accessible lessons that cater for all pupils' needs.

Westwood (1997) supports the promotion of citizenship and the social model of disability within the curriculum, as a means of shifting the emphasis away from the pupils with the disability to the roles that teachers and non-disabled peers can play in facilitating all children's' learning. However, Westwood notes some caution in ignoring the complexity of defining inclusion and its current ability to be facilitated by teachers, due to their lack of clarity and training of this subject area. If as the PE NC (2000) suggests:

"Teachers must take action…" and *"Ensure that their pupils are enabled to participate." (QCA 1999a p33)*

… a greater focus on models of best practice in teaching and learning pedagogy will need to be considered in the future.

In conclusion, if teachers of PE are to enable pupils with SEN to benefit from inclusive education the fundamental principles outlined in this chapter must be drawn together to provide a cohesive framework for practice. This will need to reflect upon the policy positions, definitions, and interpretations of SEN in PE, whilst crucially focussing on providing teachers with the teaching and learning strategies to make inclusion a reality.

Following the methodology, the study will now move towards an examination of the key themes and issues that have emerged from this, and the previous chapter (two), in relation to how answers to the four research questions outlined in chapter one can begin to be addressed. Consequently in relation to the main research question of 'how is the current training of PE teachers for inclusive settings implemented', a thorough examination of the literature to date and the research findings at each level of investigation will be analysed. As part of this process, the models of best teaching and learning practice, policy provision and implementation by teachers in schools indicated in this and the previous chapter will be examined in the context of the extent to which existing provision is demonstrating evidence or a move in the directions indicated earlier. As a result, in addition to evidence of best current inclusive practice, areas of weakness and models for future delivery and practice will be highlighted in order to provide a comprehensive overview of the present and future direction of inclusive PE for children with SEN.

C H A P T E R   F O U R :
METHODOLOGY

4.1   Background and Context

This chapter considers issues related to the establishment of the research questions, whilst examining the challenges, justifications and rationales that underpin the selected methodical approaches undertaken within this study. The studies main question of *"How is the current training of PE teachers for inclusive settings implemented?"* is approached through a triangulation of three areas of concern. These are the 'official line', 'professional opinion and practice', and the 'consumers', each containing a further sub question, that relates back to the main research question. According to Robson (1999) triangulation:

> *"… is an indispensable tool in real world enquiry. It is particularly valuable in the analysis of qualitative data where the trustworthiness of the data is always a worry. It provides a means of testing one source of information against other sources" (Robson 1999, p382).*

The need for such an approach was considered vital to this study, due to the three levels of interpretation being closely interrelated. For example, the initial basis for the research stems from the **'official line'** (statutory and professional agencies) view as a means of establishing the overarching background and context for the investigation. This involved clarification of policy directions, professional expectations of teachers, and the interpretation and implementation of inclusive PE for children with SEN. In examining this position, a critical success factor is dependant upon gauging the knowledge, understanding and practices of ITT providers (the second level of interpretation – **'professional opinion and practice'**) in ensuring that PE teachers are adequately prepared to deliver inclusive PE for children with SEN. As a result, the third level of investigation addresses the professional ability and commitment of trainee and qualified teachers (the **'consumers'**) to deliver inclusive PE for children with SEN. Consequently, this final phase acts as the ultimate benchmark against which official line, and professional opinion and practice positions are judged in relation to ensuring policy is implemented in practice.

Depauw and Doll-Tepper (2000) support this view with their desire to ensure inclusive education does not just become part of an official line 'bandwagon discourse', but impacts in practice. Thus, whilst official line policies are important, the real yardstick is ensuring teachers of PE are equipped to make a difference when they work with children with SEN. According to Dyson (2001) therefore, production of policies in government, statutory agencies, ITT institutions and schools is the easy part – the success factors rest however in the outcomes of inclusive practice for children with SEN.

Within this backdrop, the chapter addresses the methodological discussion through a combination of two inter-related themes. Firstly, an examination of the rationale behind the chosen methodological approaches engaging extensive analysis of the process of self-criticality undertaken in order to arrive at a systematic research design. This analysis offers a valuable insight into the personal dilemmas and resolutions that were considered prior to the establishment of the final research design. Secondly, the chapter provides an overview of the research design, and five-stage methodological approach that was finally undertaken. As part of this analysis, the various research tools utilised to examine the main and sub research questions are also outlined.

4.2 Rationale and Self-Criticality of Designing a Systematic Research Design

Research methodology processes and procedures need to demonstrate that they have both a systematic structure, (Robson 1999, Moore 2000, Lloyd 2000) and be able to satisfy objectives of 'transferability, credibility, dependability and conformability' (Robson 1999). The methodological processes within this study were constructed to ensure that the key objectives set out by Robson (1999) became an integral component of the research design. As a result It is argued the theoretical framework within this study can be readily reassigned to other inclusive PE settings (transferability), whilst at the same time taking note of the real world settings, themes and dilemmas associated with this area of research. Thus, the triangulation of the three areas of concern (official line, professional opinion and practice, and the consumers) recognises the inter-relationship and complexity of inclusive PE provision for children with SEN. As a result, each of the five stages of the study outlined later in this chapter (See Figure 4.1) reflect different 'real life' aspects of the current process of training PE teachers for inclusive settings related to children with SEN. In undertaking such an approach, the study offered opportunities to interpret both isolated, and holistic perspectives on a wide and varied range of issues concerned with PE teacher training, inclusion and SEN.

In relation to 'credibility' of research design, this was achieved through prolonged involvement with subjects, persistent observation, triangulation of the three levels of concern, evidence of peer de-briefing, informed consent, confidentiality of subjects, and public presentation of the data evidence. Therefore, from the initial examination of official line literature, through to the analysis of PE ITT provider's provision, and finally delivery and interpretation by PE teacher's, careful and sustained involvement with the subjects and agencies concerned is clearly evidenced. As a result, it is argued the 'dependability' and accuracy of the studies research processes are, systematic, clearly evidenced and sufficiently rigorous to be subject to external scrutiny.

In addition, consideration of bias and trustworthiness of the chosen methodologies has been addressed at each of the five stages of the research design. This has been examined with particular reference to recognition of the potential for both researcher and subject bias. In regard to Robsons fourth key objective of 'conformability', the research design examined within this chapter enables researchers and professionals external to the study the opportunity to follow and replicate the chosen methodology, within a systematic and cohesive design structure. This enables the findings to be checked against the different levels of analysis of official line, professional opinion and practice, and consumers, as well as providing a level of transparency and justification of the studies outcomes within the wider context of training PE teachers to include children with SEN.

According to Robson (1999), entering into any kind of investigation involving other people is necessarily a complex, and sensitive undertaking and to do this you need to know what you are doing. In exploring the methodological approaches within this study, it is contended that the research design stands the test of Robson's (1999) four key themes of transferability, credibility, dependability and conformability. Within this context, the next part of this chapter proceeds to a personal, and critical reflection of the rationale behind the chosen research methodology. It is envisaged this will offer a helpful insight into the many decisions that were taken in arriving at the final five stage methodological approach.

4.3   A Personal Reflection on the Research Design

In designing this study, there were many issues that had to be considered prior to arriving at an appropriate methodological approach. This involved extensive examination of potential research methodologies, at a personal level, in conjunction with my supervisor, and through the PhD upgrading process.

In attempting to arrive at a strategy that would enable me to analyse the research questions it was important to initially identify a baseline position of where the current policies, strategies, views and opinions stood on the issue of inclusion of children with SEN in PE. In order to address the main research question of **"How is the current training of PE teachers for inclusive settings implemented?"** a first step was to identify the stakeholders who had an involvement in this process. Following consideration of this question many agencies and individuals were identified as playing a role in this process such as government, statutory agencies, professional associations, ITT providers, schools, trainee and qualified PE teachers, children with SEN and parents. In order to try and structure the various stakeholders, I decided to group people into a number of areas in order to consider how to examine the various views and opinions related to the main research question.

In organising the stakeholders into groups, this helped establish three further sub questions, which will be discussed later. As a result, the stakeholders were grouped into three categories, whilst at the same time recognising that some of the agencies as part of the delivery of their functions may be involved in more than one category. In order to address the recognition of potential partnership working across more than one of the categories, a decision was made to place each stakeholder into the area in which they had major, rather than minor involvement. For example, the TTA can be recognised as playing a role both at government level as well as with ITT PE providers. However, there significant functions relate to setting policy and standards in ITT, rather than engaging directly in the delivery of ITT. As result of this process the three categories were identified as:

Official line agencies: Including government, statutory agencies, professional PE, and disability sport associations

Professional opinion and practice: PE ITT providers and schools

Consumers: *trainee and qualified PE teachers, schools, parents and children with SEN*

Following this initial grouping of stakeholders, further decisions had to be made

regarding the extent to which all of the agencies and individuals could sufficiently be

examined, whilst being cognisant of the main research question concerned with

"How is the current training of PE teachers for inclusive settings

implemented?" Therefore, a decision was made to construct further sub questions

related to each of the three stakeholder levels of official line, professional opinion and

practice, and the consumers. In deciding to undertake such a strategy, the three sub

questions would further enable opportunities to triangulate a diverse range of views,

opinions, policies and practices, whilst contributing to analysing the main research

question for the study. As a result of the identification of the three categories, a

further decision was then made to logically address each of the three levels in turn as

part of the establishment of a coherent and systematic methodological approach to

this study. Figure 4.1 provides an overview of the final five-stage research design for

the study, and the next part of this chapter gives details of how this process was

established.

Figure 4.1 Overview of the Research Design for the Study

Stage one – Official line

Review of literature and enquiry letters sent to seven official line agencies: DFES,

QCA, OFSTED, TTA, BAALPE, PEA (UK), EFDS.

Stage two – Professional opinion and practice (part 1)

Questionnaires to the 30 PE Initial Teacher Training (ITT) providers delivering secondary

undergraduate and/or postgraduate PE

Stage three – Professional opinion and practice (Part 2)

Face to face, taped and transcribed depth interviews with 5 selected PE ITT providers on the

basis of geographical location, range of OFSTED grades and mix of provision (i.e. large,

small, undergraduate, and or postgraduate provision)

Stage four – Consumers (Part 1)

Questionnaires to the 5 selected PE ITT provider's final year trainees

---

Stage five – consumers (Part 2)

Questionnaires to a random sample of PE teachers between NQT status and 2 years post

qualifying experience from the 5 selected PE ITT providers

4.4   A Critique of the Official Line Approach (Stage One)

Following the decision to consider each of the three levels of investigation in turn, the logical starting point was to examine the views and opinions of those agencies at the official line level. Particularly as they were responsible largely for giving strategic direction and policy guidance to the second and third categories of professional opinion and practice, and the consumers.

In order to begin to address the first set of issues concerned with the official line, a sub question was established of *"What are the views and policies of government, statutory agencies and PE associations in relation to the delivery of inclusive PE for children with SEN?"* This first step involved identifying which agencies played a strategic role in either policy direction, and/or had opportunities to influence provision and delivery within ITT and school based PE settings for children with SEN. As a result, seven **'official line agencies'** were identified as contributing to this process comprising government (DFES), statutory bodies (TTA, OFSTED, QCA) and PE and disability sport agencies (PEA (UK), BAALPE, EFDS).

Once the seven official line agencies were established the next decision was to consider the most appropriate method of gauging the current strategic policy, guidance, legislation and expectations related to inclusion, SEN and PE. There were many methods that could have been undertaken in order to analyse these issues. For example, questionnaires could have been sent to each official line agency in order to determine views and opinions whilst establishing policy directives, guidance, and nature of involvement in inclusive PE, ITT provision and delivery to children with SEN in schools. However, a problematic issue here would have been whom to send the questionnaires to, and the extent to which details of strategy, policy, and views and opinions would have been gained. Another possibility could have been to undertake face-to-face interviews with representatives from each of the official line agencies, however similar issues to those noted with the questionnaires were becoming apparent, as well as a concern that I was going to initially get too close to a personal, rather than strategic view of issues related to the research question.

Therefore, it was decided as a **stage one phase** to undertake a comprehensive literature review of the current official line policy view, whilst offering the opportunity for each of the seven agencies to give free responses (via an enquiry letter) to the studies research outline. In arriving at this decision it was felt that a baseline of the current position was important to establish, prior to an examination of the extent to which agencies and individuals at the professional opinion and practice and consumer levels were equipped to implement national agendas.

The first stage of the research involved examination of official line agencies documentation and policy positions related to their views and policies on the delivery of inclusive PE for children with SEN. This process comprised of two phases, one involving an enquiry letter sent to each official line agency, and secondly a review of literature (i.e. scrutiny of policy documentation, articles, web sites, definitions and interpretations of inclusion, and guidance materials) produced by the respective agencies. The intention of this was twofold; firstly to establish areas of commonality and diversity in official line policy, and secondly to use the data collected as a basis to prompt questions at the professional opinion and practice and consumer levels. In addition, the concept of inclusion in general, and related to PE, was undertaken in order to ascertain existing knowledge, understanding and literature related to inclusive education. This data was then used as a means of establishing questions for consideration at the professional opinion and practice and consumer levels of interpretation, whilst at the same time establishing from the outset a contextual overview and baseline position for the remainder of the research.

4.5   Enquiry Letters to Official Line Agencies

Seven official line agencies were posted an enquiry letter (see appendix 1),

explaining the context of the study, and inviting open comments, submission of

documentation and interpretations of inclusive PE teacher training for children with

SEN. Each official line agency was re-contacted up to a maximum of three times at

monthly intervals to prompt responses, and this process achieved a 100% return rate

from the respective agencies. The level of information received range from extensive

through to one page written submissions. According to Moore (2000), issues of

response rate and bias must be considered when relying on people to complete

questionnaires or letters, especially as the:

> "... characteristics of those who do respond, compared with those who do not
> maybe different" (Moore 2000, p 144).

This was an initial issue with the official line letters as some agencies responded

promptly, whilst others received repeat letters prior to gaining a successful full

response from each of the agencies. Therefore, in gaining a 100% response rate the

concern of Moore (2000) was minimised greatly, in that all the 'key players' had the

opportunity to respond to the studies research questions.

4.6   Review of Official Line Literature

In conjunction with the letter responses from official line agencies, an extensive

literature review was undertaken to establish areas of commonality and diversity in

relation to the training of PE teachers for the inclusion of children with SEN. Moore

(2000) supports the need to undertake literature reviews where issues and research

questions related to policies are:

> "... problematic and contentious concepts that are open to a number of
> different interpretations" (Moore 2000, p 156).

Consequently, Moore suggests that by undertaking such reviews it is possible to identify key themes and issues about the way people think and feel towards complex issues like inclusive PE for children with SEN. This was the case within this study in which through the examination of official line letter responses, and literature reviews it was possible to frame questions and contextual overviews to be explored further at the professional opinion and practice, and consumers levels of interpretation.

As part of the establishment of the initial contexts for the study, an examination and interpretation of terminology and definitions concerning the term 'inclusion' and 'SEN' was also undertaken as part of the literature review. This was seen an essential component of the first stage of the official line research process, because as Lloyd (2000) suggests there is an assumption:

> "… that there is some kind of agreement about what is meant by equality of opportunity and inclusion" (Lloyd 2000, p166).

Consequently, within the field of inclusive education many questions have been asked with regard to the ability of organisations to have parity of definition and interpretation of policies, which are fundamentally complex in nature (Farrell 1998, Ainscow 1998, Dyson 2001, Skrtic 1995). Depauw and Doll-Tepper (2000) support and extend this view by suggesting that when considering the interpretation and definition of inclusion, the extent to which agencies enter into the inclusion debate as part of a myth, reality, or response to:

> "… current bandwagon debates" (Depauw and Doll-Tepper 2000, p78)

… must be fully considered. This is one such reason why the need to establish the key issues, areas of commonality and diversity of provision through letters and literature searches was undertaken, prior to further analysis later in the study.

4.7   A Critique of the Professional Opinion and Practice Approach (Stages Two & Three)

In order to address the issues related to the second level of interpretation it was recognised the main agencies and individuals involved in this process were PE ITT providers, lecturing staff, trainee teachers and partnership schools involved in the training process. Following examination of the main research question a decision was made to focus upon the ITT part of the provision, and gauge the relationship of school based training provision via the PE training providers. In part, this decision was made as a consequence of ensuring that the focus of the study remained with the training process for which ITT providers have a primary responsibility. In addition however, as part of the upgrading process it was recognised that in order to separately examine school based views and opinions, the scope of the study was going to be too large, and it would detract from the primary purpose of focusing on the training process for PE teachers.

Therefore, the second sub question at the professional opinion and practice level was established as **"What are the processes and course contents of initial teacher training institutions related to inclusive PE for children with SEN?"** In order to answer this sub question, several further decisions had to be made regarding the most appropriate method of gaining an insight into the processes and course contents related to inclusive PE for children with SEN. It was felt that as with the establishment of a baseline position of literature, and views and opinions undertaken at the official line level, a similar approach should be implemented as part of the second level of interpretation. Consequently, a decision was made to survey the views, opinions, processes and course contents of all the secondary PE ITT providers in England. This involved gaining a list of the 30 ITT PE providers receiving funding from the TTA in the academic year 2000/2001.

Once a decision had been made to survey each of the 30 PE ITT providers, the next step was to design an approach that would gain an insight into processes and course contents that would not be too labour intensive. Therefore, it was decided that it would have been highly problematic to have either visited each of the 30 PE ITT providers, undertake face-to-face interviews, and/or observe delivery of practice. As a result, the most appropriate approach was to send a questionnaire to each of the 30 PE ITT providers (stage two) in order to gain an insight into both individual institutional approaches, whilst building a national picture of the current provision within England.

Once it had been decided to undertake a questionnaire survey, the next step was to consider the design and nature of questions to be asked. This process involved a reflection upon literature and views that were going to be gained from the official line agencies in order to ascertain the extent to which policy was being implemented, as well as whether ITT providers felt equipped to prepare PE teachers for the inclusion of children with SEN. Consequently, the stage two questionnaire (see appendix two) was constructed around a series of open and closed questions in order to gain an insight into the views and opinions of the PE training providers. Once the content had been established, a decision was made to send the questionnaire to the Heads of Department and or members of staff responsible for inclusion within each ITT provider. This was relatively easy to establish as I regularly attend national PE ITT network meetings, and have direct access to lists of the appropriate contacts.

Following the decision to send questionnaires to each of the 30 PE ITT providers, I was still of the opinion that there was going to be a need to gain further insight of PE ITT providers views and opinions through some format of more personal contact. Therefore, the earlier thoughts of either face-to-face contact, or possibly some form of either telephone interviews or supplementary questionnaires began to emerge. As part of this process I considered the logical phased approach to the research design that was beginning to emerge, which led me to think about the third level of interpretation. This related to a consideration of how I was going to gain access to the views and opinions of trainee and qualified PE teachers, schools, parents and children with SEN?

Following extensive examination of attempting to establish a logical, and coherent approach to the research design for the study, I decided that the ITT providers were going to be an important vehicle through which I could gain access to trainee, qualified teachers, and schools. Additionally, this would help me gain an insight into how official line policy was being addressed by ITT providers at the level of professional opinion and practice, whilst also enabling me to analyse its impact in delivery by PE teachers at the level of the consumers. As a consequence of this deliberation, and as part of the auditing of official line literature and National PE ITT provision the opportunity was beginning to emerge to track the impact of policy in practice through discussion with ITT providers, trainee and qualified teachers. Thus, a decision was made to identify a number of PE ITT providers for more extensive examination, following the return of the stage two questionnaires.

This decision led to the construction of a stage three phase of the research design, in which via contact with a selection of PE ITT providers a further insight into the questionnaire responses at stage two could be determined. In addition this process would help with the feed forward of information into further phases of the research design at the consumer level. As a result, it was decided that face-to-face visits should be undertaken with a selection of PE ITT providers in order to gain a rich insight into their questionnaire responses through depth interviews, whilst also seeking consent to examine the views and opinions of their trainee and qualified PE teachers. Following the return of questionnaires, it was decided there would be a need to identify criteria that could be acknowledged as fair and against which selection could be established. Consequently, the criteria for selection of follow up face-to-face interviews comprised of:

An agreement to undertake a face-to-face depth interview;

An agreement to offer access to trainee and previously qualified PE teachers;

Geographical variation within England;

Range of OFSTED grades;

Variety of PE ITT provision (encompassing the full range of provision from the full 30 providers initially surveyed by questionnaires) including large and small undergraduate and postgraduate trainee numbers

Following examination of these criteria, five PE ITT providers were finally selected for face-to-face depth interviews. A decision was made to tape and transcribe the interviews (see appendix three), especially as it was envisaged that a rich source of data was going to be gained from these discussions. Consequently, following the return of the stage two questionnaires, and agreement from the five PE ITT providers for follow up face-to-face taped and transcribed depth interviews, further consideration of the nature of the questioning needed to be examined. This process involved an identification of key themes and issues that were going to emerge from the questionnaire returns at stage two of the research design. As a result of the identification of the two phases of research at the professional opinion and practice level it was envisaged that an extensive insight would be gained in order to prepare for further analysis at the consumer level of interpretation.

The intention of the professional opinion and practice phase of the study was to gain ITT provider's perspectives on the training of PE teachers for the inclusion of children with SEN, which was seen as the 'central hub' upon which the studies research questions link the official line and consumer perspectives together. This phase of the study also focused on a relatively limited area of previous research within the field of

PE, SEN and inclusion. Prior to this study, the main body of research undertaken in the area of inclusive education has mainly centred upon the impact of inclusion from either official line (i.e. statutory or policy level) or consumer (impact of inclusion) viewpoints (Barton 1997, Depauw and Doll-Tepper 2000, Farrell 2000, 2001, Dyson 2001). Therefore, it was envisaged that through the examination of PE teacher training processes related to SEN and inclusion a rich insight would be gained on the interpretation of government policy, and its implementation by teachers within schools.

In order to examine complex issues related to inclusive PE, Depauw and Doll-Tepper (2000) suggest there must be some analysis of the extent to which:

> "... regular PE or normal PE remains the normal and dominant programme"
> (Depauw and Doll-Tepper 2000, p 138)

Thus, questions must be asked about the extent to which ITT PE provider's, and teachers examine goals for achieving inclusion or integration. (Depauw and Doll-Tepper, 2000). Therefore, the professional opinion and practice stages of the study can be seen as fundamental to the examination of whether teachers are considered adequately prepared for the inclusion of children with SEN. As a result, it is this area of concern in which Depauw and Doll-Tepper (2000) note that there is previously:

> "... little analysis of the deconstruction of regular PE occurring" (Depauw and
> Doll-Tepper (2000, p 138).

It is with these thoughts in mind, that the professional opinion and practice questions were constructed, and examined in relation to the nature of how PE subject knowledge and understanding is developed by the ITT providers, and the extent to which they embrace inclusion within both their own, and students thinking.

119

The research at the professional opinion and practice level attempted to therefore unpack such questions, concerns and issues through a combination of qualitative and quantitative data collection. The initial sampling of data from the 30 ITT PE providers, gained through the questionnaire enabled the establishment of key themes and issues to be identified, and examined in detail during the stage three face-to-face depth interviews. Moore (2000) supports such a methodological approach, and suggests it is possible to take a sample from an initially larger data group, then look in detail and infer characteristics of the whole group through face-to-face interviews. Haug (1998) also supports the notion of questionnaires, followed by in depth interviews, and argues discourses on SEN and action that take place often reinforce certain truths, while negating others. This study therefore attempted to tease out some of the general themes and issues, as indicated by Moore (2000) and Haug (1998), prior to further exploration, scrutiny and clarification in the taped and transcribed depth interviews with selected ITT PE providers.

4.8   Stage 2 – Questionnaires to ITT PE Providers

A detailed questionnaire was posted to all 30 PE ITT providers in England in order to examine their views, opinions and perspectives on the training of PE teachers for inclusive education with children with SEN. The questionnaire was initially piloted for clarity by gaining comments and responses from 10 University Lecturers working in the field of PE and teacher training. The comments and suggestions were noted prior to the questionnaire being mailed out to the 30 respective institutions. The accompanying covering letter can according to Moore (2000):

> "... improve the response rate by fifteen percentage points" (Moore 2000, p114)

... and care was taken to give a clear indication of the design, intention and time involved. The questionnaire contained a total of 43 questions that focused upon 8 themes titled: About you, About your institution, Management and co-ordination of SEN, Programme content and delivery, Links with schools and mentors, Partnerships with disability sport/special needs agencies, Values and Attitudes and Other views and opinions. Informed consent was gained from respondents, and an abstract of the findings were collated and distributed to all participants once analysed.

The questionnaires were posted to either named Heads of Department, or lecturers with responsibility for the delivery of inclusive education. Follow up letters and questionnaires were re-mailed up to a maximum of three times, if no initial response was received within one month. A total of 24 responses out of 30 PE ITT providers were finally received, representing a return rate of 80%. The total number of secondary PE student places across the 24 institutions returning a questionnaire was 2151, with cohorts ranging from 5 to 380. The postgraduate percentage of the 2151 student places was 21.48% whilst the undergraduate ratio was 78.52%.

The data from the questionnaires was collated initially by allocating each PE ITT provider a number between 1-24 in order to preserve confidentiality of the subjects and institutions involved. The data was then analysed, and represented in graph format for the closed responses, whilst the open-ended responses were used as a basis for framing the follow up questions in the face-to-face depth interviews. This supports the view of Booth et al (1997) who argues interviews help to shape our talk around a set of general findings initially gained from questionnaires. In addition, Barton and Thomlinson (1981) support the use of follow up face to face depth interviews in order to tackle the inherent assumptions and contradictions of research with questionnaires. In further considering the problematic nature of self-completion questionnaires, Moore (2000) suggests that they are unlikely to produce a great depth of information, as people tend to fill them in quickly, giving immediate, rather than considered responses. As a consequence of this view, the initial (stage two) questionnaires to all PE ITT providers were used to build a broader picture, of the key and emerging themes rather than be used to make detailed judgements on issues of depth, which can be subject to more extensive analysis and scrutiny in the face-to-face taped and transcribed depth interviews.

4.9 Stage 3 - Face to Face Taped and Transcribed Depth Interviews

Following the 24 questionnaire returns, five PE ITT providers were identified on the basis of a stratified sample, according to the set criteria noted earlier for a follow up face-to-face depth interview. The interviewees were initially contacted by telephone to seek approval for a follow up interview. The depth interviews took place in the individual PE ITT provider's institutions and consent forms were signed prior to the start of the interviews. The interviews were taped and transcribed with subjects being sent a full copy of the content of the discussions following their interviews. On average each interview lasted two hours. The discussion was framed around 14 questions (see appendix 3), which allowed the researcher an opportunity to clarify data on attitudes, feelings beliefs, and action from individual providers. The five taped and transcribed interviews were coded from A-E to preserve confidentiality, and some limited background details on each provider is given below:

PE ITT provider A: Large undergraduate four year undergraduate course in the North of England

PE ITT provider B: Large undergraduate four year undergraduate course in the South of England

PE ITT provider C: Large one year postgraduate course in the Midlands

PE ITT provider D: Small undergraduate four year undergraduate course in the South of England

PE ITT provider E: Small one-year postgraduate course in the Midlands

The face-to-face taped and transcribed interviews, offered an opportunity to explore emerging issues and themes through a qualitative methodological approach which, according to Robson (1999) is:

> "... all about developing a detailed understanding of individuals views, attitudes and behaviours" (Robson 1999, p403)

In employing such methods following the initial questionnaires, this allowed respondents to talk, often at great length about their feelings and underlying attitudes, beliefs and values towards inclusive PE and children with SEN. The responses were coded according to four factors of seeking to demonstrate credibility transferability dependability and conformability (Robson 1999) of the results in relation to the stage two questionnaires as a means of validating the findings. The content of the depth interviews also assisted with the framing of the questionnaires at the consumer level of interpretation with trainee and recently qualified PE teachers.

In relation to researcher bias, Robson (1999) offers some caution related to the trustworthiness of qualitative research, and how this can be monitored at all stages of the research process. This is of particular relevance when examining contentious issues in which a rich insight into the general and specific issues related to training PE teachers for inclusive education is gained through face-to-face depth interviews. In order to consider the inextricable links of the researchers views, and those of the subjects under investigation the interviewer spent time recording his personal responses and pre-conceptions of inclusive PE prior to discussion in the interviews.

This helped establish my thinking, and personal views as well as set in place structures, in which the researcher could compare their own views with those gained during the research. In constructing this reflective log of personal views and opinions, it assisted with consideration of the comparability, contrasts, similarities and differences of researcher and subject interpretations during the study.

4.10 A Critique of the Consumer Approach (Stages 4 & 5)

After the logical progression of examining the literature and baseline perspectives at the official line, followed by its interpretation by ITT providers at the professional opinion and practice level, the next stage was to consider the impact on delivery by teachers in schools. Prior to the PhD upgrading process, the initial intention was to consider a range of consumer views encompassing trainee and qualified PE teachers, parents and children with SEN. However on the advice of the upgrading panel, it was felt that it was going to be too extensive a study to undertake research on gaining the views of children with SEN in relation to their perceptions of inclusive PE. This is not to say that their views are less relevant than any of the other stakeholders, but merely recognises the constraints within which the size and scope of this study can be undertaken. However, the views and perceptions of children with SEN, and their advocates is something which I would wish to extend this study to consider at some point in the future, and in many ways is the next logical progression following the outcomes of this research.

The decision was made therefore, to consider the extent to which trainee and qualified PE teachers felt equipped to deliver inclusive PE to children with SEN under the sub question of **"What are the views and opinions of current student trainees and recently qualified PE teachers related to their training for inclusive education?"** This decision to consider the views and opinions of student, and qualified PE teachers was twofold. Firstly, it gave an opportunity to reflect on perceptions of readiness to deliver inclusive PE whilst in training, and once in practice. Secondly, it enables the opportunity to gain an insight into the professional development of PE teachers at different stages of their career development.

In order to ascertain the similarities and differences of perception amongst trainee and qualified PE teachers, the decision was made to split this process into two phases. A **Stage four phase** - with the trainee teachers, and a **stage five phase** with the qualified teachers. In relation to the stage four process of gaining the views and opinions of trainee PE teachers there were a number of options that were considered within the research design. Firstly, it would be relevant to use the five selected PE ITT providers at the professional opinion and practice level to determine the extent to which the views expressed by their University lecturers were being acknowledged. Secondly, it offers a further opportunity to logically proceed from the initial literature searches at the official line level, to the National and selected survey at the professional opinion and practice level, prior to tracking through the views of trainee teachers currently being prepared to deliver inclusive PE to children with SEN. Thirdly, by already gaining the consent of the five selected PE ITT providers, access to their trainee PE teachers was going to be a relatively easy process to organise.

Following consideration of the issues noted above, the next concern was which students to select. In relation to the trainee teachers on a PCE course, there were no issues to consider, as they only undertake a one-year course. However, in relation to trainees on four year undergraduate programmes it was felt that final year students would be in the best position to evaluate their ITT training, as they would of had the opportunity to undertake extensive school based training experiences, and would have engaged in lectures on aspects of SEN and inclusive provision. The next consideration was how to ascertain the views and opinions of the trainee teachers, and several options were considered. For example, trainee teachers could have been observed whilst on school based practice, or in tutorials and lectures whilst at University. This would however have proven problematic to standardise, as well for me to be available at appropriate times, and gain insights into individual views and opinions. As a result, face-to-face interviews would also have proven problematic as well as being subject to potentially small sample populations.

The decision was therefore taken to distribute a questionnaire containing similar open and closed questionnaires to all final year trainee teachers from the five selected PE ITT providers. This gave the opportunity for a large sample gathering, and offered opportunities to track key themes and issues gained from the research at the official line, and professional opinion and practice stages of the research design. Furthermore, in order to ensure a high return rate, each of the five selected PE ITT providers was offered a guest lecture on PE and SEN, at which time the questionnaires could be distributed, collected, then followed by a lecture. This method had many advantages in that it gave something back to the selected PE ITT providers and trainee teachers who had agreed to engage in this study, whilst providing high return rates for the questionnaire.

In relation to the **stage five phase** involving qualified PE teachers, similar considerations to those indicated in stage four were undertaken. However, there were further complications with regard to ready access to qualified teachers who had now left the ITT provider and could be employed anywhere in the country. As a result, it was decided to contact recently qualified teachers up to a period of two years post qualifying experience. This had two major advantages, firstly ITT providers keep data on first destination statistics and many teachers may still be in their first teaching posts. Secondly it offers the opportunity to ask teachers to reflect both upon their recent ITT and subsequent abilities to deliver inclusive PE to children with SEN as recently qualified teachers.

Consequently, it was decided as part of the logical process of measuring policy into practice, to try and identify through a questionnaire a selected number of qualified PE teacher's views on their training and current inclusive PE practice with children with SEN. The decision was taken to contact three male, and three females from each of the five selected PE ITT providers. In addition, by undertaking a questionnaire survey, this furthered the opportunities to track key themes and issues from the research at the earlier phases of the research design.

The intention of both questionnaires at the consumer level was to examine the process of training, and its resultant application with trainee and recently qualified practitioners facing the challenges of inclusive PE as part of their daily teaching practices. Consequently, subjects were asked within the questionnaires to reflect upon their PE ITT within a framework of examining the extent to which it had enabled them to satisfactorily deliver and or feel ready to deliver inclusive PE to children with SEN.

4.11 Stage 4 - Questionnaires to Final Year PE Trainees from the 5 Selected PE ITT Providers

A questionnaire comprising of a series of open and closed responses was distributed to all final year trainees (see appendix four) from the five selected ITT PE providers. Prior to distribution, a small-scale pilot of the questionnaire was undertaken with teacher training students in order to check the clarity and format of the questionnaire. The comments from the small-scale pilot study were taken on board and amended accordingly. The questionnaire comprised of 32 questions under 6 headings of: About you, Your professional development and training to date, Your links with schools and mentors, Interpreting inclusive PE, Values and attitudes and Other views and opinions. In order to increase the return rate, the researcher offered each of the five selected PE ITT providers a guest lecturer on PE and SEN. This was taken up by all providers and enabled the distribution and collection of questionnaires on the same day, resulting in high return rates. All questionnaires were completed prior to delivery of the guest lecture.

The total number of returned questionnaires from the five selected PE ITT providers totalled 202 responses, representing 85 males (42%) and 117 females (58%). The questionnaires were analysed on the basis of a random sample of 25 students from the larger institutions and full analysis from smaller providers. Each institutional questionnaire where random selection occurred was undertaken according to the male female ratio noted above. Consequently, a total of 113 trainee responses were analysed on the basis of:

PE ITT provider A: 25 trainees random selection of a large undergraduate four year BA (Hons) course

PE ITT provider B: 25 trainees random selection of a large undergraduate four year BA (Hons) course

PE ITT provider C: 25 trainees random selection of a large one year postgraduate course

PE ITT provider D: 20 trainees Full analysis of a small undergraduate four year BA (Hons) course

PE ITT provider E: 18 trainees Full analysis of a small one-year postgraduate course

Each questionnaire set from the respective PE ITT provider was analysed separately, then combined with the other providers to provide a global overview of the data set for final year trainees. The data was coded according to Robsons (1999) key objectives of transferability, credibility, dependability and conformability. The closed questions were presented in graph format, whilst the open responses were used to help frame some of the questions with the stage 5 questions to newly and recently qualified PE teachers. Moore (2000) suggests in order to be satisfactorily gauging opinion, sufficient quota samples must be undertaken in order to make more generalised assumptions regarding the wider subject group. Consequently, in administering the questionnaires directly to 5 of the 24 PE ITT respondents of final year trainees, this represented 20.8% of the total population group. In addition by administering the questionnaires on a face-to-face basis with the trainees, the high response rates have to a large extent discounted the probabilities of difference due to low return rates.

4.12 Stage 5 - Questionnaires to PE Teachers Between NQT Status and 2 Years Post-Qualifying Experience From the 5 Selected ITT PE Providers

A questionnaire comprising of a series of open and closed responses was posted to a random selection of recently qualified PE teachers from the five selected PE ITT providers. All PE teachers contacted were between NQT status and two years post qualifying experience. Prior to distribution, a small-scale pilot of the questionnaire was undertaken with recently qualified PE teachers in order to check the clarity and format of the questionnaire. The questionnaire comprised of 32 questions under 6 headings of: About you, Your initial teacher training in PE, Your experiences once you qualified, Interpreting inclusive PE, Values and attitudes and Other views and opinions. The questionnaires were sent out with an accompanying letter (see appendix five) explaining the context of the research, and confirming that a named staff member from the respective PE ITT providers had consented to passing their details to the researcher. A total of 30 questionnaires (3 males and 3 females from each of the selected providers) were posted to the recently qualified PE teachers with monthly follow up reminders up to a maximum of three contacts. The data was analysed on the basis of 19 responses, representing a return rate of 63.3%. The responses were coded according to Robsons (1999) four key objectives, and either presented in graph format for the closed questions and free responses with the open questions.

When attempting to make judgements on individual's views, opinions, and experiences of inclusion, Farrell (2000) suggests there are concerns related to this type of methodological research in that:

> *"... evaluating the effectiveness of inclusion is virtually impossible" (Farrell 2000, p 156)*

This is due to the range of SEN, inclusive experiences and contexts being so great, and the variety of available provision and delivery within schools being so diverse. Therefore, as a result it is difficult to judge whether PE teachers are experiencing similar or entirely different forms of inclusive PE provision for children with SEN. In contrast, Goodwin and Watkinson (2000) suggest however that the alternatives of not comparing or discussing inclusive provision, discounts the rich sources of data that can be gleaned from the subjects themselves who are fundamentally at the heart of the provision that is being delivered. Therefore, bearing in mind the concerns indicated by Farrell (2000), the questionnaires sort to gain data related to the PE teachers views and experiences of inclusive education, professional development, and training to date and their perceived readiness to implement inclusive activity. In addition, when analysing the data, careful examination of the comparability of individual responses was considered prior to making any more generalised assumptions regarding the nature of comments made.

4.13 Interpretation, Analysis and Triangulation of the Five Stages of the Research Design

Throughout the five stages of research, the findings were collated in order to help answer the main or sub questions, as well as assist with the design of the subsequent phases of the research process. The data was analysed separately at each of the 5 stages, in order to ascertain the views and opinions of official line, professional opinion and practice and consumer perspectives. This helped to gain a rich insight into the respective isolated perspectives, prior to the triangulation of the collective views and opinions in order to give a holistic stance to how the current training of PE teachers for inclusive settings is implemented. The process of examining one data set against another was a crucial component in comparing, contrasting and making judgements in the field of real world enquiry (Robson 1999). With this in mind, the study now turns to an analysis of the findings which will be analysed in respective chapters on the official line, professional opinion and practice and consumer perspectives. Following this examination, common themes, key issues and perspectives will be drawn together in chapter 8 of the study in order to provide a comprehensive analysis of the present position and future directions related to the training of PE teachers to include children with SEN.

C H A P T E R   F I V E :
RESULTS AND DISCUSSION OF THE OFFICIAL LINE
(STAGE ONE)

This chapter analyses the findings of the studies 'official line' research question on 'what are the views and policies of government, statutory agencies, and PE associations in relation to the delivery of inclusive PE for children with SEN'. An examination of the findings from literature searches, and views and opinions gained by the seven official line agencies is considered, with particular reference to the extent to which there are similarities and differences in interpretation and expectations of inclusive PE for children with SEN. In addition, the level to which official line agencies work in partnership to provide a coherent and consistent message for those working in the field of inclusion, SEN, PE ITT, and schools is also examined.

The desire to gain a clear insight into the initial official line level of analysis is essential to triangulating the impact, and relationships with the professional opinion and practice, and consumer levels of interpretation (See chapters 6 and 7). Furthermore, it will contribute to the evidence base for responding to the studies main research question of **"How is the current training of PE teachers for inclusive settings implemented?"**. As a consequence of this analysis, the chapter argues there is extensive evidence of inclusive policy at the official line level. However, there is less detail of collaborative working, and joined up thinking with regard to both policy development, and implementation in practice of inclusive PE for children with SEN.

The notion of 'joined up thinking ' is of particular relevance as the DFES (2002)

'Education and Skills: Delivering Results: A Strategy to 2006' states:

> *"Successful delivery will depend on strong and effective relationships with many partners. By laying out the strategic direction and ways of working, our intention is to provide the platform for ongoing dialogue and engagement with others on how best to achieve the outcomes we seek" (DFES 2002, p1).*

This standpoint of strategic direction, in partnership with others is of central concern

to Depauw and Doll-Tepper (2000) regarding their arguments on bandwagon

discourse. They advocate for example, a need to ensure models of inclusive practice

are 'infused' from strategic policy direction, through to successful implementation in

practice. Consequently, Depauw and Doll-Tepper (2000) note caution by suggesting

whilst agencies may 'say the right things', the extent to which this is then evidenced

through official line multi-agency working, genuine culture change, and enhanced

inclusive practice (Dyson and Millward 2000, Skrtic 1995, Ainscow 1999) is of

paramount importance if high quality PE experiences for children with SEN are to be

realised.

5.1   Shared Visions

The need for a clear, consistent inclusive message is further emphasised by

Avramadis and Norwich (2002) who advocate:

> *"... without a coherent plan for teacher training in the educational needs of children with SEN, attempts to include these children in the mainstream would be difficult" (Avramadis & Norwich 2002, p139).*

This call for joined up thinking, multi-agency working, and recognition of the role

which all stakeholders should play, is supported by Charles Clarke (Secretary of

State for Education and Skills) who when launching the DFES 'Delivering Results

Strategy' in December 2002 stated:

> *"This is our vision for the future. It can only be achieved if it is a shared vision, and if we all relish the challenge. The targets set high expectations. All of us -*

the government and key agencies, front line professionals, parents and young
people - must play a part if we are to meet them" (DFES 2002, p 2).

Consequently, since launching their Green paper on special needs education in

1997, the new Labour government have been intent on further promoting inclusive

education, and have advocated:

> *"... a progressive extension of the capacity of mainstream schools to provide*
> *for children with a wide range of needs" (DFES 2002, p44).*

Ainscow et al (1999) notes that:

> *"The government green paper 'Excellence for All Children: Meeting SEN'*
> *places the issue of inclusion at the centre of discussions on the development of*
> *policy and practice for pupils with special needs" (Ainscow et al 1999, p9).*

Thus, as part of a 'progressive extension' of inclusive provision, the wish to construct

a shared vision in which official line agencies jointly set the wider policy and practice

(implemented through professional opinion and practice, and the consumers)

framework has taken on even greater significance.

However, whilst noting the increased emphasis on inclusive and collaborative

provision, the Audit commission in 2002 produced a report 'Special educational

needs: a mainstream issue' which looked at how well children with SEN are being

served by the education system. The report made wide-ranging recommendations for

schools, LEA's and National Policy makers and stated,

> *"Despite the significant number involved, children with SEN have remained a*
> *low profile group" (Audit Commission 2002, p 6).*

The report went on to say

> *"Surprisingly little is known at a national level about the pattern of children's*
> *special educational needs. In England there are no common definitions of*
> *need, so while LEA's may hold detailed information on the needs of pupils in*
> *their area, this cannot be aggregated" (Audit Commission 2002, p 6, point 14).*

Thus, despite the high profile government agenda to promote inclusive education for children with SEN, the extent to which this policy is a shared official line vision, which systematically impacts at professional opinion and practice, and consumer levels appears to be rather fragmented, and in need of further collaborative work. In addressing these concerns the Audit Commission (2002) suggest,

> "Developing teachers' skills at recognising what is and what is not a special educational need could help ensure a more consistent approach to identifying needs. New national standards for the award of Qualified Teacher Status expect newly qualified teachers to 'identify and support...those who are working below age-related expectations, those who are failing to achieve their potential in learning, and those who experience behavioural, emotional and social difficulties'. While this is welcome, it may be unrealistic to expect in-depth coverage of this during initial teacher training. We therefore recommend that developing NQT's skills and confidence at identifying SEN and making appropriate responses should be a key element of the induction year. Given the range of practice across schools, this might be best achieved by working in partnership with local schools, both mainstream and special." (Audit Commission, 2002 p 11, point 33).

Thus, despite a government policy of inclusive education, which has seen more children with SEN entering mainstream schools (2001 – 67%, 1997 – 57%, 1993 – 48%), the extent to which they are treated equally, and fairly remains an area of concern. Consequently, a key area in question at the official line level is that despite a desire for shared visions and partnership working, the extent to which a coherent framework for inclusive PE for children with SEN exists is debatable. In contrast, the evidence tends to suggest (Audit Commission 2002), that whilst inclusive policy may be apparent, it has not been constructed, either as a result of multi-agency working, or through effective implementation with partners in practice. As a result, whilst the desire to extend multi agency and 'joined up' approaches may be advocated, the reality is an even greater need for the 'gatekeeper' agencies (Trend 1997) such as the DFES, TTA, OFSTED and QCA to work together to ensure that inclusive policy is implemented appropriately, monitored, evaluated, and that teachers are sufficiently equipped for its delivery - DFES support this concern by indicating an intention to

> "... develop multi-agency working. Too often different support agencies do not work effectively together" ('DFES 2001a, p 22).

The view of a lack of agencies working together is evident from the research undertaken within this study. For example, based upon the views, opinions, and scrutiny of literature from the official line agencies, notions of inclusion tend to be recognised, yet subsequently offer only limited evidence of collaborative approaches to it's development, implementation and review.

For example, whilst five of the seven official line agencies indicated policy directives related to the inclusion of children with SEN, only OFSTED indicated collaborative approaches with PE ITT national networks (professional opinion and practice), schools (the consumers) and the TTA. Therefore if strategic policy directives are to have more impact, there is going to have to be a vast increase in partnership working both across the official line level, and through collaboration with PE ITT providers and schools at the professional opinion and practice and consumer levels of interpretation.

As a result, if the DFES are seeking to provide:

> "... the platform for ongoing dialogue and engagement with others" (DFES 2002, p 1)

... on how best to achieve the outcomes of inclusive education, a first step should be a reflection upon the Audit Commissions (2002) view that surprisingly little is known about the profiles of children with SEN. Consequently, whilst at present only limited evidence of collaborative working has been found within this study, if the inclusion of children with SEN in PE is to be fully realised much work is yet to be done by the DFES in the first instance to act as the catalyst to draw all the key stakeholder agencies together. If this partnership approach was initiated it offers immense potential for the creation of a coherent framework (Vickerman 2002) within which all stakeholder agencies respective roles, responsibilities, and expectations of policy development, implementation, and review of inclusive PE for children with SEN could be comprehensively examined - rather than the present situation in which there is an almost 'un-written', isolated rule that official line agencies know their particular roles, but do not engage in collaborative face to face discussion, and joined up thinking in order to ensure a clear and coherent message is conveyed to agencies at the professional opinion and practice and consumer levels.

5.2 A Strategy For Inclusion

The DFES aims to build a competitive economy and inclusive society by: **creating opportunities** for everyone to develop their learning; **releasing potential** in people to make the most of themselves; and by **achieving excellence** in standards of education and levels of skill (DFES 2002). Thus, in the context of inclusive PE for children with SEN the relationships between official line policy, professional opinion and practice, and consumer stakeholders need to be fully considered if a cohesive and systematic approach to this area of work is to be implemented.

The DFES state, in order to meet their aims of developing an inclusive society, they will need to develop a high-class workforce and modern infrastructures for education and skills:

> "We can only implement our policies successfully with an able and motivated workforce of leaders, teachers, trainers, advisers and support staff, working with learners of all ages. We need to recruit and retain the best people, and we must invest in their development and career paths and reward them for the work they do. They should be well supported and have access to the information and communications technology that will be increasingly central to their work" (DFES 2002, p 16).

Furthermore, in order to ensure the DFES deliver their key strategic priorities they have established a set of behaviours characterising the way in they are going to work, which are:

- *We are determined to make a difference*

- *We listen and value diversity*

- *We are honest and open*

- *We innovate and challenge*

- *We learn and improve*

However, in relation to the 'behaviours for working', evidence from the research data demonstrates that the inclusive policies and contexts appear to be in place, but there is only limited evidence of engaging in collaborative discussion with both the official line agencies and those at the professional opinion and practice and consumer levels regarding its implementation. For example, the DFES (2003) have recently been working to produce a CD-Rom 'Success for All: an inclusive approach to PE and school sport' as part of their stated commitment to the joint DCMS/DFES publication 'A Sporting Future For All (2001). The development of this resource engaged a range of official line and other stakeholder partners (i.e. OFSTED, QCA, EFDS, TTA), one ITT provider and schoolteachers. This on the surface looked like a positive move towards the notion of collaborative working, addressing some of the concerns noted earlier within this chapter. However, whilst, there was evidence of agencies working together to produce the resource which is going free into all primary, secondary and special schools, there was no evidence of further strategic discussion of its implementation, and or potential to act as a resource for continuing professional development or ITT.

As a result, there was an expectation that agencies at the professional opinion and practice, and consumer levels will:

"… implement the resource on their own" (DFES verbal response).

In taking such a stance, a great opportunity appears to have been missed in ensuring that official line policy is both strategically and coherently implemented and delivered in partnership with PE ITT providers, schools and PE professional bodies. This further supports the concern of authors such as Depauw and Doll-Tepper (2000), Farrell 1998, Dyson and Millward (2000) who advocate a need to ensure that for inclusive practice to become a reality, agencies must work in partnership to both develop policy, but more essentially ensure that it is fully implemented, rather than take the 'tick box' approach of addressing inclusion at a superficial level.

5.3   Schools, ITT and the Development of Inclusive Practice

The DFES state in order to enhance inclusive practice within schools they intend to improve the:

> "...quality of ITT supported via the TTA" (DFES 2002, p16).

As a consequence, the DFES policy of progressive extension of inclusion is reliant upon ensuring that the future generations of teachers of PE are satisfactorily equipped to include children with SEN. This policy position according to the DFES is to be achieved through the TTA's implementation of revised standards for the award of QTS (The TTA 'Professional Standards Framework' (TTA 2002) 2002), which:

> "... reflect an increasing focus on aspects of inclusive practice" (DFES open letter response).

As a result, the DFES strategic policy of inclusive education relies heavily on a cohesive process of interpretation and implementation by the TTA, delivery by the PE ITT providers, and subsequent auditing by OFSTED in relation to training quality and delivery by teachers in schools. However, no evidence was gained in this study of the DFES, TTA, OFSTED, PE ITT providers and/or schools working collaboratively to ensure that the inclusion of children with SEN was being realised. In contrast, the various stakeholders tended to work in isolation to each other, rather than see the view of Charles Clarke in 2002 ("All of us - the government and key agencies, front line professionals, parents and young people - must play a part") realised.

The need for official line agencies to work with ITT providers and schools is of further significance when analysing the Audit Commission (2002) view that inclusion and SEN training for teachers should become part of their NQT year. What emerges from this statement is a concern that teachers at present are not sufficiently prepared within ITT, and that schools need to address this as part of an NQT's induction year. Thus many questions related to the TTA (2002) 'Professional Standards Framework' (TTA 2002), training by PE ITT providers, and the roles of a range of other official line stakeholders is brought into question regarding the current readiness of PE teachers to deliver an inclusive education for children with SEN. Consequently the Audit Commission (2002) appear to be advocating a strengthening of the link between official line agencies, ITT providers and schools to ensure that the policy is put into practice, rather than at present see children with SEN remaining a low profile group within schools.

The TTA Corporate Plan 2003-2006 states:

> "Our purpose is to raise standards by attracting able and committed people to teaching and by improving the quality of teachers training and induction. The TTA continue by stating "their five strategic aims have been agreed by Ministers in the context of their commitment to the delivery of better public services" (TTA open letter response)

… and encompass an intention to:

> Increase the number of able and committed people recruited to teaching

> Improve the quality of ITT and induction for NQT's

> Ensure a sufficiently wide range of good quality ITT provision to meet trainee needs and the number of training places nationally

Communicate clearly, effectively and persuasively with all audiences and stakeholders

Plan and use resources effectively, seeking to improve the quality of services

The second, third, and fourth strategic aims are of particular significance with regard to training PE teachers to include children with SEN. For example, in relation to quality improvement the TTA stated:

"... they will work with OFSTED to raise standards through inspection" (TTA open letter response).

In addition, the TTA indicated that:

"... the five strategic aims had been agreed by Ministers" (TTA open letter response)

... but did not give details on the extent of consultations with the DFES, OFSTED or other stakeholders with a vested interest in ensuring teachers are satisfactorily equipped to deliver inclusive PE for children with SEN. As a result the extent to which the TTA will, or have consulted with stakeholders is problematic to determine, other than by reading their various consultation documents sent to its stakeholder partners. Consequently, the level to which this consultation was by paper, or through open dialogue is still a grey area to determine.

In contrast, it is interesting to note however that OFSTED have indicated clear communication networks with the PE ITT providers by:

"... attending regular partnership meetings with HEI providers to reflect and share practice" (OFSTED open letter response).

However, there is no similar arrangement with the TTA who:

"... tend to engage in dialogue at individual institutional level" (TTA open letter response).

Thus OFSTED stated that in order to enhance the quality of PE and teacher training (of which inclusion is one aspect) they:

> "... wish to work with providers in an attempt to have a significant impact on raising standards in ITT" (OFSTED open letter response).

However the TTA emerge as an official line agency that awaits inspection evidence in order to make judgements on future funding and potential review of the appropriateness of the existing 'Professional Standards Framework' (TTA 2002)s, rather than engage in substantive discussion with other stakeholders.

5.4   A Positive Step Forward?

The Audit Commission (2002) suggest:

> "At a national level, the new standards for qualified teacher status, which came into effect in September 2002, represent a step forward in many respects, the standard on curriculum differentiation is particularly welcome. However, the standards fall short in their failure to reflect the wider policy context of inclusion. Although trainees are expected to learn about the SEN Code of Practice, it is surprising that there is no mention of the National Curriculum Inclusion Statement or, crucially, the Disability Discrimination Act. The latter includes important anti-discriminatory provisions, of which all staff should be aware. More generally, it is essential that trainee teachers should understand the value placed on helping children with SEN to achieve, including those who may be among the most challenging to teach; and that SEN is a core part of their teaching responsibilities, not an 'add-on'" (Audit Commission 2002, p 38, point 98).

Thus, whilst some aspects of inclusion and SEN are being addressed within ITT, the view of the Audit Commission (2002), is that the TTA have not gone far enough in ensuring the teachers of the future are satisfactorily equipped to appreciate and deliver all the issues related to an inclusive education for children with SEN. Consequently, whilst the DFES are recommending visions of shared and collaborative working approaches, the reality is that the views and experiences of agencies such as the Disability Rights Task Force (DRTF) and those expressed by Dyson and Millward 2000, Ainscow 1999, and Skrtic 1995 related to genuine culture change and a readiness to adapt existing structures are not at present being fully addressed within ITT. Therefore, whilst the new 'Professional Standards Framework' (TTA 2002) implemented in September 2002, set out with the intention of a greater emphasis on inclusion, the view from the Audit Commission (2002) is that there is still much work to be done in this area. – Particularly if the PE teachers of the future are to be equipped to fully appreciate the human rights philosophies and principles of inclusion, as well as recognise the strategies to implement it in practice.

As a result of the views from the Audit Commission (2002), Ainscow (1999), Skrtic (1991) and Dyson and Millward (2000), the need for a comprehensive and systematic review of how the inclusion of children with SEN is going to be realised needs to be undertaken. This will require official line agencies to not only set the context for inclusion, but in partnership with others establish a clear and coherent framework in which policy is implemented in practice. This will require a radical re-think of all agencies existing structures and provision and a shared desire to work together, rather than in isolation to provide a joined up approach to the inclusion of children with SEN in PE.

5.5   The Disability Rights Task Force and the Enforcement of Civil Rights

"The Disability Rights Task Force (DRTF) was established in 1997 to advise on how best to deliver the governments manifesto commitment to comprehensive and enforceable civil rights for disabled people" (DRTF 2003, p1).

A key objective was a recognition that attitudes towards disabled people needed to change if real progress was to be made, and the recommendation was that this should not be left to disability organisations and government alone, rather all agencies needed to recognise their roles and responsibilities, and work together to achieve success.

In 1999 the DRTF published a document 'From exclusion to inclusion' which identified 156 recommendations for action across all areas of peoples lives, in order to ensure that the needs and aspirations of disabled people were fully realised. In 2001 'Towards Inclusion - Civil rights for Disabled People' was subsequently published which set out the governments final response to the DRTF recommendations, and set the context for further government reform, particularly related to strengthening rights in relation to access to education.

The government recognised that:

> "... equality of opportunity for all our citizens is a prime objective for this government" (DRTF 2001, point 1.1).

... and at present indicate there are three Acts of Parliament which provide a means of enforcing rights preventing discrimination against disabled people namely; The Disability Discrimination Act (DDA) (1995), The Disability Rights Commission (DRC) (1999) and the SEN and Disability Act (SENDA) 2001. In terms of this study it is the impact and implications of SENDA (DFES 2001c) that are of particular significance to the inclusion of children with SEN within PE settings.

The DRTF suggest in relation to SENDA (DFES 2001c) for example:

> "The Act will improve the standard of education for children with SEN and will make it unlawful for education providers to discriminate against disabled pupils, students and adult learners" (DRTF 2003, p 1).

Thus, whilst inclusion has been a priority area for government since 1997, there is now a requirement that official line, professional opinion and practice, and consumer stakeholders ensure its implementation through the added pressure of legislation. As a result, in many cases this will require a fundamental re-think of existing education structures (Ainscow 1999, Skrtic 1991, Dyson and Millward 2000, Farrell 1998) in which children with SEN can now expect agencies to adapt to meet their particular needs, rather than anticipating them fitting into pre-existing structures.

This expectation and change in working will not occur in isolation however, and further emphasises the need for all stakeholders with a vested interest in inclusive PE for children with SEN to work much more in partnership to deliver the requirements of SENDA (2001). Thus, each partner will need to share their expertise openly, and be responsive to change particularly as the DRTF (1999) indicate that:

> *"In the area of education, probably more than any other issue considered by the Task Force the principle of inclusion underlined our considerations and recommendations" (DRTF, 1999, Chapter 4, point 2).*

As a result of this view, teachers of PE can be seen as a key agent of change, and consequently need to be given the necessary support and training in order to deliver this new inclusive agenda.

The extent of the work still to be done is further evident from the DRTF (1999) who note:

> *"The research findings that 61% of under 35 year olds said that they had no contact with disabled people are a reminder of how far there is still to go in achieving acceptance of disabled people as equal members of society. Inclusion of disabled people throughout their school and college life is one of the most powerful levers in banishing stereotypes and negative attitudes towards disabled people amongst the next generation. When disabled and non-disabled people are educated together, this sends powerful messages to the whole community about the potential for a truly integrated and diverse society" (DRTF, 1999, Chapter 4, point 3).*

The DRTF went on to suggest:

> *"There are constraints on achieving full inclusion and individual rights to full access to education...In granting new rights, the issue of individual versus collective rights was thoroughly debated. In some instances, more can be achieved for disabled people in the long term by laying duties on education providers to make their facilities systematically accessible than by giving specific rights of access to particular individuals" (DRTF, 1999, Chapter 4, point 5).*

This supports the view of Reiser and Mason (1990) who advocate 'social models' of disability within which organisations and teachers must look to adapt and modify their structures to accommodate individual needs, rather than the other way around ('medical models'). Many authors such as Dyson 2001, Dyson and Millward 2000, Reiser and Mason 1990, Ainscow 1999, Skrtic 1995 support this view, advocating flexibility of approach and a readiness to adapt to meet children's individual needs.

Consequently, a key recommendation emerging out of the work by the DRTF, was a new duty on schools and LEA's to plan strategically and make progress in increasing accessibility for disabled pupils to school premises and the curriculum. This supports the arguments of Ainscow 1999 and his view of 'moving schools' in which a state of constant change, reflection and intent to accommodate individual pupil needs is facilitated. This notion is further supported by Dyson and Millward (2000) and Skrtic (1995) who advocate the establishment of schools and teaching philosophies that change and adapt to meet the needs of children with SEN, rather than them fitting into static, unchanging educational provision.

This point is particularly well emphasised when the DRTF found that in relation to policies, practices and procedures:

> *"The education world tends to have written policies and procedures and*
> *acceptable practices covering the range of activities that take place in schools"*
> *(DRTF 1999, From exclusion to Inclusion, Chapter 4, point 21).*

However, the key is in seeing activities that are planned in policy statements implemented in practice through clear target setting, monitoring and evaluation of the extent to which progress has been made and evidence of flexible approaches to inclusive provision.

The DRTF 'From Exclusion to Inclusion' (1999) report, emphasises very well some of the valuable points noted earlier when it states:

*"The 1978 Warnock Report laid the ground for a transformation in the
education of children with SEN. Although, we would not claim that the
recommendations we have made will lead to a similar transformation two
decades later, they offer a real opportunity for increasing the rights of disabled
people to a quality education, free from unfair discrimination and segregation.
However, government legislation and new resources on their own will not be
effective. As important is a real change in the attitude of all those engaged in
all stages of education" (DRTF, 1999 Chapter 4, point 51).*

Consequently legislation alone will not make a difference to inclusive practice, it is

the fundamental shifting of attitudes and a readiness of PE teachers (suitably trained

and equipped) to change their existing pedagogical practices that will make the

ultimate difference in whether inclusion becomes a reality or not. This cannot

however be achieved in isolation, it has to be part of a multi-agency, coherent and

committed approach to the inclusion of children with SEN in PE.

5.6   PE, Inclusion and SEN

In tandem with attempts to equip PE teachers with the necessary skills to deliver

inclusive education, the government have recently set targets to:

*"Enhance the take up of sporting opportunities by 5 to 16 year olds by
increasing the percentage of school children who spend a minimum of two
hours each week on high quality PE and school sport within and beyond the
curriculum from 25% in 2002 to 75% by 2006 (joint target with the DCMS)"*
(DFES 2002, p11).

This strategy position is supported by Sport England (2003) who state:

*"A minimum of 2 hours of PE for every child should be provided in the National
Curriculum" (Sport England 2003, p2).*

This commitment to the recognition and value of physical activity within the school

curriculum is vital if the inclusion of children with SEN in PE is to satisfactorily be met.

Thus whilst various stakeholders can work towards equipping PE teachers with the

skills to include children with SEN, it is of no worth if it is not satisfactorily matched by

protected time within the school curriculum. – Especially as the medium of PE as a

147

subject area, has useful means of enhancing all children's wider appreciation of an inclusive society (Vickerman 2003, DRTF 1999, DCMS 2001).

In relation to using physical activity as a medium for promoting physical activity, the DCMS social exclusion units Policy Action Team (PAT 10) established a programme of research in 2001 into what works, and best practice under the heading of 'Count Me In - Research Project on social Inclusion' in sport. This research examined how social inclusion could be promoted through sport, and whilst it did not relate specifically to PE the project raised a number of issues which, support physical activity being used as a means of enhancing an inclusive society and education system. The specific intention was to learn about the evaluation and impact of a range of projects in relation to gathering evidence of 'what works' (or not) to assist with policy making in the future, and to build up experience of monitoring and evaluation for guidance in future projects. It was found through the research for example, that sport was a useful medium through which a multiplicity of groups in society could come together and gain mutual understanding and appreciation for diversity. However, some of the critical success factors relied on effective coaching and a readiness to adapt to meet particular peoples needs. This supports similar views expressed by Skrtic 1995, Ainscow 1999 and Dyson 2001 related to their notion of constantly moving schools, offering flexibility of teaching and learning approaches.

Consequently research evidence supports physical activity as a valuable medium for addressing aspects of developing an inclusive society. The critical success factors however, rely on effective teaching and coaching, a readiness to adapt to accommodate individual needs, and sufficient time within the school curriculum to address these issues. Although, another crucial factor that needs to be addressed at the official line level is the current participation rates of young people engaging in PE and school sport. For example, the Sport England Survey (1999) on young peoples participation in physical activity found only 11% of children aged 6-8 years spent two hours or more per week in PE lessons - a fall of two-thirds from the 1994 figure. In addition, for children aged 9-11 it has fallen by more than half from 46% in 1994 to 21% in 1999. Whilst this may have specific links to the implementation of the numeracy and literacy strategies at the primary phase, the emergence of the Key Stage three strategy in secondary schools may also place similar pressures on participation rates. Consequently, social inclusion may have benefits of delivery through PE, but the first step must be to attempt to raise levels of participation and engagement by schools and young people.

5.7   PE And Disability Sport Professional Agencies

The PEA (UK) and BAALPE are the two professional PE bodies that play a role in the support of PE both in schools and related to the initial, and continuing training and professional development of teachers. Consequently, at the official line level they have a central role to play in both lobbying for effective support for their members, whilst arguing for sufficient curriculum time within which PE can be addressed within school contexts. However, in relation to SEN and inclusion there involvement and engagement with other official line agencies has been rather limited. For example, both agencies have yet to establish clear policy directives in relation to inclusion, SEN and PE, and from the research evidence they state an intention to address this issue in the near future, but do not indicate when, or what this process may entail. Thus, the professional PE bodies appear to be currently in a vacuum in which they appear to either have insufficient skills and expertise to lobby agencies or support their membership in the area of inclusion and SEN.

As a consequence, the impact of any interpretation of generic SEN and inclusive government policy, and or statutory guidance being interpreted through the subject of PE is at present an area that is largely under-developed. In addition, within this study no evidence was found of either PE professional body engaging with and building upon the expertise of the EFDS who act as:

"... the united voice of disability sport in England" (EFDS 2001, p 1).

This lack of unity across the three PE and sport official line agencies is an area of concern and is in need of rapid action. As a result, if a clear, unified and coherent message is to be imparted to other official line agencies, and those at the professional opinion and practice, and consumer levels, a significant amount of work needs to be undertaken by the PE professional associations in developing collaborative working approaches that further the inclusion of children with SEN in PE.

An example of the lack of joined up thinking between PEA (UK), BAALPE and EFDS, is the development of the EFDS led course entitled 'Including young disabled people in PE'. This programme was:

"... developed by the EFDS and the Youth Sport Trust", (EFDS open letter response)

... and had no involvement from agencies such as the DFES, BAALPE, PEA (UK) and or people at the professional opinion and practice level (i.e. PE ITT providers). Therefore, whilst respective official line agencies are at liberty to work with whoever they wish, there appears to have been many missed opportunities to develop a comprehensive resource which had the involvement, expertise and backing of all the relevant stakeholders. Consequently what has developed is a rather piecemeal resource that tends to focus on sport, rather than PE and is promoted through governing bodies of sport, rather than within an educational context.

Accordingly, a recommendation from this study is for the PE and disability sport professional bodies to begin to undertake much more collaborative approaches to the support and development of all aspects of SEN and inclusion. In addition, this would

help promote a strategic alliance on many phases of inclusive activity in order to work

towards a more co-ordinated approach within official line, professional opinion and

practice and consumer partnerships – In addition, it is interesting to note that the

PEA (UK) and BAALPE have recently (June 2003) began formal discussions to

consider merging organisations to provide one national voice for PE and school

sport. This potential step forward may also help to provide a more co-ordinated

approach to the inclusion of children with SEN in PE.

5.8   Official Line Curriculum Developments in PE

The QCA in their remit letter from the Secretary of State for education note:

> "The Authority has a specific duty to have regard to the requirements of
> persons with special learning needs. The Secretary of State looks to the
> Authority to build on the work of SCAA (School Curriculum Assessment
> Authority) and NCVQ (National Council for Vocational Qualifications) in this
> area to ensure that the interests of those with special needs are taken into
> account across the whole range of its functions" (QCA 2001, Annex 2,
> paragraph 6).

Consequently, the QCA have a set of 'general principles' through which in:

> "all aspects of its work, including advice to government, on issues relating to
> the curriculum, assessment, occupational standards and qualifications, QCA
> seek to ensure" (QCA open letter response 2003):

> The appropriate inclusion of all learners at relevant levels of activity;

> Opportunities for continuity and progression for all learners;

> The achievement of the highest possible standards for all learners;

> The recognition of the achievements of all learners;

> The provision of easily accessible advice and guidance relevant to all learners

Thus, in addressing the points indicated above, QCA state an intention to promote

equal opportunities in all its work, and have produced a range of materials on this topic area, although most are generic in nature rather than specifically related to PE. However, the QCA do identify three resources that specifically address the subject of PE; which encompass a PE and school sport website; a document on assessing the PE curriculum for people with learning disabilities; and the PE NC online resources. However, in examining the NC online resources related to inclusion in PE, there are no specific documents evidenced which support any of the key stages or areas of activity related to aspects of inclusion and SEN. In contrast, what they do offer is web links to the National Grid for Learning (NGFL), but again all of the materials are generic, and not specifically related to PE. Thus, whilst there is a stated commitment to equality of opportunity and inclusive activity, the extent to which resource materials have been designed to support specific subject areas such as PE is rather limited at present.

The QCA also cited The British Educational Communications and Technology Agency (BECTA) which:

> "... has a website through which a range of government supported projects related to inclusion and SEN are addressed" (QCA open letter response).

This site whilst comprehensive, encompassing information sheets, discussion areas and the like, again does not have any documentation that is specifically related to PE. In contrast, the BECTA web site notes that the TTA has produced a needs identification CD-ROM to complement the DFES Code of Practice (DFES 2001b), in which each standard is illustrated by video case studies and associated commentaries that explore the relevance of the SEN Specialist Standards (DFES 1999). On examination of this resource however, all the case studies are classroom based, and do not offer any practical examples of inclusive PE for children with SEN. Although in contrast, the recent DFES (2003) 'Success For All: an inclusive approach to PE and school sport' CD-ROM resource does begin to address some of these concerns of moving from generic to subject specific resource materials, by

highlighting nine case studies encompassing the six activity areas of the PE NC.

In relation to the PE & School Sport website, QCA suggest this resource is aimed at:

> "... improving the quality of PE and school sport, by looking at new ways of
> ensuring that pupils have at least 2 hours of high quality PE and school sport
> each week" (QCA website 2003).

This site does offer information related to inclusive practice, and SEN by citing

evidence from real school examples, and is a useful point of reference for schools to

see different approaches to curriculum development and delivery in PE. However, it

is evident that this resource has been established in isolation with schools, and does

not draw upon the experience of other official line agencies in order to provide a

clear, coherent and substantive resource for schools and PE teachers.

Consequently, from the evidence gathered within this study the development of

inclusive PE resources for children with SEN appear to have largely been developed

in isolation, rather than through collaborative working arrangements with other key

stakeholders. As a result, this adds to the inconsistency of message and lack of

cohesive, and joined up approach currently presented by official line agencies to

those at the professional opinion and practice, and consumer levels.

5.9   Monitoring and Evaluation of Inclusive Practice

Since the creation of OFSTED in 1992 as a non-ministerial government department

whose:

> "... main aim is to help improve the quality and standards of education and
> childcare through independent inspection and regulation and provide advice to
> the Secretary of State" (OFSTED 2003).

... their role has over the years gradually expanded. For example, in recent years

OFSTED have began to take on responsibility for undertaking reviews of LEA's, further education, ITT provision, early years childcare and education, and private, voluntary and independent schools (including independent special schools). As a consequence, this has raised many areas of concern on the level to which official line agencies are imposing stringent standards and regulation on educational provision in schools and ITT provision, and the extent to which there is any level of flexibility of approach which remains in the governments drive for educational improvement.

Specifically in relation to ITT inspections, OFSTED:

> "... report on the quality of training, standards achieved by trainees and whether trainees are being accurately assessed" (OFSTED open letter response).

Whilst this scrutiny is wide ranging, it does give OFSTED the opportunity to gain a comprehensive insight into the training of PE teachers and their readiness to deliver high quality learning experiences to children in schools. In addition, through recent revisions of OFSTED inspection frameworks they now have a much greater role to play in judging the extent to which schools are providing inclusive learning opportunities for children with SEN. Consequently, part of this judgement will necessitate a reflection on the training quality of trainee teachers and the function of ITT providers.

Thus, whilst there may be general feelings of miss-trust or scepticism within the profession of the intentions of inspection, based on the studies research findings, OFSTED are in a crucial position in which they are able to measure a variety of factors that contribute towards ensuring PE teachers are satisfactorily equipped to include children with SEN. In relation to PE for example, it is evident that Her Majesties Inspector for PE ITT, does engage openly with people at the professional opinion and practice and consumer levels. This involves attending regular PE ITT National Networks in which all the training providers come together to reflect and share on practice. The study found that this dialogue is a two-way process in which

OFSTED share findings and concerns from inspection reports, but crucially also listen to the views of the ITT providers, and learn from their experiences as well. This open and often frank discussion appears to bode well for working collaboratively to raise standards in ITT, and other official line agencies would benefit from the establishment of similar working arrangements in which official line agencies, ITT providers and schools work to raise the standards of education for all children.

In the context of this study, the two issues of relevance with regard to OFSTED inspection are ITT, and school based inspection processes, and the impact they have on raising standards of general teaching quality whilst preparing PE teachers for work in the area of inclusive education. In relation to ITT for example, the purpose of inspection is (OFSTED open letter response) to:

— *Ensure public accountability;*

— *Stimulate continuous improvement in the quality of provision;*

— *Provide objective judgements on providers for public information;*

— *Inform policy;*

— *Enable the statutory link to be made between funding and quality;*

— *Check compliance with statutory requirements*

Based upon the evidence gathered within this study OFSTED are engaging openly with agencies and individuals at the professional opinion and practice, and consumer levels with the intention of enhancing quality. This collaborative working is to be welcomed, and many of the other official line agencies can learn a great deal from the manner within which OFSTED have engaged key stakeholders. In contrast however, there is only limited evidence of OFSTED working with other official line agencies (i.e. the TTA) to provide a joined up, strategic approach to aspects of inclusive provision for children with SEN, and this is an area which requires further work in the future if a coherent framework is to be established. Thus, in order for a cohesive framework for inclusive PE for children with SEN to be established, collaboration must be working both within, and across official line, professional opinion and practice, and consumer levels.

In relation to schools, the OFSTED (2003) 'Inspecting Schools Framework' indicates that they are committed to:

*The findings of inspection being **valid, reliable and consistent***

*The findings of inspection contributing to **improvement***

*The process of inspection promoting **inclusion***

*Inspection being carried out **openly** with those being inspected*

Consequently, whilst it is not the intention of this study to examine in any detail the process of OFSTED inspection in schools, it is worth noting the commitment to open dialogue and the promotion of inclusion within schools. As a result, it is apparent that the government's commitment to creating an inclusive society is being measured to some extent through the TTA (2002) 'Professional Standards Framework' (TTA 2002)s and inspection by OFSTED of ITT, and school contexts. However, whilst it is evident that in relation to OFSTED there appears to be a clear, and systematic process in place to evaluate the extent to which the government agenda is being realised, the position is less clear with regard to other official line agencies engaging in similar processes either within, or across the stakeholder network.

5.10 The Development of Official Line Multi-Agency Approaches to the Inclusion of Children with SEN in PE – Some Concluding Thoughts

In 1998 DFES published a document 'Meeting Special Educational Needs A Programme of Action', which according to David Blunkett (then Secretary of State) was based upon a recognition that:

> "The education of children with special needs is a key challenge for the nation. It is vital to the creation of a fully inclusive society" (DFES 1998b, p 1).

This document intended to set the context within which the government proposals to improve the educational achievements of pupils with SEN, were to be based, and focused upon five key points of action namely:

— *Ensuring that high expectations are set for pupils with SEN;*

— *To provide support to parents;*

— *To increase the numbers of pupils with SEN within mainstream;*

— *To emphasise the need for practical support, rather than procedural guidance;*

— *To promote partnerships in SEN at local, regional and national level*

Five years on from the 'Meeting SEN – A Programme of Action' document, the Audit Commission (2002) produced a report on the extent to which the inclusion agenda in schools for children with SEN was becoming a reality. In relation to the presence of children with SEN, the Audit Commission stated:

> "Although parents of children with SEN have the same right as others to express a preference for which school their child should attend, their choice is often limited by a lack of suitable provision locally and unwelcoming attitudes in some schools. LEA's should seek to develop a spectrum of provision to ensure that as far as possible, all children with SEN have the option of attending a local mainstream school" (Audit Commission, 2002 p 15).

Thus, from this statement it is apparent that there is still much work to be done in both the establishment of structural arrangements, and pedagogical practices to implement a successful inclusive education for children with SEN. For example, the recommendation of the adoption of a 'spectrum of provision' picks up on many of the past and present educational philosophies (Ainscow 1999, Dyson and Millward 2000, Fredrickson and Cline 2002) noted in earlier chapters in which all children should be supported along a continuum of provision rather than separating them into pre-defined groupings. This allows for greater flexibility in teaching and learning approaches, whilst enabling more extensive differentiation that caters for all children's movements along a continuum of learning need. Consequently, further efforts need to be made by official line agencies to ensure that at the professional opinion and practice and consumer levels the necessary structural and pedagogical practices are implemented.

In relation to the development of teachers skills to deliver greater flexibility of teaching approach, the Audit Commission (2002) found:

> "The more inclusive the classroom, the greater the diversity of needs among its pupils – and, in turn, the greater the challenge teachers face to tailor lessons to suit the aptitudes of each and every pupil. Many teachers feel under considerable pressure, on the one hand to meet the needs of individual pupils, and on the other to deliver a demanding national curriculum and achieve ever-better results; research suggests that many feel ill equipped for this task. We interviewed over 40 SENCO's, many of whom felt their colleagues lacked confidence in working with children with SEN" (Audit Commission 2002, p 36, point 95).

Thus, whilst the government and many other official line agencies are attempting to work towards equipping teachers with the necessary skills to support inclusive education:

> "... perceptions are consistent with academic research which indicates that staff skills and confidence in relation to SEN vary widely" (Audit Commission 2002, p 37, point 96).

Consequently, based on the Audit Commission evidence, there is still much work to be done in addressing both the structural process of inclusion, as well as the training and development of teachers to deliver the government's inclusion agenda within schools. The issues raised earlier within this chapter related to lack of collaborative working across the official line level are resulting in a fragmented approach to the implementation and delivery of a clear, consistent and coherent message for practitioners at the professional opinion and practice, and consumer levels of interpretation. Thus, the need for agencies such as the DFES to act as catalysts for joined up and collaborative approaches to inclusive PE for children with SEN is vital if the governments ambitions are ever to be fully realised.

The indication from evidence at the official line level within this chapter, is that many agencies may be 'saying the right thing' in terms of policy (although some are still to develop a policy – see PE professional bodies), they are not working collaboratively with all the stakeholders to ensure it is satisfactorily implemented. In addition, in relation to PE, it is particularly interesting to note that many of the recommendations and guidance offered by official line agencies are not at present subject specific, and consequently are not readily accessible to teachers.

This view is particularly relevant to the TTA, OFSTED, DFES, and to a large extent the QCA. – Whilst, those official line agencies who do represent PE and sport (i.e. PEA (UK), BAALPE and to a lesser extent EFDS) do not have any policies of any real depth with regard to the inclusion of children with SEN. Therefore, although some agencies (i.e. OFSTED) do consult widely with others, on the whole agencies at the official line are neither consulting across their own level, nor with agencies and individuals at the professional opinion and practice, and consumer levels. Consequently, the outcome is a fragmented, inconsistent and ineffective inclusive policy which not only impacts at policy level, but more essentially is not being implemented in practice through a collaboration of both subject specific and statutory guidance (see Depauw and Doll-Tepper 2000, Avramadis and Norwich 2002).

Based upon the research evidence at the official line level there is a great deal of work to be done in implementing a joined up approach to the inclusion of children with SEN in PE. The DFES (2003) have for example, recently created a 'Ministerial SEN Implementation Working Group' (SENWG), which draws on high-level expertise including SENCO's, headteachers, LEA officers, OFSTED, health, social services and the voluntary sector. Its main role is to advise on practical ways of improving standards of education for children with SEN or disabilities and is chaired by Baroness Ashton (Minister with responsibility for SEN).

Although this recent development is welcomed, the danger is that it may be 'more of the same' and may not result in collaboration with all the PE stakeholders to ensure policy becomes practice (See Depauw and Doll-Tepper 2000, Dyson and Millward 2000). – Perhaps what is needed at the official line level is the establishment of subject specific sub-groups of SENWG who can work in partnership, with the full backing of government level support to ensure that a clear, consistent and coherent message is delivered to all those involved in the policy and practice of inclusion for children with SEN. This would help address the current inconsistency of message at the official line level, and would benefit from joined up working arrangements with agencies and individuals at the professional opinion and practice and consumer levels of interpretation.

In noting the recommendation of greater subject specific involvement the DFES have also recently introduced:

> "… a SEN Small Programme Fund…established in 2000 to promote a one-sector approach to meeting pupils SEN. It directs funding towards projects that improve teaching and learning, and supports projects that are based on a commitment to the development of partnership working" (DFES open letter response).

The fund is designed to build a more strategic approach to working with the voluntary sector and improve the way the DFES funds projects, and offers grants of up to £50,000, although Schools, colleges, universities and health authorities cannot apply as lead agencies. This fund however does offer some potential for a range of agencies to engage with each other, both across and within official line, professional opinion and practice, and consumer levels, and could act as a starting point to provide a more co-ordinated approach to work in the area of PE, SEN and inclusion.

In summary, the Audit Commission (2002) report notes a series of wide ranging recommendations for future action if the mainstreaming of children with SEN is to take on more significance. In examining these recommendations, and the evidence gained from the studies research at the official line level, the action points offer a useful starting point for agencies to begin to evaluate their current working practices and establish a context for future action at the professional opinion a practice and consumer levels. Consequently, the Audit Commission (2002) suggests the need to:

1. Promote consistent practice in identifying and meeting children's needs
2. Promote early intervention
3. Ensure that children with SEN are able to attend a local mainstream school, as far as possible
4. Promote effective inter-agency planning
5. Enable all children with SEN to join as fully as possible in the life of their school
6. Develop the skills and confidence of staff to respond to the wide range of children's needs in classrooms today
7. Promote the effective allocation and management of SEN resources
8. Hold schools to account for their work on SEN
9. Provide a meaningful basis for monitoring schools' work on SEN
10. Recognise schools' commitment to helping children with SEN to achieve

Following the examination of evidence and recommendations from this chapter at the official line level, it is apparent that an effective starting point would be a comprehensive review of the extent to which DFES, TTA, OFSTED, QCA, BAALPE, PEA (UK) and EFDS are addressing the ten action points noted above. Furthermore, if the official line agencies were to review and address the ten action points together, this may help to formulate a clearer, more consistent message which directly impacts on practice at the professional opinion and practice and consumer levels of interpretation.

In considering the need for official line agencies to work more coherently to impact on practice, the next two chapters turn to focus on the professional opinion and practice, and consumer levels of analysis. This will enable the triangulation of the three levels of interpretation in Chapter 8 in order to answer the main and sub research questions of this study.

C H A P T E R   S I X :
RESULTS AND DISCUSSION AT THE PROFESSIONAL
OPINION AND PRACTICE LEVEL

(STAGES TWO AND THREE)

This chapter examines the findings from the professional opinion and practice level of interpretation, and focuses upon the second sub question of **"What are the processes and course contents of initial teacher training institutions related to inclusive PE for children with SEN?"** The analysis comprises data gathered from the 24 PE ITT questionnaire responses, and the five follow up face-to-face depth interviews with selected providers. Additionally, this contributes to the triangulation of views and opinions across the official line, professional opinion and practice, and consumer levels in order to provide answers to the main research question of **"How is the current training of PE teachers for inclusive settings implemented?"**

The conduct within which agencies at the 'professional opinion and practice' level implement official line policy, and effectively equip PE teachers with the necessary pedagogical practices is of primary concern to authors such as Depauw and Doll-Tepper (2000), and Westwood (1997). They view the nature of delivery and implementation as central to any effective move towards an inclusive agenda, and advocate the undergraduate curriculum is the key agent for change and development of new and existing practices. Consequently, it is argued within this chapter whilst a vast array of provision is evident there is a need for PE ITT providers to identify and co-ordinate good practice much more effectively within individual institutions, across the professional opinion and practice level, and with stakeholders at the official line and consumer levels of interpretation.

In considering the sub question at the professional opinion and practice level, the discussion within this chapter is primarily focused around the eight headings from the **stage two** questionnaires to PE ITT providers. The follow up face-to-face depth interviews **(stage three)** are subsequently used to elaborate (in italics) upon the evidence and points being made from the 24 questionnaire returns at stage two. In drawing together this data, a comprehensive picture emerges of the current ITT processes with regard to the extent to which PE teachers are equipped with the necessary knowledge, skills and understanding to include children with SEN.

As a result, what emerges from the PE ITT providers is the view that:

"Continuing professional development is essential" (PE ITT provider 22)

... with 84% either agreeing or strongly agreeing with this statement. Furthermore, only 25% of providers felt presently that trainee PE teachers entering the profession are adequately prepared to address issues of inclusion and SEN, with a further 50% indicating a neutral view. Within this backdrop, this chapter sets out to identify what the underlying issues and challenges are at the professional opinion and practice level which lead to an overwhelming perception that PE teachers entering the profession are currently not equipped to include children with SEN and will need further continuing professional development.

6.1   The Institutional Context

This section of the questionnaire sort to gain background information on the respondent of the questionnaire and details of their institutional make up.

The data from the stage two questionnaires was gained from Heads of Department, or curriculum leaders, and returns were allocated a PE ITT provider response number from 1-24 to preserve confidentiality. The data from the 24 respective questionnaires was then collated to produce one data set, offering a comprehensive

overview of the views and opinions of PE ITT providers at the professional opinion

and practice level. In relation to the face-to-face depth interviews, the transcribed

data from the five selected institutions was allocated a letter from A-E in order to

preserve confidentiality, and brief institutional details are given below.

> **PE ITT provider A:** *Large undergraduate four-year course in the North of England – (PE ITT provider: 21)*

> **PE ITT provider B:** *large undergraduate four-year course in the South of England – (PE ITT provider: 13)*

> **PE ITT provider C:** *Large postgraduate one-year course in the Midlands – (PE ITT provider: 3)*

> **PE ITT provider D:** *small undergraduate four-year course in the South of England – (PE ITT provider: 15)*

> **PE ITT provider E:** *Small postgraduate one-year course in the Midlands – (PE ITT provider: 14)*

6.2 Establishing a Context for Policy into Practice of Inclusive PE

This section seeks to provide a contextual background to inclusive PE for children

with SEN, both related to policy directives and its resultant impact in practice.

Westwood (1997) supports the promotion of citizenship and the social model of

disability within the curriculum, as a means of shifting the emphasis away from pupils

with SEN to the roles that teachers and non-disabled peers can play in facilitating all

children's learning. However, Dyson and Millward (2000) and Fredrickson and Cline

(2002) argue, there needs to be caution in ignoring the complexity of defining

inclusion and its current ability to be facilitated by teachers, due to their lack of clarity

and training in this subject area. If as the PE NC 2000 suggests:

"Teachers must take action ..." and *"... ensure that their pupils are enabled to participate ...,"* (QCA 1999a, p33)

... PE ITT providers must first seek to clarify what the underpinning philosophies of inclusive practice are, then consider through pedagogical practices the most appropriate way of ensuring teachers are equipped to facilitate this when working in schools.

Westwood (1997) has attempted to draw together the common threads of inclusive education policy, and suggests successful implementation relates to an acceptance of basic values of citizenship and principles of equal access and provision for all children. In addition, teachers and schools must have a positive attitude; supporting policy statements and most importantly plan effectively for inclusion. As a result, Farrell (2001) and Ainscow et al (1999) suggest if inclusive education is concerned with minimising the number of pupils in which the curriculum has to be disapplied, then ITT providers need to recognise how to increase teachers knowledge, understanding and skills on both the philosophy of inclusion as well as the practice of adapting the PE curriculum.

The DFES 'Schools Achieving Success' (DFES 2001a) document suggests they will help schools to meet the needs of children with SEN through a commitment to inclusion and a recognition of the responsibility placed upon teachers to enable such practice to occur. In relation to 'PE NC 2000' (QCA, 1999) PE NC begins to address some of these issues. The document suggests PE teachers should consider assessment in alternative activities, with flexible judgements and contexts in order to facilitate accessibility to the curriculum for children with SEN. This is a major policy objective that rests the responsibility of implementation and delivery with ITT providers and PE teachers to ensure they are adequately prepared to deliver such practices in order to meet the requirements of the curriculum, and recent changes in legislation (i.e. NC Statutory Inclusion Statement (QCA 1999a) SEN and Disability

Act (DFES 2001c, Code of Practice, DFES 2001b).

The expectation from official line agencies (i.e. DFES and QCA) that PE ITT

providers will implement this policy, and equip teachers with the necessary skills is

an issue of concern for agencies at the professional opinion and practice level. For

example, one PE ITT provider stated:

> "I do see guidance materials as an important thing... they should be making
> clear ... maybe un-picking aspects of the National Curriculum and making a
> clear statement. What does it mean on a practical level in the classroom or
> field situation. What sort of practices that meet the guidance which is delivery
> because the National Curriculum does need unpicking to understand it at all
> different levels" (PE ITT provider B).

The concern that statements are made at the official line, but are not supported by

clearer expectations or guidance as to what they mean in practice is further

emphasised by the view that in:

> "Catering for a good inclusive curriculum ... can we see, or can we have
> information on how schools do deal with ... and what issues come up as they
> are trying to cater for that ... we need to see I think, rather than just read" (PE
> ITT provider A)

Thus, there is a feeling official line agencies need to go beyond establishing policy

statements, and offer PE ITT providers more guidance related to setting clearer

expectations of what a vision for inclusive PE for children with SEN looks like in

reality. Consequently, as discussed in chapter 5, there is a need for agencies at the

official line and professional opinion and practice levels to engage much more

directly with each other to examine how policy impacts in practice. This view is

particularly well emphasised by one PE ITT provider when referring to official line

agencies commented:

> "Well, first of all they need to get their own act together and just join up and
> have a coherent co-ordinated programme, not something that's just
> dysfunctional or fractional" (PE ITT provider E).

To a certain extent this process has began to occur with the production of the DFES CD-ROM resource 'Success For All: an inclusive approach to PE and school sport' (2003). This has engaged agencies at the official line (i.e. DFES, QCA, OFSTED, EFDS) working with an ITT provider (professional opinion and practice) and teachers (consumers) to produce resource materials, which support PE teacher's development of their inclusive practice. Consequently, further resource-based initiatives like this should be encouraged both to encourage collaboration with all stakeholders, and enable the production of professional development materials that evidence good practice for PE ITT providers to consider. This would go some way towards addressing the free response comments from the stage two questionnaires that:

> *"More exemplification of good practice materials would benefit the profession"* (PE ITT provider 12)

… and:

> *"Guidance on teaching children with SEN in PE across the six activity areas is desperately needed" (PE ITT provider 7)*

The TTA (1999) published 'National SEN Specialist Standards' emphasising:

> *"The key to unlocking the full potential of pupils in our schools lies in the expertise of teachers and headteachers. Research and inspection evidence demonstrate the close correlation between the quality of teaching and the achievement of pupils" (TTA 1999, p1).*

The document recognised the central role teachers and schools play, and for the first time began to identify aspects of SEN provision required in order to create access to education. The key issue according to Rose (1998) however, remains the extent to which ITT providers are helping teachers with the practical skills to deliver policy objectives that strongly advocate inclusion. For example, the 'DFES SEN Programme of Action' (1998) suggests the government:

> *"… is committed to ensuring that all teachers have the training and support they need to do their job well and are confident to deal with a wide variety of SEN" (DFES 1998, p3).*

The TTA SEN Subject Specialist Standards (1999) advocate the 4/98 (DFES 1998a) (and subsequent 2002 'Professional Standards Framework' (TTA 2002)) will be the vehicle for measuring competence within ITT. However, they argue as more children with SEN enter mainstream:

> "... more teachers in mainstream schools will require the knowledge, understanding and skills to work effectively with pupils" (TTA 1999, point 9, p3).

The document then goes on to suggest

> "... all teachers, whether in mainstream schools or in special schools, will need to continue to develop their teaching, pedagogy based on the known features of effective practice in meeting all pupils learning needs" (TTA, 1999, point 10, p3)

This is a key factor in the success of inclusive PE, as the ITT providers must make judgements as to what an acceptable standard of equipping teachers with the necessary skills is, and how this can be measured in practice with pupils with SEN in schools.

The process of measuring what an acceptable standard is can be problematic, even though 4/98 (DFES 1998a) (and subsequent 02/02 (TTA 2002) 'Professional Standards Framework' (TTA 2002)s) identify SEN and inclusion as areas to be addressed. One PE ITT provider indicated:

> "Yeah. Well it is written into, you know, some of the specific 4/98 (DFES 1998a) standards... in that sense they are looking for evidence that trainees have met those standards and that the training providers have addressed the area. So I guess it is there, but it's there amongst about 80 or 90 others, and the difficulty I have with the standards is that, they are not all equal. They don't seem to be prioritised in any sense and I think that's very problematic because there's a lot to fit in a short period of time" (PE ITT provider C).

This concern expressed by one PE ITT provider supports the data gathered from the stage two questionnaires, highlighting only 29% agreed that the 4/98 (DFES 1998a) standards were ensuring students are adequately prepared for inclusive education.

Thus, individual PE ITT providers need to move beyond the 'Professional Standards Framework' (TTA 2002)s and embrace a process model of knowledge and understanding in practice, which ensures PE teachers of the future are trained to deliver inclusive education. According to Wright and Sugden (1999) this will necessitate change that is embedded at a variety of levels, and not merely tagged onto the end of a process – but more importantly involves a readiness to consult with all stakeholders, and modify and adapt practices in order that they have impact in practice for children with SEN.

This view of consultation with stakeholders is indicated by one PE ITT provider who suggested:

> "if we look at those official lines of support that you mentioned. The TTA and OfSTED perhaps could help with more guidance, and support documentation and again with this evidence of good practice because these are the people who generally do quite a bit of research into this area. More subject specific for us and now perhaps they could give us more guidance in relation to the inclusion on the new standards coming out. They do give examples, but it is very general and not subject specific. Which is something that we will probably have to do as an institution, to look at what inclusion means" (PE ITT provider A).

Therefore, in setting out the context of implementing policy into practice in inclusive PE for children with SEN, there is a strong message coming from the professional opinion and practice level that greater collaboration and clarity is required both in relation to interpretation of 4/98 (DFES 1998a) (DFEE 1998a) standards, and the development of practical guidance materials. The chapter will now turn to address in more detail some of the general points highlighted above, whilst considering potential strategies to enhance the current processes of training PE teachers to include children with SEN.

6.3 Values And Attitudes Towards Delivering An Inclusive Agenda Through PE

This section of the questionnaire set out to gain an insight into the respondent's personal values and attitudes towards inclusive PE for children with SEN.

The requirement for ITT providers to address inclusion is evident from a plethora of statutory and non-statutory educational policy documentation. The DFES (1998c) Excellence for All document supports an increasing emphasis shift to an inclusive agenda by advocating:

> "The education of children with special needs is a key challenge for the nation ...It is vital to the creation of a fully inclusive society". (DFES 1998, p1)

The key question in relation to this study however, is whether ITT providers feel they are in a position to deliver the governments vision, and reflect inclusive practices both within their courses and through their links with trainee and newly qualified PE teachers in schools. For example, one PE ITT provider commented:

> "It does make people sit up and think about it ...these are statutory orders in physical education and curriculum 2000 and it is not something you can just opt out of ... you got to deliver it if you are in a state school. On a personal level its right but also its the legality of things that you have got to address this issue otherwise you are not doing your professional job appropriately, irrespective of whether you think its correct or not". (PE ITT provider B)

This view of a recognition of the requirements of the PE NC, and the professional and legal duty of teachers was supported in the stage two questionnaires in which 79% of ITT providers agreed or strongly agreed with the view that children with SEN should be included in mainstream education, with a further 21% indicating a neutral view.

> "I think it was a good thing providing that it meets the needs of the individual children, you know, if people are integrated and accepted hopefully within society...can lead reasonably normal lifestyles and achieve and experience what most other children experience." (PE ITT provider C)

As a result of these views, support for the concept of inclusion is strong, and agencies such as the DFES, TTA, and OFSTED have taken this strategy forward with the aim of improving the educational achievements of pupils with SEN. A key publication in support of this plan was the governments 1998 'Excellence for All' Strategy (DFES 1998c). This document is of particular relevance to ITT providers as it specifically states its intentions to:

> *"... develop the knowledge and skills of staff working with children with SEN"*
> *(DFES 1998c, p4)*

In order for ITT providers and schools to address this policy, Farrell (1998) argued that if inclusive education is to be reflected, interpreted and fully embraced, schools will need:

> *"... to reconsider their structure, teaching approaches, pupil grouping and use of support" (Farrell 1998, p81)*

As part of this process the stage two questionnaires indicated 67% of PE ITT providers felt children with SEN should be consulted as part of their facilitation of inclusive PE. This view is significant in recognising that it is not only the professionals who need to be part of the process of delivering inclusive PE, but also children with SEN – especially as many of their personal experiences and insights offer valuable learning opportunities for teachers and schools. As part of this process, schools and ITT providers need to move beyond existing arrangements of integration, which may assume that:

> *"... the school system remains the same but that extra arrangements are made for children with SEN" (DFES 1998c, p 81)*

... to a system that fully embraces a person centred planning approach. This supports the views of Ainscow (1999), and Skrtic (1991, 1995), and their notions of moving schools which adapt to meet the needs of particular children:

"... what is really needed is an individual curriculum for every child" (PE ITT provider E)

If the philosophy of inclusion is to be embedded within educational policy and be widely accepted by PE teachers and pupils, the education system must become much more responsive and flexible to the needs of the individual child, rather than the child having to adapt to fit the existing restrictions of the curriculum as it stands. As 87.5% of PE ITT providers agree or strongly agree with the view that SEN issues should be integrated fully into training courses, agencies will have to be much more proactive in the training and guidance delivered to teachers – particularly as the PE NC (2000) requires teachers to set suitable learning challenges, respond to pupil's diverse needs, and differentiate assessment expectations accordingly.

This position is supported by one PE ITT provider who noted:

> *"... in a sense it goes further than we have ever done before what ... as you know with any policy the problem is implementation. So anything can look really really good on paper, but in terms of how that manifests itself in practice is a totally different matter. If we just take the HEI's first of all with the time constraints in terms of our timetabling and the hours ... to deliver aspects of the course anyway, according to areas that need addressing in terms of subject knowledge gaps we can audit that need and prioritise. I know some institutions say right this is what we are doing ... they do it the same year after year and that's not geared towards their needs. So in a sense the way we go about our own practice gives ideas and informs the practice of the students. If it doesn't then we shouldn't be doing the job that we are doing really" (PE ITT provider E)*

Thus, if PE teachers are expected to move beyond their existing practices, and adapt their teaching and learning strategies, then PE ITT providers should be doing the same both in meeting the needs of their trainees, as well as ensuring inclusive education has impact in practice rather than remain part of a policy statement.

> *"So if we're just sticking to the same thing year after year to every new cohort that comes in we'll never change. The issue then still is to prioritise that need and special educational need in terms of what the student has to have" (PE ITT provider E)*

Thus whilst some PE ITT providers are moving to positions of evaluating the currency of their present course structures, others need to initiate this critical analysis if they are to become more confident that they are equipping PE teachers with the necessary skills to include children with SEN.

6.4 Guidance and Implementation of National Curriculum PE for Children with SEN

This section of the questionnaire set out to examine respondent's views and opinions with regard to the level of guidance they perceived was available to facilitate the implementation of an inclusive PE curriculum. For example 45.5% of PE ITT providers agreed or strongly agreed with the view that NC 2000 provides PE teachers with a clear framework for the development of inclusive activities. Consequently, there is still much work to be done in supporting teachers and PE ITT providers to effectively deliver an inclusive curriculum to children with SEN.

> "I think all pupils have an entitlement to PE as far as is reasonably possible, I should try to include them in all PE lessons. But I think you have to be realistic about the extent to which it can happen in normal PE lessons" (PE ITT provider D)

The recognition of entitlement is further supported in the view:

> "The statements made have certainly I think made trainees more aware of the need for inclusive practices. It is a crystal clear statement and there was 9 pages on inclusion and there are only 10 pages of the National Curriculum. I think what's coming from the Government is a clear statement. I think it is moving in the right direction, and I think the flexibility of the national curriculum if it is interpreted appropriately and delivered appropriately will help – but we need help to do this" (PE ITT provider B)

As a result, whilst many of the PE ITT providers indicate teaching children with SEN is just an extension of any PE teachers mixed ability teaching (67%), the reality in practice is that agencies at the professional opinion and practice level need help and support in ensuring PE teachers of the future embed the statutory inclusion statement in the PE NC 2000 (QCA 1999a) as part of their everyday practice.

Therefore, whilst agencies and individuals need to be responsive to change existing

practices, (Dyson 2001, Dyson and Millward 2000, Ainscow 1999, Skrtic 1995)

stakeholders need to work much more in collaboration with each other in order to

share expertise and resources if inclusive practices are to change for the better. –

The Audit Commission (2002) support this view advocating that at present despite

the plethora of inclusive policy, children with SEN still remain a low profile group. This

view is further emphasised in the comment:

> "... in a sense the issues that we are talking about isn't a separate issue it isn't
> something that is tagged on .. it isn't something that is a separate section to the
> National Curriculum.. it is something which is part and parcel of our everyday
> work" (PE ITT provider E)

In relation to children with SEN, remaining a low profile group, and the need for

greater collaboration, the stage two questionnaire responses demonstrated

significant concern with the extent to which official line agencies provide adequate

advice to those at the professional opinion and practice level. For example, only 25%

of PE ITT providers felt PE professional associations were currently providing

sufficient support, advice and guidance regarding the delivery of PE and SEN. An

even stronger picture was given in relation to government and statutory agencies,

with only 4% indicating any satisfaction with current support and guidance being

offered, and a further 58.5% indicated a significant level of dissatisfaction with

present levels of guidance material.

In examining this view it is evident PE ITT providers take the view that at present

there is a lack of consistency of message, and guidance being offered by official line

agencies to those at the professional opinion and practice level. This supports the

position that emerged in chapter 5, in which a lack of a systematic, and coherent

message at official line level related to the inclusion of children with SEN was

apparent:

"... let's have these organisation sort of working cohesively, in a strategic way"
(PE ITT provider E).

"... as national associations I think they should have a policy on it. I think there
should be some public policy that's readily accessible in a published journal. I'd
hope to think, well I'd like to think they'd speak with one voice or, so there
wouldn't be differences between those, and the difficulty with having Baalpe,
Youth Sport Trust, PEA UK, etc.. is that there is the potential for them to say 3
different things" (PE ITT provider C)

6.5   Management and Co-ordination of SEN

In this section of the questionnaire, respondents were asked to comment on how
their respective PE ITT managed and/or co-ordinated SEN provision.

In response to the governments increasing move towards an inclusive education
system, it is evident from the stage two-questionnaire data that ITT providers have a
varied approach to the responsibility mechanisms and delivery of SEN and inclusion.
For example, 50% of ITT providers indicated they have a named person with
responsibility for inclusive PE, whilst 25% indicate that it is all staff's responsibility,
and a further 12.5% stated no one had direct responsibility. If as Farrell (2001) and
Ainscow et al (1999) suggest, it is necessary for teachers to develop opportunities to
look at new inclusive ways of involving all pupils and to draw on their skills of
experimentation, reflection and collaboration with external agencies, ITT providers
must have a systematic approach to this area of work. In addition to the mixed
approaches to responsibility for delivery and implementation, 37.5% of ITT providers
indicated lecturers had no direct experience or qualifications in SEN. This therefore
brings into question the extent to which professional opinion and practice agencies
are able to be effectively responsive to the inclusion agenda if lines of accountability,
responsibility, training, and lecturer experience are weak. As a result, the extent to
which there can be a systematic approach to equipping PE teachers with the
necessary skills to include children with SEN at both an individual institutional level,

and across all professional opinion and practice providers is questionable, and in need of auditing.

The desire for clear structures is supported by Dyson (2001), and Dyson and Millward (2000), who advocate if inclusive practice is to have impact, it requires senior management commitment, clear accountability, and training of staff in order that they can be responsive to the individual needs of pupils. Whilst Dyson and Millward (2000) note this within the context of schools, similar arrangements could be in place at the professional opinion and practice level with PE ITT providers in order to interpret policy, then ensure the necessary training and resources are given to make a positive difference in practice.

An example of the lack of systematic approach and accountability was indicated by one PE ITT provider who when commenting on how inclusion is facilitated stated:

> "... the only thing I would add is ... and I think this is a problem ... this is probably specific to this institution. We don't have anyone co-ordinating solely special educational needs on the undergraduate and the postgraduate. Its all down to me, and I am not an expert I just have an interest in the area, people have left and its gradually me who is responsible for it along with being co-ordinator of other major areas... and I think that it is a real weakness ... it might be specific to here ... we have got to have somebody because of the size of the statement in National Curriculum and the significance of it ... who is so totally focused on special educational needs and how it can be delivered to our trainees (PE ITT provider B)

This view of a lack of co-ordinated provision, and real anxiety was evident in many of the questionnaire responses, and emerges as a key area in need of radical redress by PE ITT providers. In contrast, for those providers who did have a named, experienced person responsible for inclusive PE, it was evident attempts to facilitate a systematic and co-ordinated whole department approach to the implementation of SEN, and inclusion was being undertaken. For example, PE ITT providers who had a named member of staff responsible for inclusion were able to talk much more coherently about the work being undertaken, whilst appreciating the issues and challenges faced in effectively equipping teachers with the necessary skills to deliver an inclusive education. One PE ITT provider, with a named senior member of staff responsible for inclusion noted:

"... the national curriculum is all about children working with each other any way. So I don't think it is anything special that teachers are looking at because its special needs, we are doing more and more...embedding all those sorts of issues in our practical module" (PE ITT provider A)

In addition the PE ITT provider was able to demonstrate an in-depth appreciation of pedagogical practices, and commented:

"... we need to find a balance between adapting the curriculum and the teaching over all, to suit all of the learning and then also, accommodating specific individual needs through differentiation ... in their teaching approach - I can't be 100% sure that everybody is approaching it in that way. But I would feel confident to say that the majority are looking at those issues" (PE ITT provider A)

These views support some of the current examples of good pedagogical practice identified by Ainscow 1999 and Skrtic 1995 related to agencies adopting flexible pupil, and institutionally responsive approaches.

In addressing a need to place high expectations upon lecturers, students and teachers it is important for ITT providers when considering policies and practices to recognise the view of Sugden and Talbot (1998) who advocate teaching children with SEN can be seen as an extension of mixed ability teaching. Thus, teachers should have the necessary skills to facilitate inclusive PE, and will only occasionally require specialist advice and guidance. Therefore, in relation to the delivery of inclusive PE, ITT providers need to ensure courses embed general principles of differentiation, which are facilitated and encouraged by all lecturers, alongside a named person who has responsibility for ensuring students experience a diverse range of pupil experiences during their training. Thus, PE ITT providers must get much better at recognising children with SEN as part of a continuum of learning needs, and as such they need to extend and develop their existing knowledge of differentiation and mixed ability teaching.

This view was supported by a PE ITT provider who commented:

> "... until we get to grips with the mixed ability class I think that's the hardest one rather than the disability but I think we don't cope well with the disability because we are not trained in how to. So that where we might pay lip service to it because we haven't thought about how we can modify the environment well enough, or the equipment well enough and we either give them a separate task to do, which might be necessary because of the kind of activity they are doing, or we tend say you decide what you want to do, which puts the onus on them. I don't think we think about it enough" (PE ITT provider A)

6.6 Working with Children with SEN and the Professional Development of Teachers

In the relative safety of PE ITT provision, it was intriguing to note 37.5% of students are currently not being given opportunities to teach children with SEN, with many indicating experiences would come in schools but only on an ad-hoc basis, rather than as part of a planned event. One provider indicated:

> "... we do not bring children with SEN into the University, although it would be a good idea we tend to leave any experience of this to the schools, although some students may not experience any SEN at all in some schools" (PE ITT provider 6)

Whilst the organisation of experiences for trainee teachers to work with children with SEN many be difficult to initiate, this an area in which the Audit Commission (2002) indicated required further exploration in which mainstream and special schools could support the continuing professional development of teachers.

Furthermore, by PE ITT providers leaving the opportunity of working with children with SEN merely to school experience, there are concerns in the extent to which some trainee teachers may experience sufficient depth of provision. One PE ITT provider commented:

"... the mentors will probably come up with some good ideas to compliment the issues they have been covering in the University but of course then in practice they have to go away and find out about it. And again that will depend on which school they are in, so the quality of the training will vary and it is a broad thing" (PE ITT provider A)

Consequently, another key issue in need of consideration at the professional opinion and practice level is a need for an examination of the extent to which trainee PE teachers presently receive co-ordinated and systematic opportunities to work alongside children with SEN whilst with the provider, and whilst undertaking school based experiences.

In relation to professional development training for PE ITT providers, it is evident that at present this is heavily under resourced. In the last five years from discussion with the five face-to-face PE ITT providers, it became apparent that only one national HEI PE and SEN seminar has been arranged – and that was funded by Sport England. The only other means of sharing, and discussing practice was through the PE HEI National PE network meetings, and this is recognised by many of the questionnaire respondents as a major area in need of being addressed. This could be one aspect in which official line, and professional opinion and practice agencies work collaboratively – and in partnership with experienced practitioners at the consumer levels.

Whilst it was noted earlier that 37.5% of lecturers had no specific training or expertise in SEN and inclusion, it was found 62.5% of lecturing staff had some form of SEN experience, either as an LEA adviser, through PhD experience or teaching children with SEN. As a result, PE ITT providers could audit areas of PE and SEN expertise, and then attempt to co-ordinate and disseminate existing experiences much more effectively both within their own and other institutions in order to address issues of a lack of guidance materials, interpretation of 4/98 (DFES 1998a) Standards and the need to support lecturers more effectively.

6.7 Implications For PE Training Providers and Links with Schools and Mentors

This section of the questionnaire sort to gain an insight into the mechanisms through which PE ITT providers linked with schools in order to support their trainee's development of SEN and inclusion experience. The DFES (1998) SEN Excellence for All document supports the need for students to have more direct experiences of SEN and indicate they will give:

> "… greater emphasis to SEN within teacher training and development" (DFES 1998c, p4)

In examining how they intend to implement this they suggest that this will be achieved through the 4/98 (DFES 1998a) Standards in ITT, (and the subsequent 'Professional Standards Framework' (TTA 2002) 2002). In addition, the DFES suggest:

> "To raise the standards we expect of schools and pupils, we must raise the standards we expect of new teachers" (DFES 1998c, p3)

Thus by establishing what were described as a full and detailed codification of training and competency requirements, it was envisaged student trainees would be given a thorough grounding in all aspects of the teaching profession, of which SEN is an integral and ever increasing area of prominence.

Therefore, whilst the DFES see training providers as the key focal point to ensure issues of inclusive PE are addressed, in contrast 50% of ITT providers indicated that they pass this expectation directly on to schools to deliver. However in the stage two questionnaire responses it was interesting to note only 12.5% of providers had any compulsory links with SEN schools in which students have a planned opportunity to work with children. Consequently, whilst high expectations are being placed on PE ITT providers, the Audit Commission (2002) report noted to a large extent this is not presently being satisfactorily addressed, and schools and newly qualified teachers are not ensuring a satisfactory level of involvement of children with SEN.

An example of providers passing responsibility of SEN over to schools was in the comment:

> "I also don't think it's possible to put everything into individual teacher training, and I get totally frustrated by the fact that everything comes back to training, and yet the nature of training has completely changed. Two thirds of it is school-based as you know, so we are very dependant on PE, mentors and our partners, in our partnership schools, to be as well versed in this areas as ourselves" (PE ITT provider C).

In addition, the amount of time dedicated specifically to SEN issues varied from 3 hours on a one-year postgraduate course to 90 hours on a four-year undergraduate programme, which indicates the diversity of provision currently being delivered. Although issues may be embedded throughout courses there will always be a need to have dedicated time to address specifically these questions in order to shift trainee teacher's attitudes to recognise issues which are more specific than general expectations of mixed ability teaching.

This view was supported by one of the PE ITT providers who commented:

> "I think our knowledge and understanding is not good enough because you only get so much from reading the documents, again its a matter of seeing it in practice and looking specifically in SEN how the schools tie up their policy documentation and actual implementation" (PE ITT provider A)

Thus providers at the professional opinion and practice level need to be much more proactive in developing clearer levels of accountability and expectations of what elements of SEN training should be delivered in the institution, and what can be addressed whilst on school experience. This supports the view of Lipsky and Gartner (1999) who when documenting models of good inclusive practice identify the need for clear vision, leadership, collaboration and an holistic approach to inclusive delivery.

Consequently, PE ITT providers are ultimately responsible for training, and they should take the lead in co-ordinating aspects of a trainee teachers SEN experience.

In the stage two questionnaires, 75% of PE ITT providers involved what were often described as 'recognised experts in SEN' in order to help them develop trainee's knowledge and understanding. These experts were noted as either SEN teachers in schools or individuals working in the field of PE and SEN or disability sport. Whilst many PE ITT providers indicated some use of specialist support to develop their trainees knowledge and understanding, many still commented that they would like to see:

> "More involvement of good practitioners delivering inclusive programmes in schools to either come and talk to the students formally or to come and deliver a lesson, identifying how to deal with differentiation in a physical education lesson" (PE ITT provider A)

Consequently in many of the free responses PE ITT providers recognised that whilst they do involve SEN specialists, they would like to see much more subject based analysis, rather than at present involving SEN generalists who struggle to make direct links to the PE NC.

In relation to school based training activities, it was found only 12% of PE ITT providers indicated any form of compulsory requirement to teach children with SEN. However, this position may now have changed, due to the introduction of the 2002 'Professional Standards Framework' (TTA 2002) in which inclusion has taken on greater prominence, and with OFSTED seeking to report on aspects of inclusion through inspection. This view was highlighted in one of the face to face interviews when it was indicated:

> "I've got the feeling that OFSTED are backing that up through inspection. I get the feeling they are looking at trainee lesson plans to see how they differentiate tasks and whether or not they have identified any pupils who have statements and that type of thing" (PE ITT provider B)

In addition to the compulsory teaching, 50% of PE ITT providers indicated trainees were required to undertake some form of observation of children with SEN on school experience, whilst 37.5% undertake assignments. Therefore, whilst at present compulsory levels of teaching children with SEN may be rather low, with the increasing numbers of children with SEN in mainstream schools, and a recognition of 'continuums of learning need' it would be difficult for trainees not to be gaining practical experiences whilst in school.

6.8 Partnerships with Disability Sport/Special Needs Agencies

The questionnaire sort to gain an insight to whether PE ITT providers had any links with disability sports agencies and or special needs organisations to support the development of trainee's knowledge and understanding. The PE NC Handbook (QCA 1999b, 1999c) suggests in creating access, greater differentiation on the part of teachers and the use of external agencies or teachers requiring specialist equipment will be needed in the future. This statement is fundamental in ensuring PE teachers recognise their full responsibility for planning accessible lessons that cater for all pupils' needs. However, whilst the PE NC (2000) may set out expectations of teachers, 54.5% of PE ITT providers stated they were unsure as to whether NC 2000 (QCA 1999a) had helped focus attention and give sufficient guidance and interpretation related to inclusion. Further to this 58% indicated they needed much more specialist support to embrace the new inclusion agenda. This view is emphasised in the comment:

> "I think the fact that it's there means that it's important, it raises the status of it.
> I'm not so sure how much it has given perhaps in practice, but I think if it wasn't
> there we would be in a much worse situation. But I think it takes much more
> than just pages of words in a national document for it actually to have an
> impact at classroom level. I think there has to be lots of other resources and
> stages that support that. By itself it's of limited value. But it's very critical that's
> it's in there" (PE ITT provider C).

The key to inclusive education being satisfactorily addressed in ITT is according to Westwood (1997) a recognition that there is always going to be a need for in service training for teachers to increase their knowledge and understanding and skills on adapting the curriculum. This links to the initial research question that sets out to examine how equipped student teachers are to deliver such a high profile area of work and the extent to which PE ITT providers can deliver this during a students training. One PE ITT provider commented:

"... perhaps why physical education doesn't get any better in the majority of schools is because we are not thinking hard enough or having the will or want to change our practice" (PE ITT provider A)

Thus, PE ITT providers need to take action and move beyond existing levels of provision, and begin to interpret in practice what the PE NC is expecting of teachers when working with children with SEN – rather than as a profession awaiting guidance from official line agencies.

6.9   Programme Content and Delivery

This section of the questionnaire set out to gain information on individual PE ITT provider programme content and examine the range of delivery mechanisms that were utilised. The Audit Commission (2002) indicate that it can be problematic to address all the issues related to SEN whilst in ITT, and trainees should be expected to gain more experience during their induction year. The need for continuing professional development is a significant argument to make, especially as the study found at present only 29% of providers have core modules on SEN, whilst 29% argue that they take a holistic approach, and a further 42% suggest trainees are offered optional rather than compulsory modules. This high level of optional, rather than core requirements to examine inclusive issues may be resulting in PE teachers entering the profession without a satisfactory level of understanding of how to facilitate access to their lessons for children with SEN. In addition this may be a reason for the low levels of current confidence of PE ITT providers that trainees are satisfactorily equipped to address SEN and inclusion issues.

One PE ITT provider commented:

> "I think that this area is an area that should be a priority area for CPD work. If we look at our career entry profiles that our students complete at the end of the year I should imagine that 75%-80% would put down catering for pupil diversity or differentiation or inclusion and special needs, whatever phrase they use" (PE ITT provider C)

Consequently in support of the Audit Commission (2002) view that there is still much work to be done in raising SEN from being a 'low profile group' the discussion above indicates a need to develop this area further, both whilst in training and in partnership with schools.

The TTA (2003) document 'Into induction 2003 – An introduction for trainee teachers to the induction period for newly qualified teachers' is one recent way in which PE teachers will be expected to ensure that their ITT standards are extended upon as they enter the teaching profession for the first time. The TTA state:

> "The new induction Standards will come into force from 1 September 2003 onwards, and any newly qualified teacher starting their induction on or after this will be assessed against these standards" (TTA 2003, p16)

The intention being to ensure trainees:

> "… continue to meet the standards for the award of QTS, consistently and with increasing professional competence" (TTA 2003, p16)

6.10 PE ITT Course Content

The stage two questionnaires provided a clear indication of the depth and variety of content currently delivered in relation to SEN, with 50% of providers indicating that all their training was theoretical, and only 25% of respondents offering opportunities for practical application. This was further reflected in many of the assessment tasks undertaken by students whilst in training which tended to require students to examine the academic principles of inclusion, rather than necessarily relate these to the wider process models of inclusion and its related impact on pedagogical practices.

However with the introduction of 'citizenship' as a curriculum area in its own right from September 2002, there is an ever-increasing requirement upon teachers, and ITT providers to examine inclusion issues much more in practice as they help pupils to:

> "...become informed, active, responsible citizens contributing fully to the life of their school communities" (QCA, 1999a, p126)

Thus through citizenship, teachers will need to develop children's understanding of general human rights values, and appreciation of philosophical contexts, before moving towards an analysis of implementation and delivery in practice. Consequently, this change in teaching emphasis may aid PE teachers, schools and children's understanding of the process and practice of including children with SEN in PE, and thus make teachers plan more effectively to create conducive teaching and learning environments.

In relation to the nature of module content and assessment the data gained from the stage two questionnaires was again wide and varied. Many modules comprised of a mix of teaching and learning strategies, principles of equity, assessment, differentiation, optional school placements, and independent studies. However the largest area of modular content across the professional opinion and practice level related to assessment of children with SEN with 34% of PE ITT providers indicating modules in this area, followed by teaching, learning and differentiation strategies with 17%.

With regard to the assessment of trainee's knowledge and understanding, trainees were expected to undertake the following types of assessment activities: writing Individual Education Plans (12.5%), observational analysis (25%), school based assessment tasks (25%), and historical perspectives of SEN (25%). In addition to the assessment tasks many PE IT providers indicated that trainees were expected to address issues of differentiation within their lesson planning in order to ensure that they planned each time for children with SEN:

> "... one of the prompts is differentiation, diversity, so they, they have to comment upon it in order to fulfil the requirements of the (lesson plan) form and, and in the next mentor training that we have there are just 2 agenda items actually, one is the unit of work, the flexible unit of work, and the other one is addressing individual needs and specifically we're going to talk about individual education plans" (PE ITT provider C)

The auditing and ongoing evaluation of course provision is an essential element of quality assurance procedures, and it is evident that PE ITT providers approach this in different ways with some more proactive than others. For example, some stated that in relation to measuring the extent to which the 4/98 (DFES 1998a) standards in SEN were being met they awaited OFSTED inspection for feedback (8%), others relied on links with SENCO's in schools (25%), whilst 25% indicated ongoing trainee and lecturer assessment on the delivery and evaluation of modular content. A further 17% of providers indicated that the 4/98 (DFES 1998a) SEN standards were being assessed through a combination of all of the above factors.

However in relation to making judgements on the extent to which trainees have satisfactory levels of knowledge and understanding of SEN and inclusion issues, 50% of providers indicated they relied heavily on mentors to train and make judgements. A further 25% indicated that they would be seeking evidence from trainees through portfolios of professional development that lead into their Career Entry Profiles and NQT induction year. Consequently, there is a significant burden being placed on schools to make the necessary assessment of trainee's experiences of SEN. However, one major positive is that they are being measured on their practice of SEN delivery with mentors in schools, rather than theoretical appreciation.

6.11 Creating A Framework For Inclusive PE – Concluding Thoughts

This final section of the questionnaire gave respondents the opportunity to contribute any further views and opinions they feel necessary or appropriate to the questionnaire. It is evident from analysis of the issues raised within this chapter that inclusive PE is a key issue for ITT providers to address in the coming years. In general terms inclusion is wholeheartedly supported, however existing provision is varied and there is need for further reflection and development of a much clearer systematic approach to the training of PE teachers. This is particularly apparent in that 84% of ITT providers indicated further continuing professional development will be needed once PE teachers have entered the teaching profession, and only 25% suggesting that they felt that newly qualified PE teachers were at present adequately prepared to deliver inclusive education.

The role of the ITT provider is central to the success or failure of the government's agenda for the inclusion of children with SEN, especially as they can be seen as the conduit between official line and the consumers. As more and more children with SEN enter the mainstream school environment PE ITT providers must recognise teachers and schools will face issues and challenges to their pedagogical practices on a daily basis. Therefore, there is a great need, and opportunity for PE ITT providers at the professional opinion and practice level to ensure sufficient advice and guidance is given during the training phase. However, this provision needs further organisation, both at an individual provider and professional opinion and practice level in order that a co-ordinated approach to inclusive PE can be achieved. Consequently, ITT providers need to produce clear and consistent framework approaches to PE and SEN, in order for trainees, lecturers and schools to systematically debate how to fully embed issues of inclusive education within their courses.

In meeting this co-ordinated approach, the desire to develop future PE teachers into professionals that are responsive to individual pupil need, and flexible to modify and adapt their practices is essential. One PE ITT provider suggested:

> *"If we create students who leave this institution with a positive attitude to inclusive practice, then I think we have got it right" (PE ITT provider B)*

This view of PE teachers with a positive attitude, open mind, and high expectations of children with SEN was reinforced by many of the other PE ITT providers, and could be seen as a fundamental step in ensuring inclusion gains the recognition and respect that it deserves.

CHAPTER 7 :
RESULTS AND DISCUSSION FROM THE
CONSUMER LEVEL

(STAGES FOUR AND FIVE)

7.1   Introduction and Context

This chapter examines findings from the consumer level of interpretation focusing

upon the third sub question of **"What are the views and opinions of current**

student trainees and recently qualified PE teachers related to their training for

inclusive education?" The analysis comprises data gathered from student trainees

(stage four), and recently qualified teachers of PE (stage five) from the selected ITT

providers involved in the face-to-face depth interviews at the professional opinion and

practice level (stage three).

Stage four comprises data from questionnaires to all final year students (three

undergraduate, and two postgraduate courses), with a total of 202 questionnaire

responses representing a ratio of 85 males (42%) and 117 females (58%). The data

for stage four was then analysed on the basis of a random sample of 25 students

from the larger PE ITT providers, and full analysis from the smaller institutions. This

data was scrutinised both at an individual PE ITT provider level, and as a full data set

from the five combined institutions, with a total random sample of 113 questionnaires

analysed according to:

> *PE ITT provider A: Large undergraduate four-year course in the North of
> England – random sample of 25 student responses (PE ITT provider: 21)*

> *PE ITT provider B: large undergraduate four-year course in the South of
> England – random sample of 25 student responses (PE ITT provider: 13)*

*PE ITT provider C: Large postgraduate one-year course in the Midlands –
random sample of 25 student responses (PE ITT provider: 3)*

*PE ITT provider D: small undergraduate four-year course in the South of
England – Full sample of 20 student responses (PE ITT provider: 15)*

*PE ITT provider E: Small postgraduate one-year course in the Midlands – Full
sample of 18 student responses (PE ITT provider: 14)*

*(Note: The provider letter in bold refers to the stage 3 face-to-face depth
interviews, whilst the number in brackets relates to the stage two data
collection)*

The discussion of stage four data centres around the six questionnaire headings
related to: about you, your professional development and training to date, your links
with schools and mentors, interpreting inclusive PE, values and attitudes, and other
views and opinions. This analysis forms part (a) of this chapter, followed by part (b),
which considers data gathered in stage five with PE teachers between NQT status
and two years post qualifying experience.

Following discussion in parts (a) and (b), the chapter concludes by drawing the stage
four and five consumer views together, and suggests trainee and recently qualified
PE teacher's preparation, experience, and implementation of SEN is rather mixed.
Within this backdrop however, it is possible to identify where areas of strength and
areas for further development exist and concludes by examining how these can be
addressed in order to ensure teachers of the future are suitably equipped to deliver
inclusive PE for children with SEN.

The stage five questionnaires were sent to three males, and three females from each
of the five selected PE ITT providers (stage three). The information was then
analysed on the basis of 19 responses, representing a return rate of 63.3% and
complied as one data set across the five institutions. Further to this, where
appropriate and relevant, specific individual responses will be highlighted within the

part (b) discussion. As with stage four, the analysis of stage five data centres on the six headings from the questionnaire related to: about you, your ITT in PE, your experiences once qualified, interpreting inclusive PE, values and attitudes, and other views and opinions.

In taking account of data gathered at the consumer level in stages four and five, the findings contribute towards the triangulation of views and opinions across the official line, professional opinion and practice, and consumer levels. Consequently, the discussion within this chapter contributes towards providing answers to the main research question of **"How is the current training of PE teachers for inclusive settings implemented?"**

7.2 From ITT to Induction and Continuing Professional Development

The Audit Commission report (2002) 'Special educational needs - A mainstream issue' highlighted a need for links between ITT, induction and continuing professional development to be strengthened as part of the enhancement of NQT's, SEN and inclusion training. This supports the wider recognition from agencies such as DFES, TTA, and OFSTED, that teachers new to the profession need support in transition towards their first teaching posts, and SEN is one of several key areas that should be addressed. Statutory induction arrangements for NQT'S were first introduced in 1999, and as part of the recent strengthening of the transition process, the TTA (2003) produced a booklet 'Into induction – An introduction for trainee teachers to the induction period for newly qualified teachers'.

The TTA (2003) indicate:

> *"Your initial teacher training is the first stage of your professional development. Once you have been awarded qualified teacher status (QTS) and begun your career as a qualified teacher, you will begin to consolidate what you have*

already learned and to build on your achievements. This next phase begins
with your induction period" (TTA, 2003 p3)

The TTA continue by suggesting a key element of the induction period is the

requirement to provide NQT's with 'an individualised induction programme' that

involves monitoring, support and assessment, and reflects:

> *The strengths and development priorities identified by the trainee and ITT*
> *provider towards the end of ITT as part of a Career Entry and Development*
> *Profile (CEDP) process;*
>
> *Induction standards;*
>
> *Demands of the specific post in which the NQT is starting their career*

This document (and the CEDP) can therefore be seen as the conduit between

standards for the award of QTS, and the induction standards. Thus, it seeks to help

NQT'S recognise how to implement and develop in practice (hence CEDP as

opposed to CEP previously) the ITT standards that they have been working towards

during their training. In relation to the induction standards for SEN and inclusion, the

TTA note:

> *"In order to complete the induction year satisfactorily, a newly qualified teacher*
> *must demonstrate.. They plan effectively to meet the needs of pupils in their*
> *classes with special educational needs, with or without statements, and in*
> *consultation with the SENCO contribute to the preparation, implementation,*
> *monitoring and review of Individual education plans or the equivalent" (TTA,*
> *2003, p17)*

As a result, NQT's are expected to build upon their knowledge, understanding and

application of SEN during their induction year, and as part of this process will have to

satisfactorily evidence a consolidation of their skills in this area. This supports the

desire of the Audit Commission (2002) to ensure knowledge and understanding of

SEN and inclusion is strengthened during the induction year, through partnerships

between special and mainstream schools.

As a result, the TTA (2001) argue developing practice is based upon effective and phased transition from ITT, through a CEDP, into the induction year and CPD throughout a teacher's professional career. Consequently:

"... effective teaching depends on working well with everyone who has a stake in the education of our children" (TTA, 2001, p1)

Thus trainee teachers, NQT's and experienced practitioners must work collaboratively to share their expertise in order to ensure children with SEN gain their full entitlement to the PE NC. The DFES (2001) support this and suggest all agencies (official line, professional opinion and practice, and the consumers) must work in partnership with each other to raise the profile and opportunities of children with SEN.

PART (A) RESPONSES FROM FINAL YEAR TRAINEE PE TEACHERS (STAGE FOUR)

Following the implementation of the 2002 'Professional Standards Framework' (TTA 2002) by the TTA, inclusion and SEN have become a significant area of focus for trainee teachers to address within their ITT and induction year. However, at the time of gathering data with final year PE trainees, the respondents in this study were still operating under the 4/98 (DFES 1998a) standards framework in which there was explicit note of SEN in only 3 of nearly 70 standards. As a result, the extent to which SEN was being identified and recognised as a key issue to be addressed within ITT was competing for time against many other aspects of teacher education and development.

PE ITT provider C in chapter 6 for example, highlighted the difficulty in trying to prioritise lots of different standards. – Especially as none were given any more priority than the other by the TTA. The stage four evidence in part (a) of this chapter begins by focusing upon the compilation of data from the five PE ITT providers. Although were significant variations are evident, single PE ITT provider trainee findings are examined.

7.3   The Respondents

This section of the questionnaire sort to gain information on the respondent's gender, age and institution attended. The ratio of male to female returns was relatively well balanced with 53% female, and 47% male responses, across the two postgraduate and three undergraduate ITT PE courses. These figures are in keeping with national trends for secondary PE teacher training (TTA 2000). Further to this, 91% of respondents were aged 18-24 years and dominated the data set, with 7% aged 25-30, and 2% aged 31-36 years of age. All respondents were in their final year of a four-year undergraduate degree, or in the final stages of a one-year postgraduate degree in secondary PE with QTS.

7.4   Professional Development and Training

This part of the questionnaire sort to examine the extent of trainee PE teacher's professional development and ITT to date related to PE, SEN and inclusion. The issue of whether SEN and inclusion should be addressed as either discrete blocks of work, or embedded across all elements of teacher education is an issue of considerable debate. Depauw and Doll-Tepper (2000), and Westwood (1997) advocate SEN should be 'infused' throughout the undergraduate curriculum. Consequently, trainee teachers should be encouraged by PE ITT providers to consider SEN and inclusion as an integral component of their work, and plan for these factors at all stages of their teaching and learning.

In contrast, Dyson (2001) notes caution in solely embedding principles of equality and difference within the curriculum, because whilst this appears right, the danger is that any subsequent provision is not sufficiently outcome related. Norwich (2002) reinforces the mixed views on delivery of inclusion and SEN by suggesting whilst several theories have contributed towards the modern day inclusive stance:

"There is no logical purity in education" (Norwich 2002, p 483).

Thus there needs to be recognition of a range of:

"multiple values" (Norwich 2002, p 483)

... in which no single value or principle encompasses all that is worthwhile.

From the stage four data, 60% of student trainees considered SEN themes to be embedded within their courses, whilst 25% indicated there were option modules, and a further 30% commented training came through specific core compulsory components of their course. Whilst these figures represent more than 100%, this is due to trainee responses indicating whether they felt SEN was being delivered as either core, compulsory, optional or a combination of these methods within their ITT. Consequently from the trainee responses the data supports the view of Norwich (2002) in which SEN delivery is varied. However, in order to gain insight into whether particular strategies are more effective than others, further analysis was undertaken during the stage four questionnaires to gain a comprehensive overview of the impact with trainee PE teachers.

In ensuring trainee teachers have opportunities to address SEN and inclusion, it could be argued that core, compulsory routes are the only guaranteed method of delivery. Clark et al (1997) would support this view and suggests teachers need to develop core pedagogical skills in order to change the curriculum and make it accessible to the full range of children in ordinary classrooms. However, vast individual PE ITT provider differences were found in the manner in which trainees reported their course to be tackling SEN issues. For example, in PE ITT provider A, 76% of trainees indicated there course embedded SEN issues throughout everything they do, with one respondent commenting:

> "... whatever we are doing in our university degree, the staff usually make sure we are thinking about SEN" (Trainee from PE ITT Provider A)

A similar picture found that trainee teachers from PE ITT provider C (64%) considered their course to be embedding SEN themes throughout most of their ITT.

In contrast, PE ITT provider B, and PE ITT provider E, noted that 80% and 67% respectively of SEN themes comprised of optional modules, rather than as part of core compulsory delivery. As result, this has potential for trainees to avoid particular elements of SEN and inclusion training if they so wish. Whilst it is envisaged that if PE ITT providers were of the view particular aspects of ITT were essential they would make them compulsory, many respondents commented differently. For example, some trainees indicated:

> "SEN teaching should be compulsory". (Trainee from PE ITT provider B)

> "We should not have a choice we should address SEN in our course whether we want to or not". (Trainee from PE ITT provider B).

> "We should not have opportunities to miss SEN themes if we do not like them - make them compulsory as SEN is compulsory when we're in schools". (Trainee from PE ITT provider E)

In relation to the two PE ITT providers ('A' and 'C') with high levels of embedded SEN delivery, both had senior members of staff with responsibility and significant expertise in the field of SEN. This supports discussion on management and co-ordination addressed in chapter 6, in which PE ITT providers who did not have named responsibility for SEN were less sure about how equipped trainees were to deliver inclusive education.

Thus, where PE ITT providers have made conscious decisions to train other lecturers and embed SEN throughout their course provision, the trainee teachers are acknowledging this. This approach supports the view of Dessent (1987) who advocates 'whole school' approaches to responding to individual needs, and some PE ITT providers likewise are replicating these systems. Furthermore, authors such as Clark et al (1995b); Dyson, Millward and Skidmore (1994); and Dyson and Millward (2000) note some progressive schools are embarking on intensive staff development programmes to enhance teaching and learning across the curriculum. Consequently, similar patterns are emerging in strategies to support trainee PE teachers whereby SEN is seen as an extension of a teachers mixed ability teaching and therefore should be considered as an integral component of recognising children along a continuum of learning needs (Sugden and Talbot 1998).

In contrast, at stage three when PE ITT providers 'B' and 'D' were less sure on how trainees knowledge and understanding was developing, concerns were expressed by the stage four respondents that SEN themes should be compulsory, rather than something they could potentially opt out of. This suggests that opportunities to maximise learning in SEN are being potentially, missed or not fully co-ordinated by the respective PE ITT providers. However, with the introduction of the 2002 'Professional Standards Framework' (TTA 2002) in which inclusion and SEN themes are more prominent, it will be interesting to see if PE ITT providers with high optional elements intend to review their delivery and/or change to compulsory or embedded approaches.

The total number of hours trainees spent on SEN issues during their ITT, ranged from 21% indicating between 0-5 hours, through to 2% noting they had spent over

100 hours. The majority (70%) of returns indicated however that the total number of hours spent on SEN was somewhere between 5 and 70 hours respectively. The time factors are a particular issue for the two postgraduate courses with PE ITT provider C indicating 76% of trainees spent 0-5 hours on SEN, whilst 56% of PE ITT provider E trainees spent 0-5 hours. This matches a similar picture to that gained from the stage two data with postgraduate providers. However whilst it is recognised time factors are a major concern for postgraduate courses, 49% of PE ITT provider D trainees indicated they only spent between 0-5 hours on SEN, during their four-year undergraduate course. This view expressed by PE ITT provider D trainees supports comments made in the stage three depth interviews in which it was acknowledged that time spent on SEN issues had reduced significantly alongside other pressures.

Authors such as Dyson and Millward (2000), Ainscow 1999, and Skrtic 1995 recognise vision and leadership as key components of effective inclusive provision within school contexts. Consequently, in PE ITT providers were there is a named staff member who has a clear vision and direction that is communicated to all lecturing staff and trainees, there is greater potential for SEN strategies to be effective. However, institutions who are less clear on the direction of SEN, (i.e. PE ITT providers 'B' and 'D' identified in the stage three depth interviews) appear to be having a negative impact with their trainees commenting they would like SEN to be a compulsory, rather than optional element of their course.

In addition, the lack of clarity in how SEN is delivered by PE ITT providers 'B' and 'D' may be contributing towards the reducing status of their courses through OFSTED inspection grades and diminishing student number allocations from the TTA. Cheminas (2000) supports this view noting OFSTED will be commenting on:

"... the impact of...strategies for promoting inclusion" (Cheminas 2000, p52).

In addition the DFES (2001) suggest:

"Frameworks will be developed to measure the effectiveness of...programmes for raising standards for children with SEN" (DFES 2001a, p27).

Therefore, those providers who are not fulfilling this obligation may find themselves losing student numbers in the future – especially as OFSTED inspection will take note of trainee comments as part of their inspection evidence.

Furthermore, some trainees from PE ITT provider D commented in the free response sections that they did not feel adequately equipped to address SEN and PE issues and:

"... needed more training on PE and SEN in order to feel confident to deliver" (trainee from PE ITT provider D).

Moreover, this is supported by 40% of PE ITT provider D trainees disagreeing, or strongly disagreeing with the statement that they were satisfied with their level of training in PE and SEN. This contrasts with the lower, yet still significant 24% of stage 4 PE ITT trainees who noted dissatisfaction with their ITT related to SEN.

7.5 Practical Application of SEN

The amount of time on theoretical, or practical application of SEN during ITT varied from 21% indicating an equal split, to 55% suggesting the split was at least 80% practical, and 20% theory. This data conflicts with the one given at the professional opinion and practice level, when ITT PE providers suggested the teaching of SEN was predominantly theoretical. Whilst the reasoning for this is unclear, one suggestion may be that whilst trainee PE teachers are undertaking theory lectures they are simultaneously planning for inclusion and SEN as an integral aspect of their teaching and learning activity.

This would support the embedded approach to inclusion and SEN in which trainees make links throughout all aspects of ITT, either through direction from the ITT PE provider, or via personal decision-making. Another reason may be that as differentiation was recognised by trainees as an essential requirement of lesson planning, students may have been considering SEN as an integral aspect of this process, and make their own links this way. This would support 'Policy into Practice' inclusive frameworks in which teachers must address both the philosophy of inclusion, but more importantly implement it in practice (Depauw and Doll-Tepper 2000, Vickerman 2002). Furthermore, on the basis of this analysis what does need further scrutiny on the part of PE ITT providers is a critique of whether they are currently making sufficient links between the theory and practice of SEN. PE providers must ensure that these links are made for trainee teachers, especially during their formative ITT, but this should also be subject of regular review throughout a teachers professional practice.

The range of modular content covered during trainees ITT courses was dominated by professional studies lectures on teaching, learning and differentiation which represented 48% of the returns, with a further 21% suggesting they had taken a specific PE module on SEN. In addition, 8% of trainees noted they had been involved in disability workshops organised by agencies such as the EFDS, or Youth Sport Trust focusing primarily on practical adaptations. As a result, it is evident that teaching, learning and differentiation can be seen as core principles of teacher education, identified by almost half of trainees in relation to children with SEN. A recommendation would however be for PE ITT providers to be more proactive in encouraging SEN to be considered as an extension of a teachers mixed ability teaching and differentiation (Sugden and Talbot 1998).

Consequently, trainees need to recognise that all children are part of a continuum of learning needs, and this needs to be effectively planned for. Through the implementation of teaching and learning models such as Winnick's (2000) 'Framework of alternative instructional placements' and those of Craft (1996,) and the EFDS Inclusion Spectrum more children with SEN should be enabled to access the PE curriculum.

In contrast it was re-assuring only 1% of trainees indicated that they had been involved in simulations of disability (i.e. imitating disabilities in order to gain an insight into individual needs). Anecdotal evidence from PE ITT providers during the depth interviews indicated that historically this had been much higher. However, as part of an encouragement of the social model of disability, (Reiser and Mason 1990) trainees are working much more directly with children with SEN in order to appreciate their individual needs. This supports data from the stage two, four and five questionnaires that children with SEN should be consulted as part of their facilitation of inclusive PE with at least 67% (stage two), 69% (stage four), and 84% (stage five) of respondents either agreeing or strongly agreeing with this view.

The assessment of knowledge, understanding, and application of SEN is central to PE ITT providers making judgements on the extent to which trainees are cognisant of the underpinning issues related to inclusion. The nature and location of assessment was diverse with 35% of trainees indicating they were measured on their mixed ability teaching (PE ITT provider 'B' assessment of mixed ability teaching was higher with 52%). A further 27% indicated assessment took place whilst on school experience, whilst 11% undertook an essay on equity related issues. In contrast to some trainees suggesting SEN themes were embedded throughout their training, only 2% commented they were being assessed constantly on this subject area.

Thus, whilst trainees may make some associations related to SEN, they apparently are not gaining any form of assessment feedback on the extent to which their practice is meeting principles of mixed ability teaching particularly related to children with SEN. Consequently trainee PE teachers need to become better acquainted with forms of 'curriculum adaptation' (Volger and Romance 2000), in which strategies to choose what is taught, or how it is taught can be examined.

If the views of Sugden and Talbot (1998) (teaching children with SEN is part of an extension of mixed ability teaching) are to take on more significance, more than the one third of current trainees will need to have opportunities to be trained and assessed in their mixed ability teaching. PE ITT providers could look to address this as part of their enhancement of teaching and learning in differentiation, especially as 97% of all final year trainees indicated they were required to plan for this within their PE lessons. Furthermore, PE ITT provider D was the only institution in which the requirement to plan for differentiation was less than 100%, with a figure with of 85%. Thus, a recommendation for PE ITT providers would be to consider strategies to develop trainee's appreciation of the full continuum of learning needs and explore methods of assessing their understanding on an ongoing basis. Slinger and Sherrill (2000) support such developments and argue, as part of the 'continuum of learning need', teachers must look at strategies to either change what they teach, how they teach, or who supports the inclusion of children with SEN (i.e. learning support assistants).

The need for trainees to evidence they have met the requirements of the 4/98 (DFES 1998a) standards in SEN is paramount if they are to successfully demonstrate adequate levels of subject knowledge and understanding. As part of this process, 26% of respondents indicated intentions to evidence this within their school based training activities, and 19% were seeking to document direct teaching experiences of children with SEN in schools. In addition a further 16% highlighted they would hold discussions with SENCO's whilst in school, and use the meetings as part of their gathering of SEN experience in order to satisfy the 4/98 (DFES 1998a) standards.

Consequently, all of the evidence cited by trainees was gained through school-based experiences rather than their University based practice.

This supports the discussion in chapter 6 at the professional opinion and practice level, in which PE ITT providers recognised as more ITT was becoming school, rather than University based, mentors would be playing a greater role in supporting trainees development of SEN. In addition, as part of the OFSTED (2002) inspection framework the management of ITT partnerships will be examined in order to make judgements on the crucial links between providers and schools. As part of this process, OFSTED will comment upon how the knowledge gained with the PE ITT provider is developed and extended in practice with mentors in schools. Thus providers need to have clear strategies for these links to be made, and at present in SEN, the evidence suggests this needs further attention.

7.6   Links with Schools and Mentors

This section of the questionnaire sort to gain an insight to the links that trainee PE teachers had with mentors and schools and the role this played in the development of their knowledge and understanding of SEN and inclusion.

In the stage three-depth interviews it was recognised by PE ITT providers that the nature and extent of SEN experience gained by trainees in schools varies greatly. Furthermore, this depends on the number of children with SEN in a particular school, and the support given to trainees by mentors. As part of this discussion trainees were asked to comment on whether they had opportunities to work with children in special school contexts. It was found 19% of trainee teacher's special school experience was compulsory, whilst a further 59% said there were optional opportunities to make visits if they so wished.

However, at three of the PE ITT providers, the trainee data indicated levels of optional visits to special schools were significantly higher than the average (PE ITT provider 'E' - 78%, PE ITT provider 'B' - 92%, and 76% at PE ITT provider 'C'). On further examination, this was attributed to lecturers openly encouraging trainees to experience some form of special school experience in order to extend their appreciation of the full continuum of learning needs. From analysis of the free response comments, many trainees did take up opportunities for special school experience if encouraged to do so. Consequently, those providers not encouraging this at present should consider whether to introduce this strategy as part of an enrichment of trainee's knowledge, understanding and application of SEN.

In contrast to opportunities to make visits to special schools 19% of trainees noted they had opportunities to teach children with SEN as part of a taught module whilst university based, and a further 59% indicated at present they did not have these opportunities. However, 84% of PE ITT provider 'C' trainees indicated they had opportunities to teach children with SEN as part of a compulsory taught module, which was significantly higher than other institutions. The reason for this was evidenced during the stage three depth interview whereby the provider had a link with a special school as part of a taught module. Consequently, trainees were required to teach children with SEN both as part of their University and school based practice. In addition many trainees commented on how positive this experience was, and this is one such strategy other PE ITT providers could replicate as a means of ensuring trainees experience involvement with children with SEN.

As more of ITT is passed directly to schools, the links between school and University based training should naturally increase, and there is strong evidence (87%) that trainee's have discussed SEN related issues with mentors in schools. The only significantly lower figure from any institution was PE ITT provider D, where 60% of trainees acknowledged they had discussed SEN issues with their mentors. However, this institution had recognised in the stage three depth interviews that SEN had lessened, rather than increased in recent years, and students had already noted low total numbers of hours spent on SEN. If as the DFES suggest, in order to enhance inclusive practice in schools they intend to improve the:

"quality of ITT supported via the TTA" (DFES 2002, p16)

PE ITT providers will need to review the extent to which this can be achieved if SEN issues do not have the sufficient prominence - particularly as the OFSTED (2002) inspection framework will comment upon how ITT standards are either being met or not.

7.7 Interpreting inclusive PE

This part of the questionnaire attempted to gain an understanding of trainee PE teachers understanding and definition of inclusive PE. Dyson and Millward (2000) have noted the complexity and confusion surrounding terminology related to children with SEN. In order to ascertain trainees understanding of inclusive PE for children with SEN, respondents were asked to comment upon how they would define and interpret these terms. The definitions were collated according to key words, and/or themes identified by trainees in order to gauge some of the more prominent terms used, and areas of commonality of interpretation. The notion of 'PE for all' was the highest concept identified with 55% using this term, followed by 'equality of opportunity' with 27%, and a further 25% noting the word 'differentiation'. These interpretations were similar across four of the five PE ITT providers, with only PE ITT provider A using a slightly different type of terminology. Here trainees used phrases such as 'including all pupils' (64%), 'entitlement' (16%), and 'enabling and extending' with 8%.

These terms reinforced a deeper level of understanding by recognising children with SEN right to participation in PE. In addition, through the use of the term 'enabling', trainees indicated they had examined strategies to facilitate inclusive PE and recognised the vital role they played in making inclusion a successful teaching and learning episode. Furthermore trainees from PE ITT provider A, identified that all children (including those with SEN) had a right to be challenged through PE and they described strategies they had studied in order to ensure this happened within their teaching. This type of enhanced scrutiny of inclusion for children with SEN, which moves from general equality terminology through to an examination of how it is facilitated in practice, is an aspect that other PE ITT providers should consider in order to enhance their trainees appreciation of issues related to terminology. Booth et al (2000) supports such an approach and argues:

"... inclusion is a set of never ending processes" (Booth et al 2000, p12).

Therefore, as part of the constant, and critical reflection of what can be done in practice to increase the learning and participation of diverse groups of children, teachers need to consider how as 'enablers' they can facilitate inclusion for all.

The types of support trainee teachers perceived official line agencies can offer are indicated in Figure 7.1 below. The intention of this question was to gauge how accurate trainees were in their views, whilst seeking to measure the extent to which they were familiar with the various types of support, advice, and guidance that each agency offers in practice. As a result, this analysis helps determine the extent to which PE ITT providers have satisfactorily imparted the roles and responsibilities of the official line agencies with their trainees.

Agency	Policy documentation	Practical resource materials	Advice and guidance	Other
Teacher training Agency	60%	23%	44%	2%
Office for Standards in Education	56%	24%	28%	1%
Department for Education and Skills	47%	36%	34%	1%
British Association of Advisors & Lecturers in Physical Education	32%	44%	49%	2%
Physical Education Association (UK)	26%	55%	49%	2%
English Federation for Disability Sport	36%	60%	52%	6%
Qualification Curriculum Authority	53%	32%	32%	2%

Figure 7.1 Perception of the types of support official line agencies can give to trainee PE teachers

In analysing Figure 7.1, it is evident some trainees are aware of the roles and
responsibilities of official line agencies more work is needed to clarify this whilst in
ITT. For example, the DFES and TTA only received 47% and 60% recognition of
their role in the development of policy; when this is their core remit. They set the
strategy and outline its implementation, monitoring and evaluation by other official
line and professional opinion and practice agencies. In addition the professional PE
associations and EFDS received similar mid levels of recognition of their specific
roles, and the potential support they offer to teachers. As a result, agencies such as
PEA (UK) who deal mostly with teachers and schools, and BAALPE who support
advisers and lecturers in PE either need to be more proactive in promoting
themselves, or seek further support from PE ITT providers to raise levels of
awareness of their organisations.

7.8   Values and Attitudes

Trainees were asked to respond to a series of questions in which to measure their
attitude and values towards inclusive PE for children with SEN. the questionnaire
consisted of a series of statements, to which they were asked to strongly agree,
agree, take a neutral view, or disagree or strongly disagree with.

The inclusion of children with SEN within mainstream schools has increased in prominence over recent years, supported by statutory and non-statutory legislation (i.e. SEN and Disability Act, DFES 2001c, Revised Code of Practice, DFES 2001b, PE NC 2000, QCA, 1999a). In support of this view, 62% of trainee teachers agreed or strongly agreed children with SEN should be included in mainstream schools, with a further 24% offering a neutral view (many indicating that they did not feel they had sufficient experience to take a view one way or another). The largest disagreement with the inclusion of children with SEN was PE ITT provider D with 12%. This however links to other factors with this PE ITT provider, such as low total number of hours spent on SEN, reducing SEN content, and several comments from trainees that they felt ill prepared for inclusion. Thus PE ITT providers must work towards adopting systematic approaches to their training of teachers for the inclusion of children with SEN, and consider adopting models of policy into practice frameworks to do this (Ainscow 1999, Depauw and Doll-Tepper, 2000, Skrtic 1991,1995, Vickerman 2002)

In relation to the extent to which trainees felt equipped to deliver inclusive PE for children with SEN, 43% suggested they were not adequately prepared, with a further 41% taking a neutral view. This reinforces the Audit Commission (2002) view, that NQT's need further support in their transition from ITT to schools. Furthermore, 91% of final year trainees indicated they would need some form of CPD once in schools. This level of concern supports the stage two questionnaires in which only 25% of PE ITT providers suggested their NQT's were adequately equipped to deliver inclusive PE. Thus there is a great need for all stakeholders to examine why this is the case and chapter 8 seeks to offer some strategies which official line, professional opinion and practice and the consumers can adopt to further this work.

However, whilst there may be many questions on the current readiness of PE teachers to deliver inclusion for children with SEN, 93% of trainees agreed or strongly agreed that such issues should be comprehensively addressed within ITT. In addition, PE ITT provider A trainees gave 100% support for this view, mainly due to SEN already being significantly addressed through many embedded strategies, and a recognition that to a large extent it was an effective strategy within their ITT. One trainee commented:

> "SEN should be included within ITT, and this is the case with....because we have constantly been told to think of SEN as part of a continuum of learning needs we are prepared well - but we still need more help" (PE ITT provider A trainee).

This combination of core and embedded delivery, with senior management vision, leadership and co-ordination is proving effective, and is a model which other PE ITT providers may wish to follow. Lipsky and Gartner (1999) support this view and state:

> "... while there is no single educational model or approach inclusion in schools tend to share similar characteristics and beliefs" (Lipsky and Gartner 1999, p17).

Thus PE ITT providers need to learn from the successes of each other, and work towards approaches that ensure PE teachers of the future are satisfactorily equipped to deliver an inclusive education to children with SEN.

7.9   Other Views and Opinions

This section of the questionnaire gave trainees an opportunity to offer further comments they felt were relevant to the study. The mix of views and opinions expressed in the final section of the stage four questionnaire gave an illuminating insight into the positive experiences, and concerns of trainee teachers who were about to enter the teaching profession as NQT's. Many respondents made strong representations for more practical opportunities to apply directly their theoretical knowledge base on children with SEN. In addition other trainees argued SEN should be a compulsory aspect of their ITT, and should increase in prominence, as more children are now entering mainstream education. One trainee commented:

> "SEN is not optional in schools - the PE NC gives entitlement.. likewise as trainees we should also have an entitlement to SEN training" (PE ITT provider C trainee).

A particular point of concern was that 4% of respondents were so concerned that they were not prepared for SEN teaching they were seriously questioning whether to take up a teaching post at the end of their course. As there were no follow up opportunities to examine these views, it is difficult to ascertain whether SEN was the primary factor or not. Anecdotal evidence for example suggests in any typical group of trainee teachers a percentage will be disillusioned with teaching in general, or are failing or weak students, and this may be the case with the respondents in this study. However, PE ITT providers should be encouraged to examine the reasoning behind any prospective teacher who decides to not enter the profession in order to help with their own quality assurance procedures, but more importantly attempt to ensure they do not attribute it to poor delivery.

PART (B) RESPONSES FROM THE PE TEACHERS AT NQT STATUS TO TWO YEARS POST QUALIFYING EXPERIENCE (STAGE FIVE)

Part (b) of this chapter examines the questionnaire response from recently qualified PE teachers (NQT status to two years post-qualifying experience) who were contacted via the five follow up PE ITT provider depth interviews (stage three). From the total 30 questionnaires sent out, 19 were returned as indicated below:

PE ITT provider A: Large undergraduate four-year course in the North of England – 6 responses (PE ITT provider: 21)

PE ITT provider B: large undergraduate four-year course in the South of England – 3 responses (PE ITT provider: 13)

PE ITT provider C: Large postgraduate one-year course in the Midlands – 3 responses (PE ITT provider: 3)

PE ITT provider D: small undergraduate four-year course in the South of England – 3 responses (PE ITT provider: 15)

PE ITT provider E: Small postgraduate one-year course in the Midlands – 4 responses (PE ITT provider: 14)

7.10 About You

From the 19 questionnaire responses, 7 teachers had undertaken one-year postgraduate ITT courses, whilst 12 had trained through a four-year undergraduate course. The age mix was spread more evenly than with the stage four respondents. For example, 42.10% of respondents were aged 18-24, a further 42.10% were aged 25-30, and 5.26% aged 31-36 years. Further to this, 42% of respondents were male, and 58% were female, resulting in a fairly even gender split being achieved.

7.11 Your ITT in PE

The first section of the stage five questionnaire asked teachers to reflect upon their ITT in PE. The intention was to identify similarities and differences to those given by respondents at stages 2-4 of this study. Furthermore, the stage 5 consumers are in a critical position to comment on the appropriateness of their ITT related to how equipped they are to deliver inclusive PE to children with SEN. In relation to the compulsory, optional or embedded SEN themes during their training, 11% of teachers commented these were optional, whilst 53% said they were core, and 58%

indicated they were embedded. As some respondents indicated SEN themes were delivered through a combination of core and embedded modules, the overall percentage is over 100%, and this represents a similar picture to that in the stage four questionnaires.

In relation to total number of hours spent on SEN during training, a similar picture to that at stage four emerged with responses ranging from 3 – 100 hours. The most significant figures highlighted 21% of teachers had spent around 0-5 hours on SEN, and many of these respondents had undertaken one-year postgraduate courses. These figures are similar to the stage four, and National picture gained in the stage two questionnaires. Furthermore, 26% of teachers indicated they spent 20-25 hours on SEN related issues, and as a result a comparison between stage 4 and 5 data indicates the total number of hours has not increased significantly over recent years. However, with the increasing inclusion agenda and the focus of the 2002 'Professional Standards Framework' (TTA 2002) on inclusion a changing picture may emerge in the future.

The combination of theoretical as opposed to practical application found a different pattern to that in the stage four questionnaires. For example, stage four respondents noted considerable time was spent on practical application, although this conflicted with the view from the professional opinion and practice level of interpretation. In relation to the stage five responses, 26.31% of teachers reflected all of their ITT was theory based, with a further 15.78% noting it was at least 90% theory. A further 47.34% of teachers highlighted they had done more theory than practical. Consequently, whilst the stage five data supports evidence gained in the stage two questionnaires, a reason for the difference in stage four responses may be that trainees are more forthcoming in making links between theory and practice - particularly as this is a key requirement of the current 4/98 (DFES 1998a) standards as opposed to the 10/97 (DFEE 1997c) or 10/92 (DFE 1992) frameworks which stage five PE teachers will have trained under.

As a result, with increasing amounts of ITT now being school based, and further opportunities to link theory into practice trainees are more absorbed in this type of process and it may be easier for them to make links than their PE ITT providers or teachers as they are directly experiencing this process. However if this is the case, this rather implicit association, needs to be addressed more explicitly by PE ITT providers in order to ensure these links are being made for trainees.

A similar picture relating to the nature and content of modules was found to those at stage four, with 47.36% of respondents suggesting they had undertaken courses of study on individual education plans and inclusion. A further 21.05% identified differentiation, teaching and learning content, whilst 10.52% had studied motor skill development in children. The only significant difference in modular content to that at stage four was that only 5.26% of PE teachers at stage five remember any modules that made direct links to their school based experiences. As a result, this emphasises a lack of current PE teachers having opportunities to embed their theory in practical settings during their ITT. Furthermore, only 15.78% of teachers recalled undertaking any form of modular assessment on differentiation, and 10.26% indicated they were assessed of their SEN teaching whilst on school experience. As a result, this contrasts significantly with stage four trainees who noted higher levels of practical application and assessments of SEN issues. This may as noted above be due to the changing nature of ITT, in which greater links are now being made between theory and practice in the 4/98 (DFES 1998a) and 2002 'Professional Standards Framework' (TTA 2002).

7.12 Readiness to deliver PE for children with SEN

As recently qualified PE teachers, a crucial question posed in the stage five questionnaires was 'Do you feel that your ITT course prepared you for inclusion of children with SEN in PE?' This resulted in a positive response of 16%, whilst 84% of respondents answered no. Consequently, this raises many questions on the current readiness of PE teachers to deliver inclusive PE for children with SEN. Therefore, the need for CPD (similar to that indicated in stages three, and four), is of paramount importance if PE teachers are to be satisfactorily equipped to support children with SEN. This high level of uncertainty reinforces the need to strengthen links between ITT, induction and CPD (Audit Commission 2002). As a result of this evidence, a recommendation would be for PE ITT providers to work with official line agencies and consumers to address this issue, and increase the levels of confidence to deliver PE to children with SEN. Chapter 8 will draw many of these themes and issues together for further consideration and analysis.

In attempting to identify reasons for the views that ITT does not currently prepare PE teachers for the inclusion of children with SEN, the free response comments act as a useful starting point to address this issue. For example, 57.89% of stage five respondents suggested they did not receive enough information on the range of SEN that they would have to cater for in schools, and subsequently felt ill prepared to support them. To some extent this picks up on earlier discussions of mixed ability teaching (Sugden and Talbot 1998, Dyson 1999, Farrell 1998), and the need for PE ITT providers to be much better at supporting trainee teacher's delivery of good differentiation. Likewise, trainee teachers need to be encouraged to consider children with SEN as part of a wider continuum of learning needs which they would experience within any teaching situation and plan effectively for this.

7.13 Your Experiences Once Qualified

This section of the questionnaire offered respondents the opportunity to comment on any experiences they felt relevant related to their experiences of inclusion, SEN and PE since they had qualified. A key factor to examine from the stage five respondents was a view that PE ITT providers are concentrating too much on the theory, rather than practical application of SEN in both University and school based contexts. Many current PE teachers commented that PE ITT providers should be encouraged to think carefully about strategies to enhance links between the theory and practice of SEN. Additionally, 31.57% indicated a desire to strengthen school based training experiences in order for trainees to appreciate the challenges that face teachers on a daily basis. Clark et al, (1997) supports the need for both the practicality of inclusion as well as theoretical frameworks to be addressed in tandem if inclusive practice is to be effectively achieved. Thus one without the other according to Clark only acts to provide a patchy overview of the rationale and strategies to support children with SEN in mainstream schools.

The opportunity to reflect on the early teaching experiences of stage five respondents can help with the process of establishing a framework for ensuring PE teachers are adequately equipped to support children with SEN. For example, some of the major issues faced by recently qualified stage five respondents were highlighted as challenging the more able (5.26%), struggling to work with pupils with emotional behavioural difficulties (42.10%), and a need to discuss more strategies for inclusion in schools (26.31%). In addition 26.31% of respondents indicated delivering differentiation was at times challenging to achieve, due to the vast range of pupil needs they had to cater for. This reinforces the view of Sugden & Talbot (1998) that teachers need to focus more on enhancing their strategies for mixed ability teaching in order to enable more children with SEN to access the PE curriculum.

As CPD featured so highly in relation to the stage two, three and four responses, and is acknowledged through the Audit Commission (2002) report and the TTA induction year, it is evident this as an area for prioritisation. However, from the stage five questionnaire responses some support is available to teachers once in school. For example, 10.52% of PE teachers had undertaken a course delivered by the EFDS, whilst 31.57% had undertaken some form of PE INSET through the LEA in which SEN was addressed during their induction year. Furthermore in relation to NQT meetings, 10.26% of PE teachers noted that in their induction year they had discussed specific pupils with SEN with either the LEA, and/or mentors in school. Many stage five respondents commented that the processes noted above were very positive experiences to gain, and should be extended to all NQT's induction and CPD support mechanisms.

Lipsky and Gartner (1999), and Dyson and Millward (2000) identified a number of methods through which effective inclusive practice can be delivered. A central aspect of this process involved the development of holistic approaches to the support of children, and consultation with a plethora of individuals and agencies. Bearing these views in mind, 57.89% of PE teachers at stage five indicated they had discussed issues with SENCO's, 31.57% had received advice from learning support assistants, and 31.57% had gained support from their Heads of PE. In addition many free responses indicated that successful inclusive practice had come via consultation with a range of individuals and support agencies, and this had helped ensure positive experiences for children with SEN. Thus, support mechanisms and multi-agency partnership approaches are central to any future successful delivery of inclusive PE for children with SEN (DFES 2001a).

7.14 Bringing Currency To The PE ITT Process Related To SEN

The experiences of recently qualified PE teachers bring significant currency on the extent to which ITT has satisfactorily equipped them for supporting children with SEN. As a result, the views and opinions of PE teachers who have been through ITT, induction, and on into their teaching careers offers extensive opportunities for quality assurance and feedback to ITT providers, and official line agencies. When teachers were asked to comment on any issues they felt ITT providers should address, 36.84% of respondents suggested there should be a compulsory SEN school experience. A further 42.10% suggested that more ideas on practical activities and delivery should have been given, whilst 21.05% said they required more experience of teaching the full range of SEN.

These insightful views support some of the comments made by stage two and three respondents at the professional opinion and practice level particularly related to a desire for more practical resource materials and guidance. The DFES CD-ROM 'Success For All: an inclusive approach to PE and school sport' (DFES, 2003) is one such resource, which begins to address the concerns expressed by the consumers and those at the professional opinion and practice level - as a result more initiatives such as the DFES led CD-ROM initiative should be encouraged in partnership with the experiences of PE ITT providers, trainee and qualified teachers in order to enhance children with SEN opportunities to access PE. It is recommended that through a co-ordinated partnership approach, and multi-agency working (DFES 2001a) further opportunities for professionals and agencies with PE and SEN experience should be fostered in order to extend further resource materials available for teachers.

7.15 Interpreting Inclusive PE

As with the stage four questionnaires, stage five respondents were asked to offer definitions and interpretation of inclusive PE for children with SEN, and this data was again collated in the form of key words and themes. Similar interpretations to those at stage four emerged with 42.10% using the term 'involvement of all pupils', 36.84% stating 'equality of opportunity', and 10.52% suggesting 'success through planning'. The only point of difference was recognition that success came from planning for the inclusion of children with SEN. Therefore, from the experiences of recently qualified teachers the need to emphasise that good planning leads to successful inclusion, is a point which PE ITT providers should emphasise within their training. This supports the view of Ainscow (1999) and Skrtic (1995) who argue inclusive education involves effective planning and organisation in order to produce positive outcomes for children with SEN.

In relation to the perceptions of the roles that official line agencies should play Figure 7.2 outlines the responses gained from the stage five questionnaire responses. These offer similar data to those gained from the stage four questionnaires, demonstrating no significant shift in views once qualified and working directly with official line agencies. As a result, there is a need for official line agencies and the consumers to understand each others roles much more clearly and this could come through greater partnership working.

Agency	Policy documentation	Practical resource materials	Advice and guidance	Other
Teacher training Agency	57.89%	42.10%	57.89%	15.78%
Office for Standards in Education	57.89%	10.52%	26.31%	
Department for Education and Skills	63.15%	21.05%	31.57%	
British Association of Advisors and Lecturers in Physical Education	42.10%	57.89%	42.10%	5.26%
Physical Education Association (UK)	36.84%	78.94%	26.31%	
English Federation for Disability Sport	26.31%	68.42%	57.89%	
Qualification Curriculum Authority	57.89%	31.57%	31.57%	

Figure 7.2 Perception of the types of support official line agencies can give to qualified PE teachers

7.16 Values and Attitudes

The ultimate success factor in any official line policy, implemented by agencies at the professional opinion and practice level is its impact and delivery by PE teachers in schools once qualified. The Figure below (7.3) provides analysis of the views and opinions gained from the 19 respondents across the five PE ITT providers. These act as a focal point for reflection on what they key issues and challenges are based on the interpretations of what can be considered the end product of training PE teachers to include children with SEN. As a result, it is recommended that this data is used as a starting point for all stakeholders (official line, professional opinion and practice, and consumers) to review existing and future practice in inclusive PE for children with SEN. Through an examination of all the data from the stage five questionnaires and the Figure below a clear, and full insight is offered on potential starting points for celebrating what is good, and what needs to be addressed better in relation to equipping PE teachers to include children with SEN.

Statement	Strongly agree	Agree	Neutral	Disagree	Strongly Disagree
20. Children with SEN should be included in mainstream schools	21%	66%	26%	11%	
21. Newly Qualified Teachers are adequately prepared for delivering inclusive lessons for children with SEN		21%	26%	42%	11%
22. Newly Qualified Teachers will need further training through Continuing Professional Development programmes	74%	21%	5%		
23. Children with SEN should be consulted as part of the facilitation of inclusive PE	58%	26%	11%	5%	
24. NC 2000 provides PE teachers with a clear framework for the development of inclusive activities		21%	21%	37%	16%
25. SEN issues should be integrated fully into all Initial Teacher Training courses	84%	11%	5%		
26. Teaching of children with SEN is just an extension of any teachers mixed ability teaching	16%	11%	11%	47%	11%
27. 4/98 (DFES 1998a) Standards ensure that students are adequately prepared for inclusive education		5%	32%	47%	16%
28. The TTA, Dfes and OFSTED offer adequate advice and guidance to PE teachers/trainees on SEN issues		11%	37%	37%	16%
29. Professional PE associations i.e. BAALPE, PEA (UK) offer adequate advice and guidance to PE teachers/trainees on SEN issues		16%	58%	26%	5%
30. The Code of Practice on SEN and Individual Education Plans can be related to PE with relative ease	5%	11%	32%	37%	11%
31. I am satisfied with the level of training I have received in relation to PE and SEN		11%	37%	37%	5%

Figure 7.3 values and attitudes of PE teachers at stage five

7.17 Concluding Thoughts

It is evident through examination of the views and opinions gained from the stage four and five questionnaires that training experiences, and implementation of inclusive PE for children with SEN is rather mixed. This supports the view of Norwich (2002) who advocates there are 'multiple values' related to the delivery of inclusion. Bearing this in mind however, it is possible to draw together areas of strength, and areas for further development in ensuring PE teachers are equipped to include children with SEN. As a result, The Audit Commission (2002) argues for a strengthening of links between ITT, induction and CPD to ensure teachers consolidate their knowledge, skills and application of inclusion and SEN. As part of this process the TTA (2003) require NQT's to evidence how they have built upon their knowledge and understanding and subsequently evidence this during their induction year.

The evidence gained from consumers in this chapter suggest that 'infusion models' (Westwood 1997) can have a positive impact in preparing teachers for inclusion, particularly if they are outcome related (Dyson 2001). Additionally PE ITT providers who have a named, senior member of staff responsible for the management, co-ordination and implementation of SEN within the context of 'whole school' approaches (Dessent 1987) tend to have clearer strategies and more secure trainees.

Time factors are a real issue in PE ITT, and the total number of hours spent on SEN ranged from 0-5 hours in one-year postgraduate courses, to between 5 and 70 hours on four-year undergraduate programmes. Whilst time is one factor to consider, more importantly is the manner in which PE ITT providers use this to prepare trainee teachers for inclusive education. Some PE ITT trainees report that SEN for example is a compulsory aspect of their ITT curriculum, and comment very positively on this approach. In contrast, were provision was more optional, trainees noted concern that they could potentially avoid parts of this subject area and consequently be left not equipped to deliver once in schools.

The level of dissatisfaction amongst trainee PE teachers (stage four) with their ITT related to SEN ranged from an average of 24% across the five PE ITT providers, to one institution reaching the 40% mark. These figures are alarmingly high in some cases, and providers need to work with official line agencies and the consumers to ascertain why this is the case, and draw upon the research evidence within this study.

In relation to module delivery, teaching learning and differentiation were the most common aspects of curriculum content. However, further work needs to be undertaken in order to link this much more directly to children with SEN, concepts of 'continuum of learning needs' and 'mixed ability teaching'. Additionally, as only one third of trainees indicate at present they are receiving feedback on their mixed ability teaching related to children with SEN this is an area that needs to be addressed in a much more significant way.

A recognition of the need to consult children with SEN as part of their teaching and learning gained a high positive response with 69% at stage four, and 84% at stage five supporting this view. Evidence suggests the stage five data is so high due to many teachers acknowledging the value of implementing consultative strategies with a plethora of individuals and organisations in order to support children with SEN. In relation to trainees seeking to evidence their 4/98 (DFES 1998a) standards in SEN, all of the trainees at stage four indicated this would be achieved from their school-based experiences. Thus, no one identified University based teaching and learning as a means of evidencing their practice, and this is something PE ITT providers should scrutinise further. This position was not evident in the stage five data however, when current teachers indicated that during their ITT they did not have sufficient opportunities to link their theory into practice in schools. Consequently in relation to the trainee teachers this position appears to have changed for the better, however PE ITT providers need to look to how trainees can also use their university based work to evidence competence against the 4/98 (DFES 1998a) standards.

In some PE ITT providers there is potential for trainees to have no involvement with children with SEN during their training. This could occur due to a combination of factors such as; insufficient support in schools, lack of support from mentors, or no opportunities to work with children with SEN whilst University or school based. This is a situation that again needs to be reviewed in order that all trainees actively engage in teaching children with SEN at some point during their ITT. – Especially as a high majority of stage four and five respondents support the inclusion of children with SEN in mainstream education. Consequently, some PE ITT providers may well be not fulfilling their obligations to support trainees in this part of their professional development.

In summary, there is much work to be done to address why 84% of current PE teachers from the stage five providers indicate there ITT has not prepared them to work with children with SEN in schools. A key aspect of this will necessitate professional opinion and practice working proactively with consumers, and official line agencies to determine the reasoning for such a high level of dissatisfaction. The next chapter turns to an examination of all the data gathered from official line, professional opinion and practice and the consumers in order to assimilate the findings, key themes, and issues gleaned from this study. From this analysis suggested answers to the research questions will be offered, whilst also examining strategies for how the current training of PE teachers for inclusive settings can be further enhanced.

C H A P T E R   E I G H T :
KEY THEMES FROM THE FIVE STAGES

8.1   Introduction

This chapter draws together discussion and findings from chapters 5, 6, and 7 related to the official line, professional opinion and practice, and consumers in order to triangulate responses to the main research question of **how is the current training of PE teachers for inclusive settings implemented?** The analysis comprises of the identification of themes, issues, and recommendations from the chapters noted above and incorporate the five stages of research undertaken within this study.

The three sub questions of the study are considered in turn, and key findings are identified from the official line, professional opinion and practice and consumer levels of interpretation. If we are to provide a minimum standard of access and direction for the key agencies and individuals involved in inclusive PE and SEN, then the priorities set out within this chapter whilst not intended to be detailed, are there to act as a focus for future action in the training of PE teachers. As a result, the proposed 'Eight P Inclusive PE and SEN Framework' at the end of this chapter establishes sets of priorities (via the key findings) through which the findings offer real potential to turn policies into practice.

The chapter concludes with a brief examination of recommendations for future action arising from this study, and turns as a next phase to suggest a need to hear the voices of children with SEN in order to further enhance the work undertaken within this investigation.

8.2 The Official Line: "What Are the Views and Policies of Government, Statutory Agencies and PE Associations in Relation to the Delivery of Inclusive PE For Children With SEN?"

The official line (stage one) examined the similarities and differences in interpretation of inclusive PE from the perspectives of the DFES, TTA, OFSTED, QCA, BAALPE, PEA (UK), and EFDS. The aim was to examine the views and policies of these agencies with regard to the delivery of SEN, and consequently the extent to which a clear, consistent, and coherent message is evident for all stakeholders engaged in inclusive PE. The data from stage-one substantiated extensive inclusive policies amongst most official line agencies, however there was less detail on collaboration and joined up thinking regarding its implementation in practice.

It was not surprising to see evidence of policies amongst official line agencies, due to the increased emphasis of social inclusion following the return to power of the labour government in 1997. In relation to education this has encompassed legislation such as the NC (2000) Inclusion Statement (QCA, 1999a); Revised Code of Practice (DFES 2001b); SEN and Disability Act (DFES 2001c); OFSTED Inspection Framework (2002); and the TTA (2002) 'Professional Standards Framework' (TTA 2002). However, what is of more concern is the lack of joined up thinking, and collaboration that takes place both across the official line, and with agencies and individuals at the professional opinion and practice, and consumer levels - particularly as this conflicts with the DFES (2002) strategy to 2006, which states:

> "... successful delivery will depend on strong and effective relationships with many partners" (DFES 2002, p1)

Furthermore, the DFES (2001) acknowledge:

> "Too often different agencies do not work effectively together" (DFES 2001a, p22)

… and this is proving problematic in official line agencies attempts to deliver a consistent message on inclusive PE for children with SEN. Avramadis and Norwich (2002) support this view by suggesting:

> "…without a coherent plan for teacher training in the educational needs of children with SEN, attempts to include these children in the mainstream would be difficult" (Avramadis & Norwich 2002, p139)

Thus, whilst inclusive policies at the official line may be evident, they are of limited use if they do not support similar goals, and consequently will result in disjointed or ineffective provision. This view was recognised in stage three of the study when one PE ITT provider commented:

> "Well, first of all they need to get their own act together and just join up and have a coherent co-ordinated programme, not something that's just dysfunctional or fractional" (PE ITT provider E)

Thus, 'gatekeeper' agencies (Trend 1997) need to work collaboratively to ensure their strategies compliment each other, and give consistent messages to those at the professional opinion and practice, and consumer levels. Many respondents supported this view, commenting that they required much more transparent approaches to inclusive PE for children with SEN in relation to policy directives, and supporting guidance.

In contrast to the general view of official line agencies not collaborating with each other or those at the professional opinion and practice and consumer levels, it was found OFSTED regularly engaged with stakeholders at all levels of interpretation. They indicated in stage one that they:

> "… work with partners to raise standards" (OFSTED, open letter response)

… and there is a range of evidence to support this statement.

For example, OFSTED work with the TTA and DFES at the official line to raise standards in teacher training and education. Additionally, they regularly attend HEI

PE network meetings to discuss practice, and also have opportunities to observe delivery in schools and ITT providers through their inspection work. Consequently, this level of consultation and collaboration with policy makers, ITT providers, lecturers and teachers offers a unique position to reflect on all aspects of inclusive PE practice related to SEN. Furthermore, such models of practice support the work of Ainscow (1999) and his notion of 'moving schools' in which all stakeholders collaborate to make provision relevant and effective. As a result of this partnership work and through the encouragement of open dialogue it was found OFSTED have a thorough appreciation of the respective issues from all the stakeholders, and can respond accordingly. Therefore, more of this practice should be encouraged, and one way of addressing this could be via the DFES acting as a catalyst to draw all the stakeholders together to share practice, and plan effectively for the future. The DFES SEN Working Group (SENWG) is one method in which a PE subject group could be established to implement this recommendation.

Key finding 1: There is extensive evidence of inclusive policies at the official line related to inclusion and SEN, however there is less detail on how each agency collaborates regarding its implementation in practice with each other, or those at the professional opinion and practice, and consumer levels of interpretation. The DFES SENWG should seek to establish a PE subject group to facilitate collaboration with all relevant stakeholders in order to provide joined up approaches to policy and practice.

8.3 Increasing Opportunities and Access

The government agenda to increase opportunities and access for children with SEN is evident through statutory and non-statutory legislation described earlier in this chapter. However, despite widespread legislation the Audit Commission (2002) questions the extent to which this is having the desired impact and describes children with SEN as 'still a low profile group'. The Audit Commission note teachers need further help to recognise what SEN comprises of, and they point to the TTA 'Professional Standards Framework' (TTA 2002) as a means of assisting with this process. However, the Audit Commission suggest it is unrealistic for trainees in ITT to fully appreciate all aspects of SEN and inclusive provision, and consequently suggest the induction period should be used as a means of transition and consolidation of an NQT's developing skills in SEN.

In relation to time spent on SEN during ITT, there are great pressures for PE providers and trainees on one-year postgraduate courses, whereby most courses spend around 5 hours on inclusion related issues. In contrast, four-year courses utilise between 25 and 70 hours on SEN, and as a result should be in a better position to prepare trainees for this aspect of their work. Whilst time alone cannot be a measure of quality, the TTA in partnership with PE ITT providers, the Audit Commission, schools and teachers should seek to establish where significant variations in depths of SEN knowledge, and gaps in training are evident. In undertaking this process a useful starting point would be to consider evidence from stages four and five of this study as initial areas for consideration. These include a need for higher levels of SEN school based experience; further understanding of mixed ability teaching; continuums of learning; practical application of theory; and discussion of strategies to facilitate inclusive PE for children with SEN.

In addition to pedagogical practices, the Audit Commission (2002) notes the TTA (2002) 'Professional Standards Framework' (TTA 2002) is a positive step forward in considering SEN with regard to differentiation and curriculum delivery. However, they indicate there is no acknowledgement of the wider policy contexts of inclusion and legislation within the professional standards. For example, there is no recognition of the NC (2000) Inclusion Statement (QCA 1999a), and the SEN and Disability Act (DFES 2001c), which leaves trainees with gaps in their philosophical appreciation of inclusive practice. As a result, the Audit Commission (2002) suggest that as:

> "SEN is a core part of their teaching responsibilities, not an add-on" (Audit Commission, 2002, p38, point 98)

... all aspects of inclusive practice should be embedded within teaching and learning activities both during and following ITT. This view links with the embedded, and core elements of PE ITT as opposed to optional aspects of delivery considered in stages two to five of this study. Thus it was found that were compulsory or core SEN provision was evident (i.e. PE ITT provider A, PE ITT provider C) within ITT, trainee teachers felt more equipped to address inclusion within their teaching (see consumer discussion later in this chapter).

Key finding 2: Children with SEN remain a low profile group and consequently stakeholders should seek to address strategies to resolve this through a combination of the development of trainee PE teacher's pedagogical practices, and an appreciation of the wider policy, philosophical, and legislative contexts for inclusive education.

The DRTF (2003) suggest attitudes towards disability need to change, and these cannot be left to disability organisations or government alone. Consequently, official line agencies in partnership with others need to plan strategically for the new duties placed on LEA's and schools (i.e. SEN and Disability Act DFES 2001c) in order to enhance access and opportunities for children with SEN. Furthermore, the DRTF (1999) indicate legislation alone will not make the necessary changes and a fundamental attitude shift is needed amongst all stakeholders if inclusive provision for children with SEN is to become a reality. In order to facilitate this process official line agencies need to consider how those at the professional opinion and practice, and consumer levels can address the points raised by the DRTF, as at present ITT providers, do not feel that sufficient guidance is given on this point. This will therefore necessitate greater opportunities both within PE ITT, and through Continued Professional Development to debate what inclusion in PE for children with SEN involves, whilst examining strategies to ensure that it is effectively delivered in practice.

Key finding 3: Official line agencies do not presently offer sufficient guidance on how to ensure trainees; NQT's, ITT providers, and staff in schools have opportunities to develop positive attitudes towards PE and SEN provision. This could be achieved through further development of TTA (2002) 'Professional Standards Framework' (TTA 2002)s, induction and CPD work.

8.4   Professional PE Associations and Disability Sport Organisations

An example of official line agencies needing to be more proactive in developing guidance materials and joined up approaches to support PE teachers is highlighted through the work of BAALPE and PEA (UK). The stage one research found that at present the PE professional agencies and the EFDS are in a vacuum and do not have sufficient input to official line, professional opinion and practice, or consumer levels of interpretation. For instance, at present neither BAALPE nor PEA (UK) have policies on inclusive PE for children with SEN, whilst the EFDS do. Lloyd (2000) supports the need to ensure that policy relates to practice, and suggests the most effective way to achieve this is through collaborative and joined up approaches to the delivery and implementation of inclusive education.

However there was no evidence of these agencies working together to either lobby the official line, or provide resource materials to support PE teachers in their delivery of inclusive PE. In contrast it was found that the EFDS 'Including Disabled People' course had been developed in isolation and there were many missed opportunities to link this resource into PE ITT, or CPD provision in partnership with various stakeholders. As a result, from examination of the data gathered in stages two to five, many respondents were seeking clearer guidance on what, and how inclusive PE for children with SEN can be delivered. Thus there was a demand for official line agencies to move beyond policy creation, and into the development of strategies and guidance for the implementation of PE for children with SEN. In the future, QCA PE subject officers could work with the PE professional bodies, and the EFDS to develop this area of work.

> *Key finding 4: BAALPE, PEA (UK), and EFDS currently do not work in partnership with other stakeholders to support PE teachers in the development of guidance materials to support the delivery of PE for children with SEN. In order to share areas of expertise, and provide a co-ordinated approach to supporting teachers, these agencies should work with the QCA to interpret the requirements of the NC (2000) Statutory Inclusion Statement related to PE.*

8.5   Overcoming Barriers to Participation

The Audit Commission (2002) states:

> *"LEA's should seek to develop a spectrum of provision to ensure that as far as possible, all children with SEN have the opportunity of attending a local mainstream school" (Audit Commission 2002, p15)*

Furthermore, they indicate in some instances limited provision and unwelcoming attitudes in schools are producing barriers to participation within the mainstream. From research undertaken within this study, it is evident that a combination of structural and pedagogical strategies needs to be addressed in order to begin to tackle this issue.

A natural starting point to address this for the future would be through ITT and CPD provision, and current levels of dissatisfaction may therefore be due to fragmented and inconsistent policy currently being delivered at the official line. The DFES, TTA, OFSTED, and QCA need to therefore work with the professional PE associations to ascertain how they can impact on those at the professional opinion and practice, and consumer levels of interpretation. This will require the development of guidance materials on how to eradicate barriers to participation in schools (See CSIE Index for Inclusion 2000), whilst simultaneously addressing these issues in ITT through guidance from the TTA, and inspection though OFSTED. A starting point for this

could be for official line agencies to consider the key findings from this study, and the

points for action identified by the Audit Commission (2002) below:

Promote consistent practice in identifying and meeting children's needs

Promote early intervention

*Ensure that children with SEN are able to attend a local mainstream school, as
far as possible*

Promote effective inter-agency planning

Enable all children with SEN to join as fully as possible in the life of their school

*Develop the skills and confidence of staff to respond to the wide range of
children's needs in classrooms today*

Promote the effective allocation and management of SEN resources

Hold schools to account for their work on SEN

Provide a meaningful basis for monitoring schools' work on SEN

Recognise schools' commitment to helping children with SEN to achieve

---

Key finding 5: *Official line agencies do not presently provide sufficient pedagogical,
philosophical, structural advice, and guidance to those at the professional opinion
and practice and consumer levels of interpretation. Consequently official line
agencies (possibly through the establishment of a DFES PE SENWG) need to
address the ten points of the Audit Commission (2002) report in order to produce a
clear, consistent and coherent plan to enhance the development of children with
SEN in PE.*

8.6 Professional Opinion and Practice "What are the Processes and Course Contents of ITT Institutions Related to inclusive PE for children with SEN?"

Westwood (1997) suggests the nature of delivery and implementation of teaching and learning strategies is central to any effective move towards an inclusive agenda for children with SEN. Avramadis and Norwich (2002) also highlight the need for coherent and structured plans if children with SEN are to have the same opportunities to access the curriculum as their non-disabled peers. At stage two of the study however, the extent to which PE ITT programmes are equipping teachers to include children with SEN is questionable, especially as 84% of providers felt their trainees would need CPD following their training.

Furthermore, only 25% of PE ITT providers suggested that at present their trainees were satisfactorily equipped to deliver inclusive education. Consequently, whilst authors such as Westwood (1997), and Avramadis and Norwich (2002) argue for coherence and effective teaching and learning strategies, evidence suggests that based on the views of PE ITT providers there is still some way to go in achieving such an outcome. As a result, based on the views and opinions from stages two and three concerned with the professional opinion and practice level, further examination of why PE ITT providers take the view that trainees are not currently equipped for inclusion needs to be examined - especially as the PE NC (2000) suggests teachers must take action, and ensure their pupils are enabled to participate.

In attempting to highlight good inclusive practice, Westwood (1997) has drawn the common threads of inclusive policy and practice together and identified acceptance of basic values of citizenship; equal access; provision for all children; positive attitudes; supporting policy statements; and effective planning as central to successful delivery. Furthermore, Farrell (2001) and Ainscow (1999) suggest ITT providers must recognise how to increase teacher's knowledge and understanding in both the philosophy and practice of inclusion for children with SEN. Therefore, teachers need to appreciate the wider policy contexts, as well as the teaching and learning strategies necessary to deliver inclusion.

The Audit Commission (2002) supports this view commenting that pedagogical practices are presently well grounded in the TTA (2002) 'Professional Standards Framework' (TTA 2002). In contrast however there is no recognition of the philosophy and wider policy contexts of inclusion, and this leads to potential fragmentation of the ITT standards - particularly as the standards do not satisfactorily address the points made by Westwood 1997, Farrell 2001, Ainscow 1999, or recommendations from the Audit Commission 2002. It is apparent therefore that there is a lack of coherence in the expectations placed upon PE ITT providers and trainees at present, and further work needs to be undertaken by all stakeholders in addressing this issue.

Key finding 6: 84% of PE ITT providers at stage two indicated trainees would require CPD once qualified, with only 25% suggesting at present their trainees were satisfactorily equipped to deliver inclusive PE for children with SEN. PE ITT providers in consultation with consumers, and official line agencies should seek to examine why this is the case, and draw upon the findings from this study related to philosophical, pedagogical and structural processes.

8.7   Guidance and Support

At stage three of the study, PE ITT providers A, and B, highlighted the need for more

guidance on unpicking how the policy of the PE NC (QCA 1999a), should impact in

practice. The providers were of the opinion that official line agencies should move

beyond the establishment of policy, and subsequently offer practical advice,

guidance and resource materials to support the delivery of PE for children with SEN.

Clark et al (1995a) supports such a view advocating that the practicality of inclusion,

as well as the theoretical frameworks that underpin it must be fully considered if

inclusion is to have a positive impact. For example, only 25% of PE ITT providers felt

they received sufficient support and guidance from the PE professional associations,

whilst only 4% suggested they were satisfactorily supported by the official line

statutory agencies. In support of this view comments from stage two data emphasise

the desire for more practical advice and guidance by suggesting:

> "More exemplification of good practice materials would benefit the profession"
> (PE ITT provider 12)

> "Guidance on teaching children with SEN in PE across the six activity areas is
> desperately needed" (PE ITT provider 7)

> "Catering for a good inclusive curriculum.. Can we see, or can we have
> information on how schools do deal with.. and what issues come up as they are
> trying to cater for that... we need to see I think, rather than just read" (PE ITT
> provider A)

In considering the roles of BAALPE, PEA (UK), and EFDS, many PE ITT providers

indicated that there was real potential to say different things, and thus not support

teachers in a co-ordinated manner. This view was particularly well summarised by

PE ITT provider C who stated:

> "as national associations I think they should have a policy on it (SEN). I think
> there should be some public policy that's readily accessible in a published
> journal. I'd hope to think, well I'd like to think they'd speak with one voice or, so

there wouldn't be differences between those, and the difficulty with having BAALPE, Youth Sport Trust, PEA (UK), etc. is that there is the potential for them to say 3 different things" (PE ITT provider C).

Consequently the evidence from the stage one official line data indicating a lack of coherence is being reinforced to agencies at the professional opinion and practice level. Therefore specifically in relation to the PE professional associations, and EFDS, it is necessary for these agencies to work in partnership with each other in order to effectively support PE ITT providers and teachers in schools, whilst creating a strategic alliance to lobby official line agencies.

Key finding 7: *PE ITT providers are concerned that official line agencies have the potential to create a disjointed support mechanism, especially in relation to BAALPE, PEA (UK), and EFDS. Therefore, these agencies with other official line partners should seek to develop common strategic alliances, which deliver consistent messages to ITT and PE teachers in schools.*

In responding to the desire from PE ITT providers for more practical based support the TTA (2002) suggest that research shows the:

"Key to unlocking the full potential of pupils in our schools lies in the expertise of teachers and head teachers" (TTA, 2002, p1).

They continue by suggesting the quality of teaching and achievement of pupils is closely related, consequently it is vital that PE ITT providers, trainee and qualified PE teachers are furnished with the practical skills to support children with SEN. Thus, whilst 45.5% of PE ITT providers (stage two) agree/strongly agree that PE NC (2000) provides teachers with a clear framework for inclusion there is still a long way to go as over half of providers currently disagree with this view.

Whilst there are some concerns with the PE NC (2000) and the clarity of message that is given, PE ITT provider B commented:

> *"... the new statutory inclusion statement makes people sit up and think about what is right for children with SEN" (PE ITT provider B)*

This view was one of many similar comments expressed in stage three related to the acknowledgement that if the inclusion statement was not in the curriculum teachers would be less likely to address its principles. Furthermore, 79% of PE ITT providers at stage two of the study supported children with SEN being included within mainstream contexts, with a further 21% offering a neutral view. As a result of the strong support for the principles of inclusion, 87.5% of PE ITT providers at stage two indicated that SEN should be integrated into teacher training as a core element of programmes. In order to ensure that future PE teachers have sufficient opportunities to consider this aspect of their practice, ITT providers should seek to ensure SEN is addressed as a core component of trainee's development of knowledge and understanding of SEN. This would support the view of Ainscow (1999) who advocates in his notion of 'moving schools' that inclusive practice should be developed around a number of core areas. For example, these should encompass effective leadership; involvement of all staff and students, commitments to collaborative planning, attention to the benefits of enquiry and reflection, and clear policies and practices in inclusive education.

8.8 A Curriculum for Teacher Training

The TTA 'Professional Standards Framework' (TTA 2002)s have over recent years acted as a curriculum for PE ITT providers to follow. PE ITT provider C noted some concern however that the standards offered no prioritisation as to which should have more prominence. Consequently in the 4/98 (DFES 1998a) standards, only 3 of nearly 70 specifically address SEN, and as a result the question was asked whether an equivalent amount of time should be spent on such issues. – the other view being that trainees should have greater opportunities to consider SEN and inclusion, particularly due to increasing legislation being created within this area of educational policy and practice. Therefore, due to this confusion amongst PE ITT providers only 29% of providers supported the view that the 4/98 (DFES 1998a) standards were assisting positively in the training of PE teachers for the inclusion of children with SEN. This contrasts with the purpose of the standards in which the TTA (2001) suggests they are crucial when:

> "... seeking to make sure that, at entry to the profession, each new teacher has a good foundation of knowledge and understanding, is able to perform as a skilled teacher and can operate within a clear framework of professional values and practice" (TTA, 2001a, p5).

Furthermore, PE ITT providers need to examine the reasoning behind their lack of confidence in the standards, especially as OFSTED make judgements on the extent to which they are meeting these requirements.

> **Key finding 8:** *PE ITT providers should seek to review the TTA 'Professional Standards Framework' (TTA 2002) in relation to the extent to which SEN should be addressed discretely within other standards, and/or as part of the core SEN related expectations on professional development. PE ITT providers may find that whilst SEN may be only mentioned explicitly three times, there are many other standards that relate in more subtle ways to SEN.*

Note: Since undertaking this study the revised TTA (2002) 'Professional Standards Framework' (TTA 2002) addresses inclusion and SEN more significantly than with the previous 4/98 (DFES 1998a) Standards.

In relation to PE ITT provider's management and co-ordination of SEN, 50% had a named member of staff with responsibility for this area of work, whilst 25% indicated all staff had responsibility, and a further 12.5% had no accountability at all. As a result of this mixed provision it was relatively easy to note the extent to which these management and co-ordination systems were effective in ensuring trainee PE teachers gained the necessary knowledge and skills related to SEN. As a consequence it was found that PE ITT providers who had a named senior member of staff responsible for SEN, the consistency of message to lecturers and trainees appeared to be more effective. For example PE ITT providers A, and C, with named staff articulated clearly and coherently their strategies for inclusion and SEN. Furthermore, their core and compulsory SEN course delivery were commented upon positively by trainees.

This supports the examples of good practice noted by Lipsky and Gartner (1999) who describe clear visions, leadership, and a holistic approach to the inclusion of children with SEN as essential pre-requisites to successful provision. However, another significant factor which PE ITT providers must address in order to consider fully all the issues related to SEN, is a need to ensure that the current 37.5% of lectures who have no SEN experience have opportunities to undertake some form of professional development training. This could be achieved through continued professional development programmes for lecturers, or the sharing of training experiences and expertise through the PE HEI National Network, which meets regularly to discuss professional practice.

Key finding 9: *The management and co-ordination of SEN provision within PE ITT providers is rather mixed, with over one third of lecturers having no SEN experience at all. Consequently in some institutions lines of accountability, responsibility, training, and lecturer experience are weak and ITT providers should seek to review this aspect of their work in order to ensure clear and consistent messages are portrayed at the professional opinion and practice and consumer levels of interpretation.*

In relation to the development of teaching and learning strategies 67% of PE ITT providers supported the view of Sugden and Talbot (1998) that teaching children with SEN is an extension of mixed ability teaching. This was reinforced by comments in stage three of the study that SEN and mixed ability teaching was:

> "... part and parcel of our everyday work - not something that is tagged on to the end of lesson plans (PE ITT provider A).

As a result, many PE ITT providers advocated a need to ensure trainee teachers get better at their general differentiation and mixed ability teaching in order to ensure children with SEN had full access to the curriculum. Furthermore, PE ITT provider A commented:

> "... until we get to grips with the mixed ability class I thinks that's the hardest one rather than the disability" (PE ITT provider A)

... accessibility to the curriculum for children with SEN could be potentially limited. Therefore, based on these views PE ITT provider E commented:

> "What is really needed is an individual curriculum for every child" (PE ITT provider E)

... and as a result trainees need to audit their subject knowledge gaps, and as part of their ITT and CPD seek to extend their understanding of mixed ability teaching strategies.

In relation to the requirements placed on trainees by PE ITT providers to teach children with SEN during training, only 12% insisted on any compulsory requirement to address this area of work. However, following the introduction of the TTA (2002) 'Professional Standards Framework' (TTA 2002) in which inclusion has a much higher profile than in the 4/98 (DFES 1998a) standards this picture may have changed to a more positive position. Further to this, 50% of trainees were required to undertake some form of observation of SEN whilst on school experience. As a result of this strategy PE ITT provider 6 commented:

> "Some students may not experience any SEN at all in some schools". Consequently, PE ITT providers need to establish strategies which ensure all their trainees have opportunities to teach children with SEN during their training. However, it was interesting to note that PE ITT provider A commented "perhaps why PE doesn't get any better in the majority of schools is because we are not thinking hard enough or having the will or want to change" (PE ITT provider 6)

Thus PE ITT providers must audit their training to ensure it is meeting the practical needs of trainees, and the comments in stages four and five of this study offer an illuminating insight into the extent to which this is presently being delivered. In addition, if inclusive PE for children with SEN is to become more effective all stakeholders should be prepared to radically re-think there existing structures and processes in order that they meet the needs of all concerned (Skrtic 1991,1995, Ainscow 1999).

Key finding 10: Some PE ITT providers offer no practical opportunities to teach children with SEN during their training, and as only 12% have any compulsory requirements. As a result, PE ITT providers should seek to ensure all trainees have opportunities to apply their theory and pedagogy related to children with SEN in practical settings both whilst in University and in school based practice.

Due to 50% of PE ITT providers indicating all their teaching and learning of SEN is theoretical, the extent to which there are opportunities available to apply this knowledge and understanding must be rather limited. Furthermore at stage two, 50% of providers suggested they rely totally on schools to support their trainees development of SEN, and this again needs to be reviewed in order to ensure that both structural processes and pedagogical practices are considered in a systematic and co-ordinated manner. In order to address the extent to which this is presently being achieved PE ITT provider C suggested providers should identify what issues related to SEN, inclusion, differentiation, and mixed ability teaching consistently appear in trainees CEP. PE ITT providers at the professional opinion and practice level could then use this, and in consultation with official line agencies and the consumers ensure appropriate CPD and ITT programmes are developed.

Key finding 11: Half of PE ITT providers address issues of SEN and inclusion purely in theoretical contexts. Through a national auditing of statements related to SEN on trainees CEP, a data set of all the future training and CPD issues could be drawn together. This would help identify current gaps in ITT and assist with future development of training standards and induction programmes.

8.9 Consumers: "What are the views and opinions of current student trainees and recently qualified PE teachers related to their training for inclusive education?"

In relation to trainee PE teachers, the Audit Commission (2002) advocate a need to strengthen links between ITT and induction in order to consolidate NQT's skills. The TTA (2003) support this view stating:

> "In order to complete the induction year satisfactorily, a newly qualified teacher must demonstrate.. They plan effectively to meet the needs of pupils in their classes with special educational needs, with or without statements, and in consultation with the SENCO contribute to the preparation, implementation, monitoring and review of Individual education plans or the equivalent" (TTA, 2003, p17).

8.10 Logical Purity and SEN

Avramadis and Norwich (2002) argue:

> "... there is no logical purity in education" (Avramadis & Norwich 2002, p483)

and consequently SEN provision comprises of a number of theories and perspectives, and this is demonstrated by the mixed training experiences highlighted by the stage four consumers. For example, 60% of trainees indicated their ITT comprised of embedded SEN themes, whilst 25% suggested these were optional, and a further 30% identified a combination of core and compulsory elements. However, from further individual PE ITT provider analysis it was found some PE ITT provider trainees indicated higher core/embedded approaches than others. As a result, it was evident from analysis of data, that trainees who were involved in core SEN themes and strategies during their training were commenting that they felt more engaged in a systematic and co-ordinated form of inclusive experience. This was supported by the comments that:

> "Because we had to do SEN training as a central part, my lecturers made sure I knew how and where I would need to apply it in practice when in schools" (Trainee from PE ITT provider C)

"I knew what I had to do in relation to SEN from the outset – we had specific tasks that we had to follow through in our school based training as well – and our mentors made sure we addressed these" (Trainee from PE ITT provider A)

In contrast, where this was not the case, trainees who experienced high levels of optional delivery expressed concern that their SEN training should be compulsory, and not something they could potentially opt in or out of. This supports Dessent's (1987) notion of 'whole school' approaches, in which the most effective method of delivering good inclusive practice was to ensure SEN issues are fully embedded within the curriculum, and encompass clear and consistent messages from senior management through to practitioner levels. Consequently in PE ITT providers A, and C, where senior staff had responsibility for SEN, and the delivery was through a combination of core and embedded modules trainees talked positively about this process. In contrast providers who noted they had no staff responsible for SEN (i.e. PE ITT provider B), and delivery was largely optional, trainees expressed dissatisfaction with this structure.

Key finding 12: Trainee PE teachers indicate a mixed provision of SEN delivery, however they preferred core and/or embedded approaches, as opposed to optional elements of modular delivery. PE ITT providers should ensure there are minimum expectations of core/embedded SEN themes and issues delivered to trainee teachers in order to ensure they receive a satisfactory level of SEN and inclusion training.

Whilst consumer respondents reinforced a consistent total number of hours spent on SEN to those expressed at the professional opinion and practice level, there were some differences of opinion at stage four in relation to the nature of ITT content and delivery. For example, whilst teaching, learning and differentiation were identified as core elements of curriculum delivery at the professional opinion and practice and consumer levels, trainees expressed concern that concepts of mixed ability teaching and recognition of continuums of learning were not fully embedded within these processes. Consequently consumers suggested PE ITT providers should ensure trainees receive consistent feedback on their mixed ability teaching related to SEN, through the utilisation of a range of teaching and learning models which specifically address the needs of children with disabilities. Trainees should therefore have sufficient opportunities to examine inclusive teaching and learning models such as those highlighted by Craft (1996), Winnick (2000), and the EFDS/YST Inclusion Spectrum.

8.11 Mixed Provision and Experiences

It is evident the provision and experience of SEN which stage four trainees gain varies according to a number of factors related to PE ITT providers; school based training; support from mentors; and the range of compulsory and/or optional teaching opportunities. Within this backdrop, the extent to which various groups of trainees have direct access to, and experience of working with children with SEN differs greatly. For example, 84% of trainees in PE ITT provider C indicated they had a compulsory module in University to directly teach children with SEN then subsequently follow this up with observation in school based contexts. In contrast though, 59% of trainees indicated they do not have direct opportunities to work with, and gain experience of children with SEN. Consequently, there is the potential for some trainee teachers to have no opportunities to work directly with children with SEN prior to them gaining QTS. Where this occurs it is difficult to see how trainees can fully appreciate the requirements of the NC (2000) Inclusion Statement (QCA 1999a), although at present as the Audit Commission (2000) indicates the TTA 'Professional Standards Framework' (TTA 2002) (2002) does not highlight this document explicitly as a requirement of training.

Key finding 13: *Trainee PE teachers experiences of mixed ability teaching and continuums of learning are rather mixed and need to be linked more effectively to the needs of children with SEN. PE ITT providers should be encouraged to consider using 'inclusive teaching and learning models' such as those suggested by craft (1996), Winninck (2000), and the Inclusion Spectrum (YST/EFDS) to further develop this work.*

In relation to trainees consulting mentors whilst in school, it was found between 60 to 87% of respective PE ITT provider trainees had discussed SEN issues with mentors. Therefore from the perspectives of the trainees, mentors in schools are a vital link in the development of SEN knowledge and understanding. However from analysis of the professional opinion and practice data, some PE ITT providers were unsure what mentors discussed with trainees, and how this linked to University based practice.

Therefore, PE ITT providers should work with mentors to plan this more effectively and ensure links between ITT and school based SEN are clear and consistent as presently this process is a rather informal arrangement with no prescribed structure. This is emphasised in a comment by PE ITT provider A who stated:

> "... the mentors will probably come up with some good ideas ... that will depend on which school they are in, so the quality of training will vary and it's a broad thing" (PE ITT provider A)

Thus, in order to ensure links between mentors and University are effective, there is a need for clearer expectations to be placed on the roles of both partners related to what SEN training has been undertaken and how, and why, this should be developed further in school-based practice.

In examining trainee perceptions of the roles and responsibilities of official line agencies, it is evident they are unclear on some of the functions statutory and non-statutory organisations play. For example, only 60% of trainees identified the TTA as having a policy setting remit, even though they are responsible for establishing their 'Professional Standards Framework' (TTA 2002). In addition only 47% of stage four trainees recognised the DFES as having a role to play in the setting of policy. At present trainees do not fully appreciate the place of official line agencies within the wider context of inclusion and SEN. Thus, PE ITT providers should work with official line agencies to ensure trainees appreciate the wider context of the inclusion and SEN agenda in order to recognise what roles respective agencies play and how these feed into teacher education, schools and classroom practice. This would additionally meet the desire from the Audit Commission (2002) to ensure that the present TTA 'Professional Standards Framework' (TTA 2002) should addresses wider policy and philosophical contexts, as well as pedagogical practice.

Key finding 14: Trainee PE teachers are unclear on the roles of official line agencies, and ITT providers need to ensure they establish the structural, and wider contextual perspectives of SEN in addition to any consideration of pedagogical practices.

In relation to whether children with SEN should be educated within mainstream contexts, 62% of trainees at stage four supported this statement, with a further 24% taking a neutral stance, and 12% disagreeing with this concept. On examination of the reasoning behind the neutral stance and 12% disagreement, many trainees indicated they still felt unsure and or lacking in confidence on how to deliver inclusive

PE for children with SEN. Furthermore, many of the trainees highlighting a degree of uncertainty were those who did not have large amounts of SEN experience either within their University or school based training. This picks up on the points made earlier regarding PE ITT providers ensuring that all trainees experience direct contact with children with SEN during their ITT in order to apply theoretical concepts in practical contexts.

As a result of the concerns expressed on the amount of SEN experience they gain, it was not surprising that 41% of trainees felt as they come towards the end of their ITT, their course had not satisfactorily addressed SEN and inclusion related issues. In contrast, 43% suggested they were happy with the training they had received. In comparison to the views expressed at the professional opinion and practice level in which only 25% of PE ITT providers indicated they thought trainees where satisfactorily equipped, the trainees did take a more positive stance.

However, trainees may not have the level of direct school experience to make this judgement compared to their training providers, and consequently it could be suggested that trainees are either over optimistic or, ITT providers are over cautious. In relation to whether SEN should be an integral aspect of PE ITT for example, 93% of trainees supported this view, so are indicating support for these issues to be embedded within their training. Therefore, the will and commitment to the SEN and inclusion agenda is clearly evident, but this must be matched by an effective ITT curriculum.

> **Key finding 15:** *Trainees commented that in some circumstance direct experience of pupils with SEN was rather limited, or in some PE ITT providers were non-existent. PE ITT providers should therefore ensure all trainees have opportunities to work with children with SEN during their training in order to raise levels of confidence, as well as judge the effectiveness of suggested pedagogical practices for themselves.*

8.12 The Views of Stage Five Recently Qualified PE Teachers

In reflecting upon how effective PE ITT is related to children with SEN, one vital element of data is the views and opinions of recently qualified teachers. In examining any training process from official line, through professional opinion and practice to the consumers, the ultimate measure of how effective programmes are can be judged by the responses from those who have been through the ITT process. In considering the views of Lipsky and Gartner (1999) that:

> *"While there is no single educational model or approach inclusion in schools tends to share similar characteristics" (Lipsky & Gartner 1999, p17)*

... parallel judgements can be made in relation to effective training for inclusion and SEN. Consequently it should be possible through evidence from the stage five respondents to identify models of best practice in order to determine the most appropriate methods of SEN delivery, which satisfactorily equip PE teachers to include children with SEN.

Therefore, based on the PE teacher's identification of good practice, or areas for further development a rich insight into the currency of professional development training in SEN can be gained. In addition, within the context of this study it is possible to compare the stage five views with those at stage four in order to see if any practice has changed. For example, the need for more practical application rather than pure theory was an area in which recently qualified PE teachers commented that they would have benefited from. Consequently, 47,34% of stage five PE teachers commented all of their SEN training was theory based, and they had lacked opportunities to apply this in practical teaching and learning settings. This however contrasted with stage four trainees whereby 26.38% of trainees commented all of their training was theoretical. Therefore based on this comparison there appears to be more opportunities to now apply SEN theory in practical contexts, and this in part could be as a result of the 4/98 (DFES 1998a) 'Professional Standards Framework' (TTA 2002) (stage 5 teachers operated under Circulars 10/97 (DEE 1997), 9/92 (DES 1992) requiring trainees to evidence school-based practice. Consequently since the stage five respondents have qualified, there is now more practical assessment of SEN, and PE ITT providers are seeking to address this more prominently in school based training than previously. – Particularly as OFSTED are making judgements on the application of theory to practice in school based contexts.

On further examination of the reflective comments from PE teachers on their ITT related to SEN, a number of further points were highlighted which should be considered by official line and professional opinion and practice agencies when establishing frameworks for ITT. For instance, 31.57% of stage five respondents suggested school experience needed to be strengthened to make more explicit links between University, and school based provision of SEN and inclusion. Consequently they were of the view that many opportunities had been missed to apply their training directly in schools, (see earlier key findings) because the ITT providers and mentors had not sufficiently attempted to join the theory and practice together. Therefore, based on the recommendations of the PE teachers

"... training providers should have mechanisms for identifying what aspects of SEN can be delivered in University, and how mentors can help us apply these

*in practice when in schools - Our mentors often didn't know what we had done
on SEN" (Stage five respondent).*

As a result, PE ITT providers should ensure that when they have meetings with
mentors in schools that they are clear on what content they have covered, and the
expectations on schools to help trainees apply and evidence this in practice.

Key finding 16: *The links between university based SEN practice and school based
application with mentors is weak. PE ITT providers should seek to produce more
explicit expectations of Universities, schools, mentors and trainees in order to ensure
all parties are clear on how SEN practice should be developing.*

A further point to note in considering PE teachers experiences was the question of
what major issues they had faced related to SEN since leaving training. These
comments could subsequently be used by official line and professional opinion and
practice agencies to address these issues whilst in training. For example, 42.10% of
stage five PE teachers suggested that teaching children with emotional behavioural
difficulties had been particularly challenging, and they would have benefited from
more advice and guidance in this area. In addition, 26.31% of PE teachers stated
they would have liked more opportunities to talk about strategies for inclusion, as this
would have given them opportunities to direct discussion with lecturers and mentors
around their concerns and/or experiences to date. Thus PE ITT providers should
plan for some less prescribed training opportunities in SEN whereby either
experienced professionals share their practice, or trainees could address particular
specific concerns they have through open dialogue.

> **Key finding 17:** *PE teachers indicated they would have benefited from more open dialogue on strategies that could be utilised to facilitate inclusive practice for children with SEN. PE ITT providers should seek to offer a series of open discussions/workshops in which general issues and concerns related to SEN, inclusion, and PE can be addressed.*

The TTA (2001) suggest:

> "... effective teaching relies on working effectively with everyone" (TTA 2001a, p1)

... and the stage five PE teachers were asked to comment on what support mechanisms they had utilised to help them in their work with children with SEN. As a result, 31.57% indicated they had consulted with learning support assistants, 57.89% had looked for support from SENCO's and 31.57% had spoken with their Heads of PE. Whilst Heads of PE and SENCO's could have been expected to offer support, it was positive to see teachers recognising the vital role learning support assistants can play in children with SEN access to the PE curriculum. This view supports those of Dyson 2001, Dyson and Millward (2000), Ainscow 1999, and Skrtic 1995, who all recognise successful inclusion relies on holistic, multi-agency and professional approaches to the delivery of effective pedagogical practice for children with SEN.

> **Key finding 18:** *Stage five teachers identified the central role learning support assistants can play in facilitating access to PE for children with SEN. Official line, and professional opinion and practice agencies should seek to ensure that trainees are aware of how to utilise a range of professionals to deliver effective inclusion.*

8.13 How Equipped are Teachers to Deliver Inclusive PE to Children with SEN?

The stage four respondents indicated at present that only 24% felt adequately equipped to deliver inclusive PE, with one set of ITT provider responses as high as 40%. Consequently, it is evident there is still much work to be done to address their specific training needs, and raise levels of confidence. This contrasts with the even more dramatic figures of 16% of stage five PE teachers suggesting they were adequately prepared, and 84% noting their dissatisfaction with their ITT related to SEN and inclusion. Therefore, as with the stage four comments there is a miss-match between the ITT curriculum as it stands, and the views and opinions of teachers once they apply their training in practice with children with SEN. As a result, all the stakeholders at the official line, professional opinion and practice, and consumer levels should work together to address their respective positions and experiences. The DFES SENWG in partnership with the official line, professional opinion and practice, and consumer stakeholders could seek to address many of the points raised within this study in order to identify were the gaps are in PE ITT.

> *Key finding 19:* Levels of dissatisfaction on the extent to which trainee and qualified PE teachers felt equipped to teach children with SEN ranged from 24% - 40% (trainees), and up to 84% (recently qualified teachers). The DFES SENWG should establish a PE specific group to consider the reasoning for this, using the recommendations from this study as prompts for further debate.

8.14 Summary: How is the Current Training of PE Teachers for Inclusive Settings Implemented?

It is evident from examination within this chapter that inclusive PE is a key issue for all stakeholders to address in the coming years. In general terms inclusion is wholeheartedly supported, however existing provision is varied and there is need for further reflection and development of a much clearer systematic approach to the training of PE teachers. This is particularly apparent in that 84% of ITT providers indicated that further CPD will be needed once PE teachers have entered the teaching profession, and 25% suggest newly qualified PE teachers were not at present adequately prepared to deliver inclusive education. This contrasts even more dramatically with up to 40% of trainees, and 84% of recently qualified PE teachers indicating they did not feel equipped to deliver inclusive PE to children with SEN.

The role of the PE ITT provider is central to the success or failure of the government's agenda for inclusion, and providers must recognise that teachers and schools will face these issues and challenges on a daily basis. Therefore, there is a need for sufficient advice and guidance to be given during the training phase in order that a co-ordinated approach to inclusive PE can be achieved. According to Westwood (1997), and Norwich and Avramadis (2002), ITT providers and teachers need a clear and consistent framework approach to PE and SEN facilitated through official line co-ordination in order to create a systematic approach to the philosophy, process and practice of inclusive education. The suggested framework below aims to expand upon and seek clarity for all stakeholders, and provide a set of factors that should be addressed if they are to embrace the fundamental rationale of inclusion for children with SEN in PE.

The 'Eight P Inclusive PE and SEN Framework' (Vickerman 2002) encourages agencies and individuals at the official line, professional opinion and practice, and consumer levels to begin to recognise and spend time analysing their roles,

responsibilities and delivery through eight key features. The framework identifies how

each feature links to the key findings, whilst extending the debate to highlight

significant issues and themes discussed within this chapter.

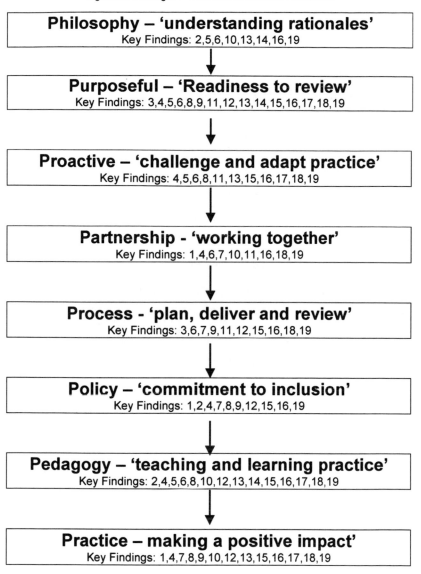

Figure 8.1 The Eight 'P' Inclusive PE and SEN Framework

Philosophy – 'understanding rationales'
Key Findings: 2,5,6,10,13,14,16,19

Purposeful – 'Readiness to review'
Key Findings: 3,4,5,6,8,9,11,12,13,14,15,16,17,18,19

Proactive – 'challenge and adapt practice'
Key Findings: 4,5,6,8,11,13,15,16,17,18,19

Partnership - 'working together'
Key Findings: 1,4,6,7,10,11,16,18,19

Process - 'plan, deliver and review'
Key Findings: 3,6,7,9,11,12,15,16,18,19

Policy – 'commitment to inclusion'
Key Findings: 1,2,4,7,8,9,12,15,16,19

Pedagogy – 'teaching and learning practice'
Key Findings: 2,4,5,6,8,10,12,13,14,15,16,17,18,19

Practice – making a positive impact'
Key Findings: 1,4,7,8,9,10,12,13,15,16,17,18,19

8.15 The 'Eight P Inclusive PE and SEN Framework'

The 'Eight P' framework encourages stakeholders to systematically work through the features noted above in order to review and seek clarity to the inclusion of children with SEN in PE. This process could be undertaken either as individual stakeholders (i.e. trainee, NQT, lecturer) or by official line, professional opinion and practice, or consumer agencies working singularly or collaboratively to extend and develop their practice. The first feature to consider is a need to recognise the *philosophy* behind inclusion and its relationships to basic, and fundamental human rights. This requires consideration of how human rights are supported as a society through statutory and non-statutory guidance such as the 2001 Disability and SEN Rights Act (DFES, 2001c), and the PE NC (2000) Statutory Inclusion Statement (QCA 1999a). Furthermore, it requires stakeholders to spend time engaging in understanding philosophical theories and principles such as those advocated by Skrtic (1995), Ainscow (1999), Dyson (2001), Dyson and Millward (2000), Reiser and Mason (1990) prior to consideration of how to apply these in practice.

In order to facilitate this debate stakeholders must embrace a *purposeful* approach to fulfilling the requirements of inclusive PE. Time should be spent initially examining philosophical standpoints in order to gain a clear appreciation of the rationale and arguments behind inclusive education. For example, the Audit Commission (2002) suggests at present the TTA (2002) 'Professional Standards Framework' (TTA 2002) does not satisfactorily address the wider contexts of SEN (i.e. philosophical standpoints). Consequently, stakeholders should be resolute in ensuring they examine philosophical issues and how they feed into the wider inclusion debate. In order to achieve these recommendations stakeholders must be *proactive* in the development, implementation, and review of inclusive PE and SEN, and consult actively with each. This would ensure the views and opinions of all stakeholders are considered in order to address the current issue of lack of coherence. This additionally compliments recommendations from the DFES (2001) to work together to create co-ordinated, and coherent (Avramadis and Norwich (2002 provision through *partnership* and collaborative approaches.

Inclusive PE for children with SEN requires a recognition and commitment to modify, adapt, and change existing teaching and learning strategies, policies and practices in order to facilitate full access and entitlement to the curriculum (Ainscow 1999, Skrtic 1991). The development of inclusive PE must therefore be recognised as part of a *process* model that evolves, emerges and changes over time, and as such needs regular review by all stakeholders. This process needs to reflect the three central aspects of official line policy, professional opinion and practice, and the views of consumers discussed within this study.

In summary, official line agencies, professional opinion and practice, and consumers must ensure inclusion is reflected within their *policy* documentation, as a means of monitoring, reviewing and evaluating delivery. This also seeks to publicly state how agencies are going to respond to inclusive practice, and can be used as a means of holding people to account (Depauw and Doll-Tepper 2000, Lloyd 2000). However stakeholders must ultimately recognise the need to move policies through into the *pedagogical* practices of lecturers, trainee teachers, NQT's, and school staff in order to ensure they have the necessary skills to deliver inclusive PE to children with SEN. Consequently, whilst philosophies, and processes are vital they must in due course be measured in terms of effective and successful inclusive *practice* that values person centred approaches to the education of children with SEN. This discussion will be developed further in chapter 9 to offer recommendations for future action, whilst celebrating areas of strength in the training of PE teachers for the inclusion of children with SEN.

8.16 A Final Say From The Children

The key themes highlighted in the 'Eight P Inclusive PE and SEN Framework' act as a focus for drawing conclusions to the main research question of **how is the current training of PE teachers for inclusive settings implemented**. Furthermore, chapters five, six, and seven identify detailed responses to the sub questions at the official line, professional opinion and practice, and consumer levels of interpretation. Consequently, these findings can be used by the respective agencies and individuals to review policies and practices, and plan for any future action arising from the recommendations of this study.

In interpreting the 'Eight P Inclusive PE and SEN Framework' as basis for determining the current training process for PE teachers, the next stage is to consider what else we need to know in order to enhance our existing knowledge and understanding which has been gained from this study. Dyson (2001) supports this view suggesting:

> "... there is an inevitable desire for unequivocal guidance on what to do next"
> (Dyson, 2001, p28)

... and therefore it would be remiss of this study not to offer suggestions for future action and research related to inclusive PE for children with SEN.

In chapter 4 (methodology) one of the initial intentions of the consumer level of interpretation was to examine the views of children with SEN in order to appreciate their views, opinions, and feelings towards inclusive PE. However, due to the size and scope of this study the decision was made not to address this element within this investigation. Therefore, the next stage of any research would be to focus upon hearing the voices of children with SEN in order to enhance current knowledge and understanding of inclusive PE.

8.17 Let The Children Have Their Say

Depauw and Doll-Tepper (2000) suggest:

> "... successful inclusion requires decision-makers, and individuals with a
> disability to have choice (informed choice) and to have choices" (Depauw &
> Doll-Tepper, 2000, p139)

... with regard to the nature of their involvement in physical activity. In order to

facilitate choice there is a need for agencies and individuals to work within a culture

which offers a commitment to improve the expertise of teachers, and offer flexible

learning and instructional environments to meet the individual needs of children with

SEN (Hofman 2003).

Consequently, in gauging the views of children with SEN, Farrell (2000) indicates that

an integral aspect of teachers and pupils having informed choice and decision

making must firstly focus upon questions such as:

> "What do pupils with SEN prefer, special or mainstream school? This is a
> potentially interesting and under researched area. What are pupils' reflections
> on the assessment process? Did they have choice in the provision they were
> offered? What changes would they like to see in their provision?" (Farrell,
> 2000, p157)

In examining questions and concepts of empowerment and consultation, Farrell's

(2000) suggestions can be considered in keeping with existing social models of

disability (Reiser and Mason 1990) which are grounded in beliefs that people

(children and adults) should have opportunities to empower themselves - thus

ensuring the views of children with SEN are considered fully in any planning,

delivery, and evaluation of inclusive practice. Thus, the role of individuals and

agencies at the official line, professional opinion and practice and consumer levels

should be to seek to avoid erecting barriers that might either block this process or

disregard the vital role that they play within in examining the inclusion process

(Christensen and James 2000).

Pensgaard and Sorensen (2002) suggest for example, there is a great need to examine concepts of empowerment and offer guides to research with individuals with disabilities. Furthermore, they suggest:

> "The role that perceived control plays in the lives of human beings is an important area of investigation within an empowerment perspective"
> (Pensgaard & Sorenson 2002, p 55)

… and as a consequence should play a significant role in any interpretation or suggested models for the delivery of inclusive practice.

Hutzler et al (2002) supports this view, linking the concepts of inclusion and empowerment, based on the belief that personal empowerment of children with disabilities is an integral component in helping to understand the inclusion process. In their study on examining the views and opinions of children with disabilities for example, they found over half of the negative physical activity experiences of children with SEN attributed failure as due to a lack of empowerment. As a result, children with SEN advocated the use of consultation as a means of addressing this issue in the future, and authors such as Mayall (2000) suggest consultation and empowerment of children with SEN are important mechanisms in understanding the issues that matter to children.

8.18 Future Directions

It is evident from the examination above, that establishment of mechanisms for consultation and empowerment are a vital ingredient to gaining a full appreciation of all the perspectives of inclusive PE for children with SEN. Therefore, the next logical steps in the progression and extension of work in this study would be to move the research in this direction. In considering potential approaches to address this, the work undertaken by Goodwin and Watkinson (2000) regarding children with disabilities descriptions of good days, and bad days and their involvement of inclusive PE serves as a valuable starting point for future action - especially as it

addresses many of the issues highlighted by the authors above in relation to

consultation and empowerment of children with SEN.

In conclusion, the involvement and consultation of children with SEN as part of their

schooling cannot be better emphasised than through a quote from Luke Jackson

(aged 13 in his autobiography 'Freaks, Geeks and Asperger Syndrome: A User

Guide to Adolescence):

> *"I used to have a teacher who helped me at school, but at the time I didn't have a clue what she helped me with...whatever level of understanding the child you are working with has got, then I reckon you should still try to involve the child so that they know what is going on". (Luke Jackson, 2002, p115)*

GLOSSARY OF KEY TERMS

BAALPE	British Association of Advisers and Lecturers in Physical Education
BECTA	The British Educational Communications and Technology Agency
CEDP	Career Entry and Development Profile
CEP	Career Entry Profile
DES	Department for Education and Science
DFE	Department for Education
DFES	Department for Education and Skills
DOE	Department of Education
EAL	English as an Additional Language
EFDS	English Federation for Disability Sport
HEFCE	Higher Education Funding Council for England
HEI	Higher Education Institution
ITT	Initial Teacher Training
LEA	Local Education Authority
NC	National Curriculum
NGFL	National Grid for Learning
NQT	Newly Qualified Teacher
OFSTED	Office for Standards in Education
PE	Physical education
PEA (UK)	Physical Education Association (United Kingdom)
PCE	Postgraduate Certificate in Education
QCA	Qualification Curriculum Authority
QTS	Qualified Teacher Status
SEN	Special Educational Needs
SENCO	Special Educational Needs Co-ordinator
SENWG	Special Educational Needs Working Group
TTA	Teacher Training Agency
UCET	University Council for the Education of Teachers
UNESCO	United Nations Education, Cultural and Scientific Organisation
YST	Youth Sport Trust

REFERENCES

Ainscow, M, (1994), Special Needs in the Classroom: A Teacher Education Guide, Jessica Kingsley Publishers/UNESCO Publishing, London

Ainscow, M, (1995), Special Needs Through School Improvement: School Improvement Through Special Needs, in Clark, C; Dyson, A, Millward, A, (eds), Towards Inclusive Schools, David Fulton, London

Ainscow, M; Tweddle, D, (1998), Encouraging Classroom Success, David Fulton, London

Ainscow, M, (1999), Understanding the Development of Inclusive Schools, Falmer Press, London

Ainscow, M; Farrell, D; Tweedle, D; Malkin, G, (1999), Effective Practice in Inclusion and in Special and Mainstream Schools Working Together, HMSO, London

Artiles, A, (1998), The Dilemma of Difference: Enriching the Disproportionality Discourse with Theory and Context, Journal of Special Education, Vol. 32(1), p32-36

Audit Commission (2002), Special Educational Needs: A mainstream Issue, HMSO, London

Avramadis, E; Norwich, B, (2002), Teachers Attitudes Towards Integration/Inclusion: A Review of the Literature, European Journal of Special Needs Education, Vol 17, No 2, p129-147

Auxter, D; Pyfer, J; Hueltig, C; (2001), Principles and Methods of Adapted Physical Education and Recreation, (Ninth Edition), McGraw-Hill, New York

Ballard, K, (1997), Researching Disability and Inclusive Education: Participation, Construction and Interpretation, International Journal of Inclusive Education, Vol. 1(3), p243-256

Barton, L, (1997), Inclusive Education: Romantic, Subversive or Realistic? International Journal of Inclusive Education, Vol. 1 (30 231-242

Barton, L, (ed) (1998), The Politics of Special Educational Needs, Falmer Press, London

Block, M; Volger, E, (1994), Inclusion in Regular Physical Education: The Research Base, Journal of Physical Education, Recreation and Dance, Vol. 65(1), p40-44

Booth, T, (1993), Raising standards: Sticking to First Principles, in Dyson, A; Gains, C, (eds), Rethinking Special Needs in Mainstream Schools Towards the Year 2000, David Fulton, London

Booth, T, (1995), Mapping Inclusion and exclusion: Concepts for All? In Clark, C; Dyson, A; Millward, A, (eds), Towards Inclusive Schools, David Fulton, London

Booth, T; Ainscow, M; Dyson, A, (1998), England: Inclusion and Exclusion, in a Competitive System, in Booth, T ; Ainscow, M, (eds), From Them to Us : An International Study of Inclusion in England, Routledge, London

Booth, T; Ainscow, M; Black-Hawkins, K; Vaughan, M; Shaw, L, (2000), Index for inclusion: Developing learning and participation in schools, Centre for Studies on Inclusive Education, Bristol

British Association of Advisers and Lecturers in Physical Education (1989), Physical Education for Children with Special Educational Needs in Mainstream Education, White Line Publishing Services, Leeds

Carroll, H, (1972), The Remedial teaching of Reading: An Evaluation, Remedial Education, Vol, 7(1), p10-15

Centre for Studies in Inclusive Education (2000), www.inclusion.uwe.ac.uk

Cheminas, R, (2000), Special Educational Needs for Newly Qualified and Student Teachers: A Practical Guide, David Fulton Publishers, London

Christensen, P; James, A, (2000), Research with Children: Perspectives and Practices, Falmer Press, London

Clark, C; Dyson, A; Millward, A, (1995a), Towards Inclusive Schools: Mapping the Field, in Clark, C; Dyson, A; Millward, A, (eds), Towards Inclusive Schools, David Fulton, London

Clark, C; Dyson, A; Millward, A; Skidmore, D, (1995b), Dialectical Analysis, Special Needs and Schools as Organisations, in Clark, C; Dyson; A; Millward, A, (eds), Towards Inclusive Schools, David Fulton, London

Clark, C; Dyson, A; Millward, A; Skidmore, D, (1997), New Directions in Special Needs: Innovations in Main Stream Schools, Cassell, London

Clark, C; Dyson, A; Millward, A; Robson, S, (1999), Theories of Inclusion, Theories of Schools: Deconstructing and Reconstructing the Inclusive School, British Educational Research Journal, 25(2), 157-177

Collins, J, (1972), The Remedial Hoax, Remedial Education, Vol. 7(3), p9-10

Corbett, J; Slee, R, (2000), An International Conversation on Inclusive Education, in Armstrong, F; Armstrong, D; Barton, L, (eds), Inclusive Education: Policy Contexts and Comparative Perspectives, David Fulton, London

Coupe, J, (1986), The Curriculum Intervention Model (CIM), in Coupe, J; Porter, J, (eds), The Education of Children with Severe learning Difficulties: Bridging the Gap Between Theory and Practice, Croom Helm, London

Craft, D, (1996), A Focus on Inclusion in Physical Education, in Hennessy, B, (ed), Physical Education Sourcebook, Human Kinetics, Champaign

Croll, P and Moses, M (2000), Ideologies and Utopias: Education Professionals Views of Inclusion, European Journal of Special Needs Education, p1-12

Daniels, H; Garner, P, (1999), Introduction, in Daniels, H; Garner, P, (eds), World Yearbook of Education 1999: Inclusive Education, Kogan page, London

Department for Culture, Media and Sport; Department for Education and Employment (2001), A Sporting Future for All: The Governments Plan for Sport, HMSO, London

Department for Culture, Media and Sport (2002), Game Plan: A Strategy for Delivering Government's Sport and Physical Activity Objectives, HMSO, London

Department of Education (1870), The Education for All Handicapped Children Act (1870), HMSO, London

Department of Education (1944), The Education Act (1944), HMSO, London

Department of Education (1970), The Education (Handicapped Act) 1970, HMSO, London

Department of Education and Science (1978), Special Educational Needs: report of the Committee of Enquiry into the Education of Handicapped Children and Young People (The Warnock Report), HMSO, London

Department of Education and Science (1981), The 1981 Education Act, HMSO, London

Department of Education and Science (1984), Initial Teacher Training Approval of Courses, Circular 3/84, HMSO, London

Department of Education and Science (1984), Initial Teacher Training Approval of Courses, Circular 24/89, HMSO, London

Department of Education (1988) Education Reform Act, HMSO, London,

Department of Education and Science (1992), Initial Teacher Training Approval of Courses, Circular 9/92, HMSO, London

Department of Education (1994) Code of Practice on the Identification and Assessment of Special Educational Needs, HMSO, London

Department for Education and Employment (1997a), Excellence for All Children: Meeting Special Educational Needs, HMSO, London

Department of Education and Employment (1997b), Initial Teacher Training Approval of Courses, Circular 9/97, HMSO, London

Department for Education and Employment (1997c), Teaching High Status, High Standards, Circular 10/97 (DFEE 1997c) Requirements for Courses of Initial Teacher Training, HMSO, London

Department for Education and Employment (1998a), Teaching: High Status, High Standards – Requirements for Courses of Initial Teacher Training, Circular 4/98 (DFES 1998a), HMSO Publications, London

Department for Education and Employment (1998b), Meeting Special Educational Needs: A Programme of Action, DFES Publications Centre, London

Department for Education and Employment (1998c), Excellence for All Children: Meeting Special Educational Needs, HMSO, London

Department for Education and Employment (1999), Meeting Special Educational Needs: A Programme of Action – A Summary, DFES Publications Centre, London

Department for Education and Skills (2001a), Schools Achieving Success, London, HMSO

Department for Education and Skills (2001b), Special Educational Needs Code of Practice, HMSO, London

Department for Education and Skills, (2001c), Special Educational Needs and Disability Act, HMSO, London

Department for Education and Skills, (2001d), Statistics of Education: Special Educational Needs in England, January 2000, Circular 12/01, HMSO, London

Department for Education and Skills, (2002), Education and Skills: Delivering Results - A Strategy to 2006, HMSO, London

Department for Education and Skills, (2003), Success for All: An Inclusive Approach to Physical Education and School Sport, HMSO, London

Depauw, K and Gavron, S (1995), Disability and Sport, Human kinetics, Champaign

Depauw, K and Doll-Tepper, G (2000), Toward Progressive Inclusion and Acceptance: Myth or Reality? The Inclusion Debate and Bandwagon Discourse, Adapted Physical Activity Quarterly, 17, 135-143

Dessent, T, (1987), Making the Ordinary School Special, Falmer press, London

Disability Rights Task Force, (1999), From Exclusion to Inclusion, HMSO, London

Disability Rights Task Force, (2001), Towards Inclusion – Civil Rights for Disabled People, HMSO, London

Disability Rights Task Force, (2003), www.drtf.org

Dunn, L, (1968), Special Education for the Mildly Retarded – Is much of it Justifiable? Exceptional Children, Vol. 35, P5-22

Dyson, A; Millward: A, Skidmore, D, (1994), Beyond the Whole School Approach: An Emerging Model of Special Needs Practice and Provision in Mainstream Secondary Schools, British Educational Research Journal, Vol. 20(3), p301-317

Dyson, A, (1999), Unpublished Paper Examining Issues of Inclusion, Department of Education, University of Newcastle

Dyson, A; Millward, A, (2000), Issues of Innovation and Inclusion, Paul Chapman, London

Dyson, A, (2001), Special Needs in the Twenty – First Century: Where We've Been and Where We're Going, British Journal of Special Education, Vol 28, No 1, pp 24-29

English Federation for Disability Sport, (1999), Including Disabled Pupils in Physical Education – Core Module, EFDS, Manchester

English Sports Council (1997), Disability Task Force Recommendations on the Future structure and Integration of Disability Sport in England, English Sports Council, London

Farrell, M, (1998), The Special Education Handbook, David Fulton Publishers, London

Farrell, P, (2000), The Impact of Research on Developments in Inclusive Education, International Journal of Inclusive Education, April 2000, 153-164

Farrell, P, (2001), Special Education in the Last Twenty Years: Have things really got better?, British Journal of Special Education, Vol 28, No 1, pp 3-9

Feiler, A; Gibson, H, (1999), Threats to the Inclusive Movement, British Journal of Special Education, Vol 26, No 3, pp 147-152

Fredrickson, N; Cline, T, (2002), Special Educational Needs, Inclusion and Diversity, Open University Press, Birmingham

Fuchs, D; Fuchs, L, (1994), Inclusive Schools Movement and the Radicalisation of Special Education Reform, Exceptional children, Vol. 60(4), p294-309

Galloway, D; Goodwin, C, (1979), Educating Slow-Learning and Maladjusted Children: Integration or Segregation, Longman, London

Giangreco, M; Dennis, R; Cloninger, C; Edelman, S; Schattman, R, (1993), "I've Counted Jon": Transformational Experiences of Teachers Educating Students with Disabilities, Exceptional Children, Vol. 59(4), p359-372

Goodwin, L, and Watkinson, J, (2000), Inclusive Physical Education from the Perspectives of Students with Physical Disabilities, Adapted Physical Activity Quarterly, 17, 144-160

Haug, P, (1998), Norwegian Special Education: Development and Status, in Haug, P; Tossebro, J, (eds), Theoretical Perspectives on Special Education, Norwegian Academic Press, Kristiansand

Higher Education Funding Council for England (1984), Assessment of the Quality of Education: Circular 3/93, HEFCE, London

Hofman, R, (2003), Staff Development and Commitment for a Successful Inclusion Policy, International Journal of Inclusive Education, 17(2), 145-157

Home Office (1995), The Disability Discrimination Act, HMSO, London

Hutzler, Y; Fliess, O; Chacham, A; Auweele, Y, (2002), Perspectives of Children with Physical Disabilities on Inclusion and Empowerment: Supporting and Limiting Factors, Adapted Physical Activity Quarterly, 19, 300-317

Inner London Education Authority, (1985), Educational Opportunities for All? (Fish report), Inner London education Authority, London

Ito, C (1999) Inclusion-Confusion, www.wm.educ/ttac/articles/inclusion/htm

Jackson, L, (2002), Freaks, Geeks and Asperger Syndrome: A User Guide to Adolescence, Jessica Kingsley Publishers, London

Keogh, B; Gallimore, R; Weisner, T; (1997), A Sociocultural Perspective on Learning and Learning Disabilities, Learning Disabilities Research and Practice, Vol 12(2), p107-113

Lipsky, D, Gartner, A, (1999), Inclusion and Schools Reform: Transforming America's Classrooms, Paul H Brookes, Baltimore

Lloyd, C, (2000), Excellence for all Children – False Promises! The Failure of Current Policy for Inclusive education and Implications for Schooling in the 21st Century, International Journal of Inclusive Education, April 2000, 133-152

Mayall, B, (2000), Conversions with Children: Working with Generational Issues, in Christensen, P; James, A, (eds) (2000), Research with Children: Perspectives and Practices, Falmer Press, London

Mintzberg, H, (1979), The Structuring of Organisations, Prentice Hall, New York

Mintzberg, H, (1983), Structure in Fives: Designing Effective Organisations, Prentice Hall, New York

Mittler, P, (1985), Integration: The Shadow and the Substance, Educational and Child Psychology, Vol. 2(3), p8-22

Moore, N, (2000), How to do Research: The Complete Guide to Designing and Managing Research Projects, (3rd ed), Library Association Publishing, London

National Curriculum Council (1989), Circular Number 5: Implementing the National Curriculum – Participation by Pupils with Special Educational Needs, National Curriculum Council, York

Norwich, B, (1994), Differentiation from the Perspective of Resolving Tensions Between Basic Social Values and Assumptions about Individual Differences, Curriculum Studies, Vol. 2(3), p289-308

Norwich, B, (2002a), Education, Inclusion and Individual Differences: Recognising and Resolving Dilemmas, British Journal of Education Studies, Vol. 50(4), p482-502

Norwich, B, (2002b), LEA Inclusion Trends in England 1997-2001: Statistics on School Placements and Pupils with Statements in Special Schools, Centre for Studies on Inclusive Education, Bristol

Office for Standards in Education, (2000), Secondary Physical Education: Main Findings, OFSTED, London

Office for Standards in Education, (2002), Handbook for the Inspection of Initial Teacher Training (2002-2008), OFSTED, London

Office for Standards in Education, (2003), Inspecting Schools: Framework for Inspecting Schools Effective from September 2003, OFSTED, London

Oliver, M, (1988), The Social and Political Context of Educational Policy: The Case of Special Needs, in Barton, L, (ed), The Politics of Special Educational Needs, Falmer, London

Oliver, M, (1990), The Politics of Disablement, Macmillan, London

Pensgaard, A; Sorensen, M, (2002), Empowerment Through the Sport Context: A Model to Guide Research for Individuals with Disability, Adapted Physical Activity Quarterley, 18, 48-67

Physical Education Association of the United Kingdom (2000) Draft PEAUK Policy on Equal Opportunities, Unpublished

Pijl, S; Meijer, C; Hegarty, S, (eds), (1997), Inclusive Education: A Global Agenda, Routledge, London

Place, K; Hodge, S, (2001), Social Inclusion of Students with Physical Disabilities in General Physical Education: A Behavioural Analysis, Adapted Physical Activity Quarterly, 18, 389-404

Porter, G, (1997), Critical Elements For Inclusive Schools, in Pijl, S; Meijer, C; Hegarty, S, (eds), (1997), Inclusive Education: A Global Agenda, Routledge, London

Pring, R. (1996) Just Desert in Furlong, J, and Smith, R. (eds) The Role of Higher Education in Initial Teacher Training, Kogan Page, London

Qualification Curriculum Authority (1999a), The National Curriculum for England: Physical Education Key Stages 1 – 4, QCA, London

Qualification Curriculum Authority (1999b), The National Curriculum – Handbook for Primary Teachers in England, QCA, London

Qualification Curriculum Authority (1999c), The National Curriculum – Handbook for Secondary Teachers in England, QCA, London

Qualification Curriculum Authority (2001), Including All Learners: Key Principles to Guide QCA's Work, QCA, London

Qualifications Curriculum Authority, (2003), www.qca.org.uk/menu.htm

Reiser, R; Mason, M, (1990), Disability Equality in the Classroom: A Human Rights Issue, Inner London Education Authority, London

Reynolds, D; Teddlie, C; Hopkins, D; Stringfield, S, (2000) Linking School Effectiveness and School Improvement, in Teddlie, C; Reynolds, D (eds), The International Handbook of School Effectiveness Research, Falmer Press, London

Richter, K; Adams-Mushett, C; Ferrara, M; McCann, B, (1992), Integrated Swimming Classification: A Faulted System, Adapted Physical Activity Quarterly, Vol. 9, p5-13

Robson, C, (1999) Real World Research: A resource for Social Scientists and Practitioner Researchers, Blackwell Publishers Ltd, Oxford

Rose, S (1998) Lifelines: Biology, Freedom, Determinism, Penguin, London

Rouse, M; Florian, L, (1996), Effective Inclusive Schools: A Study in Two Countries, Cambridge Journal of Education, Vol. 26(10), p71-85

Rouse, M; Florian, L, (1997), Inclusive Education in the Market Place, International Journal of Inclusive Education, Vol. 1(4), p323-336

Sebba, J; Sachdev, D; (1997), What Works in Inclusive Education, Barnardo's, Ilford

Sherrill, C, (1998), Adapted Physical Activity, Recreation and Sport, (5th ed), McGraw Hill, Dubuque

Skrtic, T, (1991), The Special Education Paradox: Equity as the Way to Excellence, Harvard educational Review, Vol. 61(2), p148-206

Skrtic, T, (1995), The Functionalist View of Special Education and Disability: Deconstructing the Conventional Knowledge Tradition, in Skrtic, T, (ed), Disability and Democracy: Reconstructing (Special) Education for Post-modernity, Teachers College Press, New York

Slininger, D, Sherril, C, Jankowski, C, (2000), Children's Attitudes Towards Peers with Severe Disabilities: Revisiting Contact Theory, Adapted Physical Activity Quarterly, 17, 176-198

Sport England (1997), Task Force on the Future of Disability Sport, Sport England, London

Sport England (1999), Young People and Sport in England, Sport England, London

Sport England (2003), www.sportengland.org/resources/bibs/bibliogs.htm

Sugden D; Talbot, M, (1998), Physical Education for Children with Special Needs in Mainstream Education, Carnegie National sports development Centre, Leeds

Swann, W (1985) Is The Integration of Children With Special Educational Needs Happening? Oxford Review of Education, 11(1), p3-18

Swann, W (1988) Trends In Special School Placement To 1986 – Measuring, Assessing and Explaining Segregation, Oxford Review of Education, 14(2), pp139-161

Swann, W (1992) Segregation Statistics, London Centre for Studies on Integration, London

Tansley, A; Guidford, R, (1960), The Education of Slow Learning Children (2nd ed), Routledge and Kegan Paul, London

Teacher Training Agency (1997a), Consultation on Standards for Special Educational Needs Co-ordinators, Teacher Training Agency, London

Teacher Training Agency (1997b), Survey of Special Educational Needs Training Provided by Higher Education, Teacher Training Agency, London

Teacher Training Agency (1998a), Framework for the Assessment of Quality and Standards in Teacher Training, Circular 4/98 (DFES 1998a), Teacher Training Agency, London

Teacher Training Agency (1998b), Survey of Special Educational Needs Training Provided by LEA's and National SEN Organisations, Teacher Training Agency, London

Teacher Training Agency (1999), National Special Educational Needs Specialist Standards, Teacher Training Agency, London

Teacher Training Agency (2000), Initial Teacher Training Performance Profiles: At a Glance (September 2000), Teacher Training Agency, London

Teacher Training Agency and Office for Standards in Education (2001), Inspection arrangements for Initial teacher Training 2002/2003 onwards - Consultation, Teacher Training Agency, London

Teacher Training Agency (2001a), Handbook to Accompany the Standards for the Award of Qualified Teacher Status and Requirements for the Provision of Initial Teacher Training, Teacher Training Agency, London

Teacher Training Agency (2001b), Standards for the Award of Qualified Teacher Status and Requirements for Initial Teacher Training – Consultation Document, Teacher Training Agency, London

Teacher Training Agency (2002), Qualifying to Teach: Professional Standards for Qualified Teacher Status and Requirements for Initial Teacher Training, Circular 02/02 (TTA 2002), Teacher Training Agency, London

Teacher Training Agency (2003a), Into Induction 2003: An Introduction for Trainee Teachers to the Induction Period for Newly Qualified Teachers, Teacher Training Agency, London

Teacher Training Agency (2003b), The TTA Corporate Plan for 2003-2006, TTA, London

Thomas, G; Walker, D; Webb, J, (1998), The Making of the Inclusive School, Routledge, London

Tomlinson, S, (1982), A Sociology of Special Education, Routledge and Kegan Paul, London

Tomlinson, S, (1985), The Expansion of Special Education, Oxford Review of Education, Vol. 11(2), p157-165

Trend R (1997) Qualified Teacher Status: A Practical Introduction, Letts Educational, London

United Nations Educational, Scientific and Cultural Organisation (1994), The Salamanca Statement and Framework for Action on Special Needs Education, Salamanca, UNESCO

United States of America Federal Government, (1975), Public Law 94-142, Education for All Handicapped Children, US Federal Government, Washington DC

Universities Council for The Education of Teachers (1997a), Initial Teacher Education: TTA/OFSTED Quality Framework: A Critique, Occasional Paper Number 9, November 1997, UCET, London

Universities Council for The Education of Teachers (1997b), UCET response to the Green Paper "Excellence for All Children (1997), UCET, London

Vincent, C; Evans, J; Lunt, I; Steedman, J; Wedell, K, (1994), The Market Forces? The Effect of Local Management on Special Educational Needs Provision, British Educational Research Journal, Vol. 20(3), p261-278

Vislie, L; Langfeldt, G, (1996), Finance, Policy Making and the Organisation of Special Education, Cambridge Journal of Education, Vol. 26(1), p59-70

Vickerman, P (1997), Knowing your Pupils and Planning for Different Needs, in Capel, S, Learning to Teach Physical education in the Secondary School, Routledge, London

Vickerman, P, (2002), Perspectives on the Training of Physical Education Teachers for the Inclusion of Children with Special Educational Needs: Is There an Official Line View?, Bulletin of Physical Education, Vol. 38(2), p79-98

Vickerman, P; Hayes, S; Wetherley, A, (2003) Special Educational Needs and National Curriculum Physical Education, in Hayes, S; Stidder, G, (eds), Equity in Physical Education, Routledge, London

Volger, E; Romance, T, (2000), Including a Child with Severe Cerebral Palsy in Physical Education: A Case Study, Adapted Physical Activity Quarterly, 17, 161-182

Westwood, P, (1997), Commonsense Methods for Children with Special Needs, Routledge Press, London

Winnick, J, (1987), An Integration Continuum for Sport Participation, Adapted Physical Activity Quarterly, Vol. 4, p157-161

Winnick, J, (2000), Adapted Physical Education and Sport, (3r^d Edition), Human Kinetics, Leeds

Wright, H; Sugden, D, (1999), Physical Education for All – Developing Physical Education in the Curriculum for Pupils with special Educational Needs, David Fulton Publishers, London

JMU
Liverpool John Moores University

APPENDIX 1
LETTER TO OFFICIAL LINE AGENCIES

Dear Sir/Madam

I write to you in connection with my PhD that I am undertaking at the University of Leeds under the supervision of Professor David Sugden.

I am researching the training of physical education teachers to include children with special educational needs (SEN) within mainstream settings. As part of this process I wish to examine the views of what I have termed the official line (ie DFES, TTA, OFSTED), professional opinion and practice (ie ITT institutions and lecturers) and the consumers (ie PE teachers and children with SEN).

I have a particular interest in this area as I work as a Senior Lecturer in Physical Education at Liverpool John Moores University, which has a wide variety of ITT courses in physical education.

It is with this in mind that I write to you along with other official agencies (DFES, TTA, QCA, and the PE and Disability associations). The aim being to ascertain if the Office for Standards in Education has any policies, documentation or views to express and share related to the training of physical education teachers for the inclusion of children with SEN.

In addition I would welcome any views and or policies that OFSTED has in relation to four key issues related to the competence of teachers:

- General competence in the teaching profession.
- Competence related to the subject of physical education.
- Competence related to special educational needs.
- Competence in physical education and special needs.

I realise that I am asking for a lot, both in terms of views and or policies, but would really appreciate you assistance with my request.

Kind Regards

Philip Vickerman

Philip Vickerman BSc (Hons)   MEd **Programme Manager, Sports Development, School of PE, Sport & Dance**
IM Marsh Campus Barkhill Road Liverpool L17 6BD   Telephone 0151 231 5253 Facsimile 0151 729 0030 Email P.Vickerman@livjm.ac.uk

APPENDIX 2 QUESTIONNAIRE TO PE HEI

APPENDIX 2 QUESTIONNAIRE TO PE
HIGHER EDUCATION INSTITUTIONS (HEI)

*TRAINING THE PHYSICAL EDUCATION TEACHER FOR THE
INCLUSION OF CHILDREN WITH SPECIAL EDUCATIONAL NEEDS
(SEN) WITHIN MAINSTREAM SETTINGS*

Instructions: Please complete each section in as much detail as possible.
There are some sections that will require reference to your programme
documentation

SECTION A: About You

1. Name: --

2. Job Title: --

3. Brief outline of duties:

4. Please tick if you wish to receive an abstract of the findings　　[ ]

SECTION B: About Your Institution

5. Institution: --

6. Total FTE secondary PE students on Teacher Training:　　[ ]

7. How many are　　[ ]　**8. How many are**　　[ ]
postgraduates?　　　　　**undergraduates?**

9. Date of last OfSTED [/ /] **10. Grade for the institution** [ ]
visit

11. Total FTE lecturer posts delivering PE teacher training:　　[ ]

SECTION C: Management & Co-ordination of SEN

APPENDIX 2 QUESTIONNAIRE TO PE HEI

12. Tick the statement(s) that best reflects your institution's management and
co-ordination of disability and SEN:

a) Head of Department   [ ]   **b) Named person within the**   [ ]
                                      Dept

c) All Staff   [ ]   **d) No overall responsibility**   [ ]

e) Other (please specify):   ------------- ---

13. If any lecturing staff hold professional qualifications in SEN,
please specify the qualification, and number of staff:

14. List any SEN and PE training courses/seminars that PE
lecturers have attended:

15. How are such training courses/seminars cascaded to the
whole department?

APPENDIX 4 QUESTIONNAIRE TO TRAINEE PE TEACHERS

SECTION D: Programme Content & Delivery
(nb if you deliver more than one programme (ie: undergraduate and postgraduate), please use the additional copied sheets at the end of this questionnaire to respond to each programme

16. *Please list all courses that your institution offers for secondary PE:*

17. *Indicate whether the programme contains any of the following:*

   a) Option   [   ]   **b) Core**   [   ]

   c) Embedded themes throughout the programme   [   ]

   18. Total hours dedicated within the programme to SEN and PE   [   ]
   issues

19. *How much of this time is:*

   Theoretical   [%]   **Practical**   [%]

   e) Other (please specify):   ---

20. *Please name any modules/parts of modules that focus upon PE and SEN issues, and the contact time students receive on each module. It would be helpful if module outlines are attached to this questionnaire, (eg: differentiation, teaching and learning in PE, Level 1 module, core, 25 contact hrs)*

21. *Please give details of any assessment tasks that relate specifically to PE/SEN*

22. *How does your programme meet the requirements of 4/98 standards on SEN?*

23. *How do you measure whether 4/98 standards related to SEN have been met?*

24. Do you have disabled students on your PE initial teacher training programmes?

Yes [ ] **No** [ ]

SECTION E: Links With Schools & Mentors

25. *Does the institution use SEN schools for school experiences as either a compulsory or optional requirement for students?*

    Compulsory   [ ]   **Optional**   [ ]

26. *Does the institution offer students opportunities to teach children with SEN as part of taught modules?*

    Yes   [ ]   **No**   [ ]

27. *Please give details of any use of SEN specialists within mainstream or special schools that you use to develop students knowledge and understanding*

28. *Please give details of any school based tasks that students are required to undertake related to PE and SEN*

SECTION F: Partnerships with Disability Sport and/or Special Needs Agencies

29. *Does the institution have any links with disability sport agencies such as the English Federation for Disability Sport?*

    Yes   [ ]   **No**   [ ]

30. *Do you ever invite disabled people to your institution to talk to students in relation to disability and special needs issues?*

    Yes   [ ]   **No**   [ ]

31. *Please list any journals or publications related to PE sport, disability and needs that your institution subscribes to*

32. *What further resource materials would you and your programmes benefit from in order to enhance the understanding of PE and SEN issues?*

APPENDIX 4 QUESTIONNAIRE TO TRAINEE PE TEACHERS

SECTION G: Values & Attitudes
Please rate the following statements from **1 (strongly agree)** through to **5 (strongly disagree)**

33. **Children with SEN should be included in mainstream schools**   *1*   *2*   *3*   *4*   *5*

34. **Newly Qualified PE Teachers are adequately prepared for delivering inclusive lessons for children with SEN**   *1*   *2*   *3*   *4*   *5*

35. **Newly Qualified PE Teachers will need further training through Continuing Professional Development programmes**   *1*   *2*   *3*   *4*   *5*

36. **Children with SEN should be consulted as part of the facilitation of inclusive PE**   *1*   *2*   *3*   *4*   *5*

37. **National Curriculum 2000 provides PE teachers with a clear framework for the development of inclusive activities**   *1*   *2*   *3*   *4*   *5*

38. **SEN issues should be integrated fully into all PE initial Teacher Training courses**   *1*   *2*   *3*   *4*   *5*

39. Teaching of children with SEN
is just an extension of any PE
teachers mixed ability   1   2   3   4   5
teaching

40. 4/98 standards ensure that
students are adequately
prepared for inclusive   1   2   3   4   5
education

41. The TTA, DfEE and OfSTED
offer adequate advice and
guidance to PE institutions on 1   2   3   4   5
SEN issues

42. Professional PE associations,
ie: BAALPE, PEA(UK), offer
adequate advice and guidance   1   2   3   4   5
to PE institutions on SEN
issues

43. The Code of Practice on SEN
and Individual Education
plans can be related to PE   1   2   3   4   5
with relative ease

SECTION H: Other Views & Opinions
Please add any further points that you feel are relevant to this questionnaire

APPENDIX 4 QUESTIONNAIRE TO TRAINEE PE TEACHERS

Thank you for your time. Please return the questionnaire by
Friday 13th July 2001.

APPENDIX 3
FACE-TO-FACE
INTERVIEW QUESTIONS

Thank you for agreeing to take part in an interview following the return of your questionnaire. I would like to inform you that the content of the discussion will be taped and transcribed and may be used in the final thesis.

Can I assure you however that the content of the interview will be kept confidential, and both you and the University will remain anonymous.

The interview is part of my PhD studies at the University of Leeds, which involves five stages, which are briefly detailed below. (A copy of the full research proposal is available for your information)

Stage one: Literature review and questionnaires to 'Official Line' agencies to ascertain statutory and professional association views and opinions in relation to the research question.

Stage two: Questionnaires to the 30 Higher Education Institutions delivery either undergraduate or postgraduate physical education teacher training courses. This is termed 'Professional Opinion and Practice.

Stage three: Face to face taped and transcribed interviews with 5 selected 'Professional opinion and Practice' Higher Education Institutions.

Stage four: Questionnaires to final year students from the 5 selected Higher Education Institutions. This is termed the 'Consumers'

Stage five: Questionnaires to 'Consumers' from the 5 selected Higher Education Institutions who are between NQT Status and two years qualifying experience.

APPENDIX 4 QUESTIONNAIRE TO TRAINEE PE TEACHERS

General themes and issues to be discussed during the face to face interviews

Please note these are for initial guidance and may be subject to some slight variations depending on the discussion during the interviews

What are your views on inclusive PE for children with SEN

How does the PE NC 2000 inclusion statement support the process of supporting children with SEN in PE

How do you think PE and SEN should be addressed within your programmes – should it be discrete, embedded throughout or a combination of all of these

Official line support: What support do you see statutory agencies such as TTA, OFSTED and PE associations (ie Baalpe, PEAUK) being able to give to you or PE teachers

In your opinion do you think your students have sufficient knowledge and understanding of PE and SEN issues to go out into schools

How do students gain this knowledge and understanding of PE and SEN

In what ways do students have opportunities to apply PE and SEN issues during their course

One of the general issues that has come out of the questionnaires is the need for more resource materials for people to use within Higher Education Institutions – What do you think?

Professional opinion and practice – what would help you in the HEI sector deliver good PE and SEN training

What role do schools and mentors play in the delivery of PE and SEN

Do you have specific assessment tasks either school based and or in HEI that address these issues

How much can you realistically cover on your programme within the time limits, constraints and pressures that exist

Do you think there is a need for CPD on PE and SEN when NQT's get into schools

Consumers – What would help students and or qualified teachers out in schools

APPENDIX 4 QUESTIONNAIRE TO TRAINEE PE TEACHERS

TRAINING THE PHYSICAL EDUCATION TEACHER FOR THE INCLUSION OF CHILDREN WITH SPECIAL EDUCATIONAL NEEDS (SEN) WITHIN MAINSTREAM SETTINGS

Instructions: Please complete each section in as much detail as possible.

SECTION A: About You

1. *Are you:*

    Male [ ]   Female [ ]

2. **Name of University you are attending:** --

3. *Is your course:*

    Undergraduate [ ]   Postgraduate [ ]

4. **Please indicate your age group:**

18-24	25-30	31-36	36+
[ ]	[ ]	[ ]	[ ]

SECTION B: Your Professional Development & Training to date

5. *Indicate whether your course contains any of the following PE/SEN themes:*

    a) Option [ ]   b) Core [ ]

    c) Embedded themes throughout the course [ ]

APPENDIX 4 QUESTIONNAIRE TO TRAINEE PE TEACHERS

[ ]

6. **Please estimate the total number of course hours that you have spent on SEN and PE issues to date**

7. *How much of this time was:*

                  [%]   [%]
      Theoretical   **Practical**

8. *Please name any modules/parts of modules that focus upon PE and SEN issues that you have undertaken during your training to date*

9. *Please give details of any assessment tasks that you have undertaken that relate specifically to PE/SEN*

10. *How do you intend to meet the requirements of 4/98 standards on SEN in relation to PE?*

11. *Please list any SEN/PE courses, training or experience that you have gained outside of your formal University programme:*

SECTION C: Your Links With Schools & Mentors

12. *Have you had an opportunity for any school experiences as either a compulsory or optional requirement within a special school?*

Compulsory   [ ]   Optional   [ ]

13. *Has your course given you opportunities to teach children with SEN as part of taught modules?*

Yes   [ ]   No   [ ]

14. *Please give details of any school based tasks that you are required to undertake related to PE and SEN*

15. *Do you discuss PE & SEN issues with mentors in schools?*

Yes [ ]   No [ ]

16. *Are you required to plan for differentiation within your PE lessons?*

Yes [ ]   No [ ]

APPENDIX 5 QUESTIONNAIRE TO RECENTLY QUALIFIED PE TEACHERS

17. *Please state your definition/interpretation of inclusive PE for children with SEN*

18. *Please indicate the type of support you see the following agencies offering to trainee and qualified PE teachers*

	Policy Docum ent	Practic al Resour ce Materi als	Advice / Guidan ce	Other
Teacher Training Agency	[ ]	[ ]	[ ]	[ ]
Office for Standards in Education	[ ]	[ ]	[ ]	[ ]
Department for Education & Skills	[ ]	[ ]	[ ]	[ ]
British Association of Advisors and Lecturers in PE	[ ]	[ ]	[ ]	[ ]
Physical Education Association UK	[ ]	[ ]	[ ]	[ ]
English Federation for Disability Sport	[ ]	[ ]	[ ]	[ ]
Qualification Curriculum Authority	[ ]	[ ]	[ ]	[ ]

19. *If you have ticked 'other' please indicate what additional role/functions you see each of these agencies taking:*

Other – *please state*

APPENDIX 5 QUESTIONNAIRE TO RECENTLY QUALIFIED PE TEACHERS

SECTION E: Values & Attitudes
Please rate the following statements from **1 (strongly agree)** through to **5 (strongly disagree)**

20. Children with SEN should be included in mainstream schools

        1   *2*   *3*   *4*   *5*

21. Newly Qualified PE Teachers are adequately prepared for delivering inclusive lessons for children with SEN

        1   *2*   *3*   *4*   *5*

22. Newly Qualified PE Teachers will need further training through Continuing Professional Development programmes

        1   *2*   *3*   *4*   *5*

23. Children with SEN should be consulted as part of the facilitation of inclusive PE

        1   *2*   *3*   *4*   *5*

24. National Curriculum 2000 provides PE teachers with a clear framework for the development of inclusive activities

        1   *2*   *3*   *4*   *5*

25. SEN issues should be integrated fully into all PE initial Teacher Training courses

        1   *2*   *3*   *4*   *5*

26. Teaching of children with SEN is just an extension of any PE teachers mixed ability teaching

        1   *2*   *3*   *4*   *5*

APPENDIX 5 QUESTIONNAIRE TO RECENTLY QUALIFIED PE TEACHERS

27. 4/98 standards ensure that students are adequately prepared for inclusive education

1   2   3   4   5

28. The TTA, DfEE and OfSTED offer adequate advice and guidance to PE teachers/trainees on SEN issues

1   2   3   4   5

29. Professional PE associations, ie: BAALPE, PEA (UK), offer adequate advice and guidance to PE teachers/trainees on SEN issues

1   2   3   4   5

30. *The Code of Practice on SEN and Individual Education plans can be related to PE with relative ease*

1   2   3   4   5

31. *I am satisfied with the level of training I have received in relation to PE/SEN*

1   2   3   4   5

SECTION F: Other Views & Opinions
Please add any further points that you feel are relevant to this questionnaire

APPENDIX 5 QUESTIONNAIRE TO RECENTLY
QUALIFIED PE TEACHERS

Thank you for your time. Please return the questionnaire as advised by your tutor.

APPENDIX 5 QUESTIONNAIRE TO RECENTLY QUALIFIED PE TEACHERS

APPENDIX 5 QUESTIONNAIRE TO RECENTLY QUALIFIED PE TEACHERS

APPENDIX 5 QUESTIONNAIRE TO RECENTLY QUALIFIED PE TEACHERS

APPENDIX 5 QUESTIONNAIRE TO RECENTLY QUALIFIED PE TEACHERS

TRAINING THE PHYSICAL EDUCATION TEACHER FOR THE INCLUSION OF CHILDREN WITH SPECIAL EDUCATIONAL NEEDS (SEN) WITHIN MAINSTREAM SETTINGS

Instructions: Please complete each section in as much detail as possible.

SECTION A: About You

1. Are you?   Male   [ ]   Female   [ ]

2. What University did you attend?   ---

3. *Was your course?*

          Undergraduate   [ ]   Postgraduate   [ ]

4. Please indicate your age group:

18-24	25-30	31-36	36+
[ ]	[ ]	[ ]	[ ]

SECTION B: Your Initial Teacher Training in Physical Education

5. *Did your course contain any of the following PE/SEN themes?*

          a) Option   [ ]   b) Core   [ ]

          c) Embedded themes throughout the course   [ ]

APPENDIX 5 QUESTIONNAIRE TO RECENTLY QUALIFIED PE TEACHERS

6. **Please estimate the total number of course hours that you think you spent on SEN and PE issues**   [ ]

7. *Estimate how much of this time was:*

                    [%]   [%]
        Theoretical   **Practical**

8. *Please name any modules and or key points that you remember in relation to any work you did on PE and or SEN issues whilst in training*

9. *Please give details of any assessment tasks that you remember undertaking that specifically related to PE/SEN*

10. Do you feel that your initial teacher training course prepared you adequately to support the inclusion of children with SEN in PE? (Please provide supporting evidence)

Yes [ ]   [ ]
                                           No

Comments:

11. *What have been the major challenges in general for you since qualifying as a PE teacher?*

12. *Please describe any teaching experiences that you have had or are currently engaged in since qualifying that requires you to include children with SEN within PE*

13. Please list any SEN/PE courses, training or continuing professional development
     experiences that you have gained since qualifying

14. Who or what is your major source of advice and support in relation to assisting you
     with the inclusion of children with SEN?

15. Please indicate what you see as the key issues that Initial Teacher Training Institutions
     should address in order to prepare PE teachers adequately for the inclusion of children
     with SEN in PE.

16. Are you required to plan for differentiation within your PE lessons?

                              [ ]   [ ]
              Yes   No

SECTION D: Interpreting Inclusive PE

17. Please state your definition/interpretation of inclusive PE for children with SEN

18. Please indicate the type of support you see the following agencies offering to qualified PE teachers

	Policy Document	Practical Resource Materials	Advice / Guidance	Other
Teacher Training Agency	[ ]	[ ]	[ ]	[ ]
Office for Standards in Education	[ ]	[ ]	[ ]	[ ]
Department for Education & Skills	[ ]	[ ]	[ ]	[ ]
British Association of Advisors and Lecturers in PE	[ ]	[ ]	[ ]	[ ]
Physical Education Association UK	[ ]	[ ]	[ ]	[ ]
English Federation for Disability Sport	[ ]	[ ]	[ ]	[ ]
Qualification Curriculum Authority	[ ]	[ ]	[ ]	[ ]

19. If you have ticked 'other' please indicate what additional role/functions you see each of these agencies taking:

Other – please state

----

20. Children with SEN should be included
   in mainstream schools

   1   2   3   4   5

21. PE Teachers are adequately prepared
   for delivering inclusive lessons for
   children with SEN

   1   2   3   4   5

22. Qualified PE Teachers will need further
   training through Continuing
   Professional Development in order to
   include children with SEN

   1   2   3   4   5

23. Children with SEN should be consulted
   as part of their facilitation of inclusive
   PE

   1   2   3   4   5

24. National Curriculum 2000 provides PE
   teachers with a clear framework for the
   development of inclusive activities

   1   2   3   4   5

25. SEN issues should be integrated fully
   into all PE initial Teacher Training
   courses

   1   2   3   4   5

26. Teaching of children with SEN is just
   an extension of any PE teachers mixed
   ability teaching

   1   2   3   4   5

27. 4/98 teacher training standards
ensured that you were adequately
prepared for inclusive education   *1*   *2*   *3*   *4*   *5*

28. The TTA, DfES and OfSTED offer
adequate advice and guidance to PE
teachers/trainees on SEN issues   *1*   *2*   *3*   *4*   *5*

29. Professional PE associations, ie:
BAALPE, PEA (UK), offer adequate
advice and guidance to PE teachers on
SEN issues   *1*   *2*   *3*   *4*   *5*

30. *The Code of Practice on SEN and
Individual Education plans can be related
to PE with relative ease*   1   2   3   4   5

31. *I am satisfied with the level of
training I received in relation to PE/SEN*   1   2   3   4   5

SECTION F: Other Views & Opinions
Please add any further points that you feel are relevant to this questionnaire

Thank you for your time. Please return the questionnaire in the enclosed self addressed envelope.

Lightning Source UK Ltd.
Milton Keynes UK
UKOW050418260112

186071UK00002B/34/P